Cracking the
NYSTCE®
New York State Teacher
Certification Exam

The Princeton Review

Cracking the NYSTCE®

New York State Teacher Certification Exam

The Staff of The Princeton Review

Second Edition

Random House, Inc.
New York

www.PrincetonReview.com

The Princeton Review, Inc.
2315 Broadway
New York, NY 10024
E-mail: booksupport@review.com

ISBN 0-375-76517-4

Editor: Suzanne Markert
Production Editor: Patricia Dublin
Production Coordinator: Effie Hadjiioannou
Illustrations by: The Production Department of The Princeton Review

Manufactured in the United States of America.

9 8 7 6 5 4 3 2 1

Second Edition

ACKNOWLEDGMENTS

The Princeton Review would like to thank Editor Suzanne Markert, Production Editor Patricia Dublin, Production Coordinator Effie Hadjiioannou, and the following people, without whom this book could not have been created: Anna Konstantatos, Jennifer Spitzer, Jill Pearson, Stephen White, Alex Freer-Balko, Ed Wright, Gabrielle Maisels, Jeff Rubenstein, Jeff Soloway, Beth Stanitski, Jennifer Arias, Kevin Crossman, Raymond Asencio, Rodi Steinig, Victoria Printz, Melissa Kavonic, and Ian Stewart.

CONTENTS

PART I

Orientation

1

Introduction

INTRODUCTION

The Princeton Review started in 1981 with an SAT course for 19 students. Now we help over two million students a year. Over the past quarter century we have grown into the largest test preparation company in the United States. We work with students at all levels to prepare them for college entrance exams, graduate school tests, and professional development exams. Our goal is to help you pass the New York State Teacher Certification Exam (NYSTCE). And we can help you because our methods work.

WHAT IS THE NYSTCE?

Anyone who wishes to become a certified teacher in the state of New York must take and pass the NYSTCE. Depending on what grade level and subject you will be teaching, you will need to pass some of the following exams:

- Liberal Arts and Sciences Test (LAST)
- Elementary and Secondary Assessment of Teaching Skills—Written (ATS-W)
- Content Specialty Tests (CST)
- Language Proficiency Assessments (LPA)
- Assessment of Teaching Skills—Performance (ATS-P)

You will need to pass the ATS-W and LAST, as well as the CST (if applicable), before you can apply for your first certification. If you are unsure about what tests you need to take, or if you have any other questions regarding the teacher-certification process in New York, visit the New York State Education Department website (www.nysed.gov). You will also find links on this site that will allow you to register for the necessary certification exams.

Because this book is designed specifically to prepare you for the LAST and ATS-W, other elements of the NYSTCE will not be discussed elsewhere in this book. However, you should not assume the lack of discussion on the CST, for example, means that you don't have to take that exam prior to applying for certification. Be sure you understand what exams you have to take and when you have to take them. As mentioned earlier, this depends on what grade level and subject you wish to teach.

WHAT WILL I SEE ON THE LAST AND ATS-W?

The **LAST** is a four-hour exam that consists of 80 multiple-choice questions and one essay assignment. The exam is designed to test your knowledge of math, science, history, literature, the arts, and communication skills. While it sounds overwhelming, it really isn't as bad as you might think. The knowledge you are required to demonstrate is generally at a pretty basic level. You certainly don't have to know as much about biology as a biology major would; but you might, for example, have to answer a question that tests a basic understanding of scientific method. In fact, for most questions you will be given all the information you need to answer the question, in the form of a short reading passage, picture, or graph. Keeping this in mind, the most fruitful method of preparation for the LAST is to improve your general test-taking skills and to review the basics in areas of the test where you feel less comfortable. This preparation guide is written with that strategy in mind.

The **ATS-W** is also a four-hour exam that consists of 80 multiple-choice questions and one essay assignment. However, the ATS-W tests your ability to apply your own teaching experience and what you've learned in your teacher education courses to real-life examples. You'll need to draw upon some general teaching theory, but you can answer most questions by referring to your own experience in the classroom and your common sense. Because this test measures your ability to apply prevailing theories of education to real-life examples, your preparation should consist of reviewing theories of cognitive, social, and moral development, and adopting the proper frame of mind when answering questions. You will take one of two versions of the ATS-W—Elementary or Secondary—but this book will prepare you for both. Likewise, the included practice test includes both Elementary- and Secondary-level questions, and will prepare you equally well for each.

So How Are the Tests Scored?

Both the LAST and the ATS-W are scored on a scale of 100–300, with a passing score of 220. The exam is a **criterion-referenced exam**, which means that you don't have to be concerned with how anyone else scores on the test. If you get enough correct answers and you write a good essay, then you pass. It's also very important to remember that since any score of 220 or above is as good as any other score in that range, you don't need to get every question right. Instead, you will want to focus on taking the test in a way that gives you the best possible chance of getting a passing score.

THE LAST

As we just said, you need to get a score of 220 or higher to pass the LAST. While the people who make the test, NES (National Evaluation Systems), don't publish their scoring information, we have a good idea of how they come up with your score. Each of the four question types (math/science, history/social science, arts/literature, and communication skills) on the test is given a scaled score from 100–300. Those four scaled scores are averaged, along with the written portion of the test. Provided that you earn a passing score on the test as a whole, your score on any subsection of the test is completely unimportant.

One vital point: There is no penalty for picking a wrong answer on a multiple-choice question, so you should never leave any question blank. Even if you have no idea what the correct answer is, take a guess.

The Structure of the Test

The LAST has questions that cover everything from math and science to arts and literature. Sounds a little like a game of Trivial Pursuit, huh? The difference is that a majority of the questions are reading comprehension or diagrams, so that often getting the right answer is as simple as finding it in a passage or picture. The test questions break down approximately as follows on the next page.

- Math and Science: 20 questions

- History and Social Sciences: 20 questions

- Arts and Humanities: 20 questions

- Pure Reading Comprehension and Communication Skills: 20 questions

Regardless of any particular question being "technically" a history, science, or literature question, in most cases the question will be asking you to retrieve information from an accompanying passage, picture, or graph. So while the test writers describe the exam as measuring four types of skills, there is a fifth skill that is measured throughout the test. That skill could be described as "looking stuff up."

The writing assignment will give you a question along with two opposing viewpoints on the topic. You'll need to analyze the arguments, take a stand on the topic, and defend your position. There are two major elements involved in preparing to write a passing essay. First, you will want to make sure that you are comfortable with your writing mechanics and with how you organize and present your essay. Second, you will need to give careful consideration to how you will manage your time. You have four hours to complete both the multiple-choice and essay portions of the test, but you are free to decide for yourself how much time you wish to spend on each part of the exam and in what order you would like to complete each part. We recommend that you spend roughly one hour on your essay and up to three hours on the multiple-choice questions. The following strategy is one possible approach to taking the test:

1. Write the essay (1 hour).

2. Do the multiple-choice questions (2.5 hours).

3. Review your essay once more for grammar and spelling (15 minutes).

4. Review your answer sheet to make sure you've answered all the questions. Go back to any questions you want to try a second time (15 minutes).

How to Increase Your Score

There are a few key tricks to beating the LAST.

POE (Process of Elimination)

POE, Process of Elimination, will be your best friend on the LAST. Because the right answer is going to be one of the listed answer choices, there are two ways to go about finding the right one. First, if you know the answer to the question, then all you have to do is find it and color in the corresponding bubble on your answer sheet. Second, if you *don't* know what the answer to a question *is*, you can often identify what the answer *isn't*. Let's look at the following question as an example:

The capital of Malawi is

(A) Washington, D.C.
(B) Paris.
(C) Tokyo.
(D) Lilongwe.

Perhaps you know the answer to this question without even looking at the answer choices because you studied Africa in a college course or you've memorized world capitals. But even if you don't know the answer, you should know enough to eliminate choices (A) through (C) because those cities are obviously not in Malawi. For better or worse, on a multiple-choice test you can get credit for knowing things that you didn't really know simply because you were able to eliminate the other choices. Here's another example:

The President of the United States at the time
that atomic bombs were dropped on Hiroshima
and Nagasaki was

(A) Josef Stalin.
(B) Franklin D. Roosevelt.
(C) Winston Churchill.
(D) Harry S. Truman.

Assuming that you're not a History Channel aficionado or a World War II buff, you might not be 100 perecent sure of the answer. However, you will most likely be comfortable eliminating answer choice (A) (Stalin was the leader of the Soviet Union at this time) and answer choice (C) (Churchill was the prime minister of Great Britain at this time). So you have narrowed it down to two choices.

Should you take a guess? Absolutely. We already told you that there is no penalty for getting a wrong answer, so you should definitely take this fifty-fifty shot. In fact, if you are able to figure out about half the questions on your own and can narrow the other half down to two choices, you will have an excellent chance of passing the LAST. And in case you're wondering about the answer to the question above, because Franklin Roosevelt died about four months before the two atomic bombs were dropped on Japan, the correct response to the question is (D).

Remember, even if you have no idea what the answer to a question is, never leave a question blank.

POOD (Personal Order of Difficulty)

Questions on the LAST aren't arranged in any particular order of difficulty, so you get to decide which questions you think are easy and which ones you think are hard. It's very important that you start off by working on the questions that you think are easy because you want to make sure you don't get stuck on a hard question and waste time. If you have finished your essay and answered all the easy-to-medium multiple-choice questions, then it's not such a big deal if you run out of time since all that's left are the hardest questions. Running out of time when there are easy questions left unanswered is one of the main reasons that people don't pass the test.

To avoid this pitfall, we recommend that the first time you go through the multiple-choice questions on test day you actively look for questions that you want to answer first. Depending on your personal preferences and your relative strengths and weaknesses, this could mean saving the math and science questions for last or skipping over questions that involve a lot of reading until everything else is finished. Whatever strategy you choose, you'll want to make sure that you don't get too hung up on any particular question.

Pacing

How much time should you spend on a difficult question before moving on? That is up to you. You have four hours to take the entire test, including writing the essay. Assuming you spend just over an hour writing and proofreading your essay, you will have only over two minutes per question on average for the multiple-choice section. On your first time through the multiple-choice questions, you should save for later any questions that look like they would take much more than two and a half minutes. Any question that looks like it is going to take more than five minutes is likely a question you will want to guess on and then come back to later if you finish everything else. The few really time-consuming questions on the LAST are only going to make a huge difference if you get stuck on them and end up having to rush through the rest of the test.

Remember, save the hard stuff for the end.

Standard Formatting

Somewhere between 50 and 75 percent of the questions on the LAST look the same. Well, not exactly the same, but they follow a standard format. You'll be given a short passage, the topic of which will fall into one of the four subject areas, followed by two, three, or (rarely) four questions about the passage. The secret? You won't need to know anything other than what is on the page to answer the questions. For example:

> Instead of trying to reproduce exactly what I see before me, I make more arbitrary use of color to express myself more forcefully.... To express the love of two lovers by the marriage of two complementary colors.... To express the thought of a brow by the radiance of a light tone against a dark background. To express hope by some star. Someone's passion by the radiance of the setting sun.

> —Vincent van Gogh, 1888

46. Which of the following accurately expresses how Van Gogh uses color in a painting?

(A) He tries to create an exact reproduction of his subject.
(B) He uses it more profoundly, to express things in a way that they might not appear to the average viewer.
(C) Van Gogh uses only contrasting colors.
(D) He decides on color based on his mood at the time of the painting; solemn moods are depicted with dark colors, and joyful moods require bright colors.

You can be sure that many people are going to be intimidated by this question. Even if you don't know Vincent van Gogh from Evander Holyfield, you can still answer the question. The trick to doing well on this test is to not panic if the information seems unfamiliar and instead to focus on what the passage tells you. In this case, Van Gogh is more or less saying that he picks colors to convey tone or emotion. Van Gogh is not necessarily representing things in paintings as they actually look, but instead is using color and contrast to communicate a greater meaning. So how about those answer choices?

(A) This is something that Van Gogh is not doing. Note how the first sentence explicitly states that he is not trying to reproduce exactly what he sees.

(B) This is the credited response. He uses color in a much more figurative sense.

(C) Although there is one reference to use of contrasting colors, it would be unwise to select an answer choice that says that Van Gogh uses *only* contrasting colors. Being aware of the use of absolute terms such as *only*, *all*, *never*, and *must* is fundamental to your success on this exam.

(D) Choice of color is not dictated by Van Gogh's mood at the time of the painting. Instead, the theme of the painting is what dictates his choice of color. This is a close second choice, but a careful comparison of what this answer choice says with what the quote from Van Gogh says should steer you away from this choice.

If you approach questions on unfamiliar material the way we approached this question on Van Gogh, you'll be on your way to being a great test taker.

Read the Question First

Many of the questions on the LAST will consist of a reading passage that is two to four paragraphs long followed by two or three questions. Especially when you are looking at a longer passage that is accompanied by only one or two questions, you should consider reading the questions first.

By reading the question first (and not the answer choices), you will have a much better idea of exactly what it is you have to know to answer the question. And since you should be much more interested in being able to answer the question than in understanding everything there is to know about the corresponding reading passage, it's a good idea to adopt this commonsense approach whenever possible.

Roman Numeral Questions

On the LAST you will find a great number of questions that contain Roman numerals.

12. Which of the following could be considered factors contributing to the Cold War between the United States and the Soviet Union after the end of World War II?

   I. A rise of communism in other nations
  II. The nuclear arms race
 III. The Vietnam War
 IV. A woman is first appointed to the U.S. Supreme Court

(A) I and II only
(B) I, II, and III only
(C) I, II, and IV only
(D) I, II, III, and IV

First of all, notice that all four answer choices contain both Roman numerals I and II. There is no way that either of those can be wrong because if they were then there would be no right answer. So, the first Roman numeral you should consider is III. Could the Vietnam War be considered a factor contributing to the Cold War between the United States and the Soviet Union? Absolutely. The conflict in Vietnam was a conflict between the two ideologies represented by the United States and the Soviet Union. Since III appears to be part of the credited response, you should eliminate all answer choices that do not contain III. Cross out answer choices (A) and (C). Now you have to evaluate statement IV. Does it make sense that the appointment of a woman to the United States Supreme Court would affect the Cold War? Not really. So the answer you'll want to pick should contain Roman numerals I through III: answer choice (B).

Some Roman numeral questions might accompany a chart or a table.

	Cause	Effect
I	Vehicles emit high levels of carbon monoxide gases.	Space exploration has slowed down substantially.
II	Soil erosion causes a loss of topsoil on farmland.	There is a potential for reduced crop production.
III	The ozone layer is being depleted at an alarming rate.	Annual snowfall totals have increased across the globe.
IV	Burning fossil fuels for power has caused the release of sulfur dioxide into the air in the past few decades.	Acid rain is formed and harms plant life, water supplies, and animals.

34. Which of the above direct cause and effect relationships are accurate?

(A) I and II only
(B) I, II, and III only
(C) II, III, and IV only
(D) II and IV only

In I, there doesn't seem to be much of a relationship between carbon monoxide levels in the atmosphere and space exploration. Go ahead and eliminate answer choices (A) and (B). Since both remaining answer choices contain both II and IV, you don't need to check those because they have to be right. That leaves you with III. Since there doesn't seem to be a relationship between ozone levels and annual snowfall rates, the most appropriate answer choice to this question is answer choice (D).

To summarize, here's a general strategy to approach Roman numeral questions:

- If a Roman numeral is in all available answer choices, then you don't have to check it because it has to be right.
- If you decide that one of the Roman numeral statements is correct, cross out all answer choices that do not contain that Roman numeral.
- If you decide that one of the Roman numeral statements is incorrect, cross out all answer choices that contain that Roman numeral.
- Anytime you cross out an answer choice, apply the first rule to the remaining answer choices.

THE ATS-W

As on the LAST, you need to get a score of 220 or higher to pass the ATS-W. And, just as on the LAST, the ATS-W score is generated by taking an average score from four subsections of the multiple-choice section (knowledge of the learner, instructional planning and assessment, instructional delivery, and the professional environment) and from an essay assignment. Although you will be given a 100–300 score on each subsection of the test, these subscores are unimportant because you only need to pass the test as a whole.

Don't forget that there is no penalty for picking a wrong answer on any multiple-choice question. Because of this, you should never leave any questions blank. Even if you have no idea what the correct answer is, take a guess.

THE STRUCTURE OF THE TEST

The ATS-W tests your knowledge of the various theories and approaches that are used in the practice of teaching. Questions will frequently be presented in terms of "real-life" scenarios that will require you to choose an appropriate action based on your knowledge of sound teaching practices. The distribution of multiple-choice questions by topic is roughly:

- Knowledge of the Learner: 20 questions
- Instructional Planning and Assessment: 20 questions
- Instructional Delivery: 20 questions
- The Professional Environment: 20 questions

Because this test measures your ability to apply knowledge rather than simply provide information (thereby utilizing a higher level of Bloom's taxonomy of learning), you should not devote your study time to memorizing the names and positions of various theorists. Instead, you should focus on learning material in such a way that it can be applied to real-life situations. For example, instead of remembering that Piaget claimed that children in the preoperational stage lack conservation skills, you should instead think in terms of what a child at any particular grade level can or cannot do. A first grader who mistakenly thinks that a volume of water has changed because it was poured from one container into another container of a different shape is not a child who is lagging behind his peers intellectually. Instead, this is a specific example of a child in the preoperational stage who has not yet mastered conservation problems. In the course of your preparation for this exam, always keep in mind that your ability to apply knowledge is what you will have to demonstrate. So rather than memorize Erikson's stages of psychosocial development, it would be more important for you to have an understanding of what developmental issues children of various ages are likely to face. The content we expect you will need to know for this exam will therefore be presented in terms of age groups rather than in terms of the theories themselves.

The writing assignment will present an educational goal and ask you to explain why the goal is worthy and to outline two strategies you would use to achieve it. It is vital for you to understand that you are expected to agree with whatever goal is mentioned in the writing assignment. You have four hours to complete both the multiple-choice and essay portions of the test, but you are free to decide for yourself how much time you wish to spend on each part of the exam and in what order you would like to complete each part. We recommend that you spend roughly one hour on your essay and up to three hours on the multiple-choice questions. The following strategy is one possible approach to taking the test:

1. Write the essay (1 hour).

2. Do the multiple-choice questions (2.5 hours).

3. Review your essay once more for grammar and spelling (15 minutes).

4. Review your answer sheet to make sure you've answered all the questions. Go back to any questions you want to try a second time (15 minutes).

How to Increase Your Score

All the strategies outlined earlier in the discussion of the LAST (POE, POOD, Roman numeral questions, Pacing) also apply to the ATS-W. Additionally, there is an important frame of mind that you will need to adopt when approaching the content of the ATS-W.

Throughout the ATS-W portion of this preparation guide, we will be speaking in terms of what a "good" teacher would do. For the purposes of this guide, a "good" teacher is a teacher whose approach to a problem is consistent with the principles and strategies that would earn a credited response on the ATS-W. During our discussions of what a "good" teacher is and what a "good" teacher does, keep a couple of very important things in mind:

- We are not interested in judging whether any particular teacher is "good" or "bad," nor do we mean to denigrate anyone's efforts as a teacher. Instead, we are attempting to place in the simplest possible terms how you should be thinking when considering answer choices.

- Whether the approaches that NES attributes to a "good" teacher could actually be accomplished in the school where you teach is not relevant to this test. The kinds of answer choices you should be picking on the multiple-choice questions should reflect what a "good" teacher would do in an "ideal" situation. Don't worry about whether logistics, budget, or the policies of your administration would eliminate an answer choice. Instead, your focus should always be on what you think NES wants you to say. It, after all, has the final say in what answer is going to be counted as the correct one.

Although we will go into all of these features in greater detail throughout the book, here's a rundown of the attributes of a "good" teacher according to NES.

A Good Teacher

- Uses developmentally appropriate practices
- Helps students feel good about their successes
- Is sincere in her/his praise of students
- Alters her/his approach depending on what will work best for the individual student
- Teaches to higher levels of Bloom's taxonomy
- Avoids stereotyping students based on race, gender, or socioeconomic status
- Teaches to students who have a variety of learning styles
- Recognizes achievement in all means of intelligence
- Is sensitive to various skill levels and individual needs in the classroom
- Is flexible in her/his approach
- Is sensitive to the needs of her/his students
- Incorporates student interests and learning objectives into the creation of lesson plans
- Provides opportunities for group learning
- Uses a wide variety of assessment techniques
- Has a well-managed classroom where most time is spent on tasks
- Utilizes smooth transitions from one task/topic to another
- Provides a positive classroom environment free from negativity and bias
- Never reprimands or humiliates students in front of her/his peers
- Avoids sarcasm
- Respects the chain-of-command within the school, district, and state
- Works cooperatively with parents and other teachers but always maintains a share of responsibility for the success of her/his students

- Refers parents to proper higher administration whenever required, but avoids unnecessarily "passing the buck"

- Is always looking for opportunities to improve as a teacher

- Makes strong connections in the community

- Upholds the laws pertaining to education in all circumstances

For many multiple-choice questions on the ATS-W, you should be in pretty good shape if you keep in mind that you are looking for what the test writers want you to say. Just remember that you should be picking answers that serve the best interests of your students and the school above your own interests.

MY TEST IS IN THREE DAYS—WHAT DO I DO?

If you don't have time to review everything in this book in the kind of detail that you would like, focus on the following areas:

- Review the introduction.

- Study the chapters on writing the essays.

- Study the chapter on scientific reasoning.

- Take the practice tests at the end of the book.

However, to get your best possible results on the LAST and ATS-W, you cannot afford to skip anything in this book. While there is certainly room to study *more* than what is outlined in this book (you could, for example, review a U.S. history textbook or go over your notes from your Educational Psychology course), there is no shortcut to our approach. You can only do your best if you take the time to absorb the important information contained in the following pages. Now let's get cracking!

PART II

Content Review

2

Basic Writing Skills

BASIC WRITING SKILLS FOR THE LAST AND ATS-W

The writing assignment is a crucial part of both the LAST and the ATS-W: The essay makes up 20 percent of your total test score, and there is some question as to whether a candidate can earn a passing grade on the test as a whole without earning a passing grade on the essay. While there are unique elements in both the LAST and the ATS-W writing assignments that we will discuss shortly, the two exams are similar in that they require you to demonstrate a command of basic writing skills. Accordingly, the next several pages are designed to review some basic writing mechanics.

GRAMMAR REVIEW

Grammar rules are so numerous that not many people can use them all perfectly. Your focus for the LAST and ATS-W, however, should be to have a good command of some of the more basic rules of grammar. Before test day, make sure you understand the rules discussed in this chapter.

Subject-Verb Agreement

Each sentence in your essay should contain both a subject and a verb. The subject of your sentence should contain a noun (a person, place, or thing), and the noun and verb should agree. Here are some examples of subject-verb agreement:

Teachers agree . . .
Students learn . . .
The author creates . . .
The problem explains . . .
The assignment was . . .

The nouns (people, places, and things) and pronouns (words that take the place of nouns) in your sentences must match the verbs in your sentence. Singular nouns need singular verbs. Plural nouns need plural verbs.

Here are some more examples:

Singular Nouns and Verbs	Plural Nouns and Verbs
the dog barks	the dogs bark
everyone waits	the congressmen wait
each drives	they drive
nobody hopes	the members hope
happiness is	emotions are

Add the correct form of the verb in italics to each of these sentences.

1. Your strategy is a good one, but you forgot that the cats _____ after they eat. (*to sleep*)

2. Sunshine _____ me happy. (*to make*)

3. Aunt Mary and Uncle Fred _____ in a beautiful condo on the beach. (*to live*)

4. Do you think that he _____ your novel? (*to like*)

Did you come up with these answers?

1. sleep

2. makes

3. live

4. likes

Not only will you want to be sure you are consistent in your subject-verb agreements in your essay, but you may also be asked to spot this type of error in a multiple-choice question on the LAST.

Transitions

Transitions bring you from point A to point B smoothly. Some common transition words and phrases include:

> however, because of, furthermore, therefore, on the other hand, despite, as a result, and, nor, or, for, but, although, while, otherwise, next

Try connecting the following sets of ideas using transition words and phrases such as those above.

1. John was a genius. _____ it was no surprise that he was awarded the school's highest honor.

2. _____ their concepts are quite different, biology and chemistry are both considered natural sciences.

3. The mayor didn't know how to handle the six feet of snow that had accumulated. _____ he knew that something had to be done quickly.

Here are some suggested answers:

1. Therefore/Consequently/As a result

2. Although/Despite

3. But/However

Parallel Construction

Make sure all of the verbs (the action words) you use are in the same tense. Here's a sentence that makes a parallel construction error:

Rachel ran into the building, then she was unlocking the front door to her apartment.

Ran is in the past tense. It means that the action happened at an earlier time. But **was unlocking** means that she was doing it right then in the present tense. The two tenses don't match. Instead, the sentence should read:

Rachel ran into the building, then she unlocked the front door to her apartment.

Here are some other examples of parallel construction errors. See if you can fix them.

1. George is the president of the Barbra Streisand fan club. He loved leading each of the monthly meetings.

2. I found the tissues under the sink. You say that they are in the pantry.

3. Frannie will turn off the computer when she is finished with it. She turned off the monitor as well.

Did you come up with these answers?

1. George was the president of the Barbra Streisand fan club. He loved leading each of the monthly meetings.

    -or-

    George is the president of the Barbra Streisand fan club. He loves leading each of the monthly meetings.

2. I found the tissues under the sink. You said that they were in the pantry.

3. Frannie will turn off the computer when she is finished with it. She will turn off the monitor as well.

    -or-

    Frannie turned off the computer when she was finished with it. She turned off the monitor as well.

Punctuation

Periods end a complete thought (a complete thought contains both a subject and a verb). **Commas** indicate pauses, separate items in a series, and separate nonessential phrases from the rest of a sentence. **Semicolons** separate two related and complete thoughts in a sentence, and separate groups of words in a series that already contain commas.

Parts of Speech

Adjectives are words that describe or modify nouns. Some examples of adjectives are *orange*, *big*, *fast*, and *hairy*. **Adverbs** describe or modify verbs and other adjectives. Adverbs usually, but not always, end in the letters *ly*. Some examples of adverbs are *quickly*, *frantically*, *bravely*, *artfully*, and *never*.

Choose the correct words in italics for each sentence below:

1. Frank Menches, of Akron, Ohio, was *alleged/allegedly* the *first/firstly* person to use ground beef in a sandwich when his concession stand ran out of sausages.

2. The wolf prowled *hungry/hungrily* through the woods, following *close/closely* behind Red Riding Hood.

3. It is easy to identify the *correct/correctly* written sentence if you have *adequate/adequately* familiarized yourself with the rules of grammar.

Here are the answers:

1. allegedly, first

2. hungrily, closely

3. correctly, adequately

Placement of Modifiers

Modifiers must be placed as closely as possible to the word they describe. Can you tell what's wrong with the following sentence?

Having been afraid of the dark since he was a boy, the forest was very scary for Hubert.

While we can figure out what the author means by this sentence, the sentence is not grammatically correct. The problem with the sentence is that the modifier ("Having been afraid of the dark since he was a boy") is next to, and thus modifying, the wrong noun. As the sentence is written, it says that the forest has been afraid of the dark since he was a boy. The correct version should look like this:

Having been afraid of the dark since he was a boy, Hubert thought the forest was very scary.

Errors with misplaced modifiers can be hard to spot sometimes because we are used to reading and listening for what people mean to say, not for what they actually say. The people grading your essay, however, will not be so forgiving. To help you get comfortable with spotting and avoiding these types of mistakes, here are a few more examples of sentences with misplaced modifiers:

Running frantically for the subway, Teresa's coat pocket was caught on the turnstile.

Was Teresa's coat pocket running frantically for the subway? That's what this sentence says. It should read:

Running frantically for the subway, Teresa caught her coat pocket on the turnstile.

Burrowing through the woodwork, I hated those termites.

Who was burrowing through the woodwork? Write the sentence so it says what it's supposed to say. It should read:

Burrowing through the woodwork, those termites inspired my hatred.

The hungry falcon spied the field mouse, soaring through the sky in search of prey.

What was soaring through the sky in search of prey? Not the field mouse. The sentence should read:

The hungry falcon, soaring through the sky in search of prey, spied the field mouse.

Grammar Checklist for Essay Writing and Multiple-Choice Questions

Most grammar errors you will encounter will come from the following list:

Subject-Verb Agreement

(Singular subjects get singular verbs; plural subjects get plural verbs.)

Wrong: **One** of the musicians besieged by screaming fans **are** trying to run away.
Right: **One** of the musicians besieged by screaming fans **is** trying to run away.

Parallel Construction

(Use a consistent verb tense throughout your sentence.)

Wrong: **To eat** at Shultzy's is **like finding** peace on Earth.
Right: **Eating** at Shultzy's is **like finding** peace on Earth.

Pronoun Agreement

(Use singular/plural and gender-appropriate pronouns accordingly; do not use a singular pronoun if it will create ambiguity.)

Wrong: After **Cara and Neesha** argued for a while, **she** agreed that investing the money was best. (Ambiguous)
Right: After **Cara and Neesha** argued for a while, **they** agreed that investing the money was best. (Inserting either "Cara" or "Neesha" in place of "they" also works.)

Faulty Comparison

(Make sure your sentence is comparing the two things you intend to compare.)

Wrong: **The peaches** at Adam's fruit stand are far superior to **David**. (You don't mean to compare peaches with David, but that's what this sentence is doing.)
Right: **The peaches** at Adam's fruit stand are far superior to **the peaches** at David's fruit stand.

Run-on Sentence

(Don't forget to use periods at the end of a complete sentence.)

Wrong: I was pretty nervous when I showed up at the tryouts, and then I saw that I was the shortest person there, and I got even more nervous.
Right: I was pretty nervous when I showed up at the tryouts. **Then** I saw that I was the shortest person there, and I got even more nervous.

Misplaced Modifier

(Put the modifying phrase next to the noun it modifies.)

Wrong: Having rested all day, **a nap** did not seem interesting to Tony.
Right: Having rested all day, **Tony** was not interested in taking a nap.

Quantity Words

(How many things are you talking about? Can they be counted or not?)

When comparing two things, use *better, taller,* or *more*. When comparing more than two things, use *best, tallest,* or *most*.

Wrong: Between ham and bacon, I like bacon most.
Right: Between ham and bacon, I like bacon **more.**

Wrong: Of all the players on the team, Fred is taller.
Right: Of all the players on the team, Fred is the **tallest.**

If it's something you can count (such as jellybeans, students, or pencils), use *number*. If it's something you can't count (such as gravy, love, or freedom), use *amount*.

Wrong: That's a huge amount of jellybeans!
Right: That's a huge **number** of jellybeans!

3

The LAST Essay

ORGANIZATION AND PRESENTATION OF THE ESSAY FOR THE LAST

THE LAST ESSAY ASSIGNMENT

In Chapter 2, we reviewed some basic writing mechanics that NES will be evaluating in your essay. In addition to being required to demonstrate a proficiency in grammar, spelling, and sentence structure, you will also be graded on your ability to organize and present a cogent argument. The purpose of this chapter is to give you the tools you will need to evaluate the arguments in the essay assignment and to enable you to present your ideas in an organized fashion.

The first step in writing a strong essay on the LAST is to understand exactly what the nature of the assignment is. The writing assignment consists of the following three parts:

- A question that is up for debate
- An argument in favor of the issue presented
- An argument against the issue presented

Here's an example of what an essay prompt may look like on the LAST.

Should the possession of handguns by private citizens be made illegal in the United States? The arguments below present opposing views on this question.

In favor of making illegal the possession of handguns by private citizens in the United States. The presence of handguns in the United States poses a significant threat to the safety of its citizens. Thousands of people are killed or seriously injured by handguns every year in this country. Countless innocent lives are lost due to the presence of handguns in private homes—either from accidental shootings or from domestic disputes that have escalated to violence. Armed criminals threaten the safety of law-abiding citizens in both urban and rural areas. Further, with suicide rates at an unacceptable level, any means to facilitate suicide should be strictly controlled by the government. Therefore, out of the interests of public safety and welfare, private citizens should not be allowed to own handguns.

Opposed to making illegal the possession of handguns by private citizens in the United States. The United States Constitution is very clear on the matter of gun ownership: Citizens of the United States have the right to bear arms. Thousands of law-abiding citizens responsibly keep and use firearms for legitimate activities such as hunting. Although gun accidents are of course tragic, the rights established in the Constitution are quite clear. These rights are important because private citizens should have the freedom to protect themselves in their homes. Without handguns, many citizens would feel defenseless and would be left vulnerable to burglaries or home invasions. Finally, it is important to remember that the constitutional provision that grants citizens the right to bear arms was inspired by the concern that the government's power might need to be kept in check by the citizenry. Where would we be today if our forefathers did not have firearms with which to fight in the revolution?

Should it be legal for citizens of the United States to possess handguns?

In an essay written for a general audience of educated adults:

- evaluate the opposing arguments related to this question;

- state your position on whether it should be legal for citizens of the United States to possess handguns; and

- defend your position with logical arguments and appropriate examples.

The mistake that most essay writers make on the LAST, especially when faced with a topic that is particularly controversial, is that they get so tied up in the topic they fail to meet the requirements of the writing assignment. Many people make the mistake of thinking that the essay is simply asking the writer to state his or her point of view on the topic. A closer reading of the assignment reveals that an important part of the essay is to evaluate the opposing arguments related to the question.

Evaluating the Opposing Arguments

Evaluating an argument is not the same thing as saying whether you agree or disagree with the argument's conclusion. Instead, an evaluation of an argument should focus on the logic of the argument and the relevance and persuasiveness of the evidence that the author offers in support of the claim. Your essay, therefore, should include some discussion of the following two questions:

- Does the evidence the argument uses necessarily support the main point, or are there other plausible interpretations of the evidence that might support a different conclusion?

- Does the argument fail to mention other relevant information that might weaken the argument?

Let's look at the arguments regarding whether the possession of handguns should be illegal to see how you might apply these questions to your essay.

In favor of making the possession of handguns illegal:

1. Thousands of people are killed or seriously injured by handguns every year in the United States.

Supporting a point with statistical evidence is a pretty common method for developing an argument. The author is of course making an implied claim that the fact that handguns are legal has something to do with this undesirable outcome. There are, however, two arguable assumptions behind this piece of evidence. First, the author does not establish that making handguns illegal will have any impact on the number of people killed or injured by handguns. An important issue to consider in your essay would be whether the prohibition of handguns would necessarily keep them out of the hands of criminals. If the people who are responsible for the vast majority of deaths and injuries due to handguns are those who will continue to have handguns regardless of their legality, then it would be foolish to expect that making handguns illegal would significantly reduce these injuries and fatalities. Second, the author fails to consider that the *net effect* of having legal handguns available might be that some lives are saved and some injuries are avoided due to people being able to protect themselves from people who would otherwise cause them harm. If the argument is truly motivated by a concern for public safety, it would be important to consider whether society as a whole would be safer with the presence of legal handguns.

2. Fatalities result from accidental shootings and domestic disputes when a handgun is present in the home.

This evidence relies on the principle that if fatalities result from an accident involving a product or from the use of a product to commit a homicide in the course of a domestic dispute, then it should be made illegal. In evaluating this argument, it would be useful to consider whether our society accepts this principle as being universally true. Clearly, fatalities result from accidents involving other items in the home, such as power tools, but we don't consider that fact to be compelling evidence in favor of making power tools illegal. Similarly, there are fatalities in domestic disputes that are the result of assaults with kitchen knives, but we wouldn't consider it to be a rational response to make kitchen knives illegal.

While this line of reasoning does establish that the inherent danger of an item is not generally regarded as sufficient to make the item illegal, there is of course an important distinction among handguns, power tools, and kitchen knives: Handguns do not have the same kind of everyday domestic function that power tools and kitchen knives do. This is the kind of distinction you should be highlighting when stating and defending your own position on the topic. However, with respect to the task of evaluating the evidence in the argument, it's important to point out that as a society we are accustomed to evaluating issues based on multiple factors, and one specific feature or consequence of something is not always sufficient to compel us to act or behave in a certain way.

3. Armed criminals threaten the safety of law-abiding citizens.

The argument reasons that if handguns are made illegal, then armed criminals will cease to be a threat. There is a rather dubious assumption that criminals will necessarily observe the prohibition on handguns and that making handguns illegal will therefore prevent criminals from acquiring them. It may very well be the case that if handguns were made illegal, then *only* criminals would have handguns. Further, if it truly is a problem that armed criminals threaten the safety of law-abiding citizens, another possible solution to that problem would be to issue handguns to everybody. Simply stated, the fact that a problem exists does not necessarily mean that there is only one possible way to solve the problem, nor does it mean that a proposed solution will necessarily work.

4. Any means used to facilitate suicide should be strictly controlled by the government.

Note the use of the word *any* here, and consider what this principle would mean were it invoked. Should buildings larger than two stories be made illegal because someone might jump off of one? In evaluating arguments, be especially sensitive to the use of absolute wording or statements of policy or principle to which, as a society, we make exceptions every day. Suicide is undoubtedly a tragic thing, but we are accustomed to balancing competing considerations in establishing rules for society.

As with the analysis of the claims regarding household accidents and domestic disputes, there is room to discuss the difference between a handgun and a tall building. It could be argued that while the evidence offered is too absolute to be persuasive, the cost to society of suicides resulting from handgun use is greater than the benefit of having handguns be legal. The process of weighing these competing considerations will be an important element of your essay.

Opposed to making the possession of handguns illegal:

1. The right to bear arms is protected by the United States Constitution.

The largest danger is that you could write volumes examining this simple claim. First of all, the part of the Constitution that provides this right is the Second Amendment. This brings up the point that the Constitution contains Amendments, an indication that the Constitution is a document that has been historically subject to change and has been modified and improved over the course of our nation's history. Further, precedence exists in the Constitution in which specific provisions have been overturned when it was revealed that those provisions had a net negative effect on society (there was a Constitutional Amendment prohibiting the possession and sale of alcohol, but that Amendment was later reversed by the introduction of another Amendment). So, the fact that the right to bear arms is a part of the Constitution does not necessarily indicate that the idea is beyond contestation. Certainly, a citizen's right to bear arms is already restricted to some degree: Your next-door neighbor does not have the right to have assault rifles and artillery pieces in the backyard. So, while the Second Amendment does exist, we accept that the Constitution can be changed and that certain provisions are subject to some degree of interpretation.

2. Firearms are used for legitimate purposes such as hunting.

Notice how a claim about firearms in general is being used to support an argument about handguns. How many hunters are out hunting for deer or ducks with a .38 special? This evidence can be dismissed for the most part because it does not seem to apply to the argument at hand. Competitive target shooting with a handgun could very well be considered a legitimate purpose, and if you choose to discuss that in greater detail in your essay you would want to weigh that consideration versus some of the other issues raised in the two arguments.

3. Citizens should have the right to protect themselves in their homes.

Does this claim necessarily mean that handguns should be legal? Can citizens be afforded a sufficient amount of self-protection without having handguns available? These issues are important to consider because the principle as stated would allow a citizen to protect his or her home with landmines or flamethrowers. Again, we are accustomed to accepting some restrictions on our freedoms in the interests of what is best for society. Given that a citizen who wishes to have a firearm for home protection could opt for a shotgun or a rifle, it's not entirely clear why the right to protect oneself in one's home is sufficient to establish that handguns should not be made illegal.

4. The government's power might need to be kept in check by the citizenry.

This is an interesting appeal to the rationale behind the introduction of the Second Amendment to the Constitution: The framers of the Constitution were influenced a great deal by their own experiences in the American Revolution. The colonists were able to successfully overthrow the authority of the British Crown because they had the tools to resist what they considered to be a tyrannical ruler. While this rationale was clearly applicable to late eighteenth-century America when the weapons used by the army and weapons used by private citizens weren't all that different, it doesn't resonate as that compelling a rationale in the argument against making handguns illegal. Whether you have a handgun isn't going to make all that much of a difference if you find yourself having to keep the government's power in check: A handgun isn't going to be much of a match for a government with access to tanks and machine guns. Unless the argument against making handguns illegal is part of an argument in favor of granting citizens access to any types of weapons, this particular piece of supporting evidence isn't all that convincing.

Stating Your Opinion

First of all, you should understand that it doesn't matter which side of the argument you choose to defend as far as your essay score is concerned. What's important is how you arrive at your decision.

As you've seen from the analysis of the two arguments, a lot of attention has been paid to demonstrating that the reasons given in support of each argument are not as absolutely true as the arguments for each side would have you believe. What you are left with, then, is a task which requires you to evaluate the relative strengths of competing considerations: In this case, you are weighing the interests of public safety against the protection of individual rights. You've also probably arrived at the conclusion that you don't completely agree with either side of the argument.

The remainder of your essay should be spent developing your own position. To do this, you will need to examine to what degree the competing interests revealed in the two arguments can be reconciled. For example, you may decide to take the position that it should be legal for individuals to possess handguns in the interest of maintaining individual rights, but that those rights should be accompanied by the individual's accepting responsibility for having a handgun up to the point of being held criminally responsible for injuries or deaths resulting from the use of that handgun. To the degree that the competing interests cannot be reconciled, you will need to take a position with respect to which set of interests are the more important ones. Is a threat to public safety an acceptable consequence of broad freedoms? Your essay should address this issue.

Finally, you should feel free to introduce other considerations that you think are important in evaluating the question. Does the presence of handguns in the United States have any role in the general level of violence in this country? Do police act differently because handguns are prevalent in our society? While the arguments presented in the essay assignment will surely touch on some of the main considerations in evaluating the question at hand, they will not necessarily cover *all* angles. If you think an important consideration is missing from the essay assignment, then you should present it when defending your own position.

A Typical Essay Outline for the LAST

I. **Introductory paragraph**

State the question that is to be answered, briefly summarize the primary considerations on which each argument relies, explain that the two arguments as presented are not entirely convincing, and establish your position (which will generally involve picking one side with certain modifications).

II. **Evaluate the first argument**

Examine the evidence used to support the argument's position. Evaluate whether the evidence offered might also be consistent with opposing points of view and consider whether the argument has missed other important factors that would weaken the connection between the evidence and the argument's main point. Depending on the scope of the evidence you are discussing, this may take more than one paragraph.

III. **Evaluate the second argument**

Exactly what you did in part II, but of course focusing on the content of the second argument. Again, this may take more than one paragraph depending on the scope of the evidence provided in the argument.

IV. **State your opinion**

Reconcile the competing considerations to the degree that you can. If you cannot completely reconcile the competing considerations, choose which considerations you find to be more compelling and defend your choice. If there are relevant considerations that neither argument has mentioned, bring them up now. Your final position will most likely be somewhere in between the two extremes presented in the writing assignment. This part of your essay may also take more than one paragraph, depending on the degree to which you were able to reconcile the competing considerations and on whether you think there are important considerations that neither argument addressed.

V. **Conclusion**

Briefly summarize your position by stating that while neither argument is entirely convincing as presented, they do bring up key issues fundamental to answering the question. Given the relative importance of the considerations presented and whatever additional considerations you have presented, it is clear that one answer is better than the other provided that certain other conditions are present.

A Sample Essay

The issue of gun ownership is an issue that inspires much controversy. While some people argue that the possession of a firearm is a constitutional right that must be upheld, others maintain that gun possession poses a major threat to personal safety. Although both sides are compelling, in the final analysis, I believe that personal safety comes first.

I agree with the first author, who takes seriously the threat guns pose to personal safety. I agree that countless individuals are injured or killed by handguns every year, although I think this author's point would be better supported by statistics reflecting these fatalities. I also agree that having guns in the home increases the likelihood of accidental shootings, but I think the author should have mentioned the possibility of accidents involving children. Parents who fail to store firearms properly are putting their children in jeopardy. I believe the author's weakest point is the one he makes about criminals. It would be foolish to suggest that outlawing guns would prevent criminals from obtaining guns, since criminals don't necessarily follow laws to begin with. Furthermore, in all likelihood, outlawing guns would have no effect on the number of suicides, since individuals could find other ways to end their lives. I agree with this author's platform, but I feel he could provide better support for his conclusions.

I disagree with the second author, who favors upholding the constitutional right to bear arms. While I recognize gun ownership is a constitutional right, I would argue that the Constitution has contained many unethical statutes in the past, including the right to own slaves. Just because something is constitutional doesn't mean it is right. Author two cites personal protection as a reason for possessing guns in the home, but handguns are more likely to be fired accidentally than they are to be used for protection. Furthermore, this author fails to make a distinction between handguns and other firearms when he asserts that citizens use guns for all sorts of legitimate reasons, including hunting. Handguns are not used for hunting; they are weapons designed to kill people, not animals. The author's final point is also fundamentally flawed. We are living in an entirely different social and political climate than that of our forefathers. We are not fighting a revolution, nor did our forefathers secure American independence through the use of handguns. Author two must find better support for his claims if he is to adequately defend his position.

It is clear from my critique of these authors where I stand on the issue of handguns. I think the possession of handguns is a right that should be overturned. It is far too easy for children to get a hold of handguns and injure themselves or others. Consider all of the shootings that have occurred in schools over the last few years. While I agree that the rights of individuals should be protected, I believe it is the government's job to defend the lives of its citizens by making handguns illegal.

While neither argument is entirely convincing, I agree with the first author that the best way to protect our citizens would be for Congress to ban handgun possession. If our personal safety isn't secured first, our personal liberty won't matter.

A FEW MORE WORDS OF ADVICE

The model essay above gives you an idea of how this essay can be written, but it is by no means the only way. If you feel you need additional help with writing this essay, you can try reading various newspapers and magazines that analyze events and issues. For example, the *New York Times* is a wonderful resource and can expose you to a sophisticated writing style; the paper's Editorial and Op-Ed pages are particularly helpful for understanding how to compose a critical argument to a complex issue.

4

The ATS-W Essay

ORGANIZATION AND PRESENTATION OF THE ESSAY FOR THE ATS-W

THE ATS-W ESSAY ASSIGNMENT

As with your LAST essay, your ATS-W essay will need to exhibit a command of the writing mechanics discussed in Chapter 2. This essay will differ from the essay you write for the LAST in that your ATS-W essay will require you to draw on your experience as an educator and on what you've learned in your education courses.

The ATS-W essay assignment will provide you with an educational goal and ask you to do the following three things:

- Explain why the goal is an important one.

- Present two strategies you would use in pursuit of the goal.

- Explain why your strategies would be effective in achieving the goal.

You should not under any circumstances disagree with the goal described in the essay assignment. Whether you personally agree or disagree with the goal set forth in the writing assignment, keep in mind that the writing assignment will be graded based on the assumption that the educational goal set forth in the assignment is a worthy one.

Here's an example of what an essay prompt might look like on the ATS-W.

GOALS FOR EDUCATIONAL EXCELLENCE

Goal 7: **Be aware of the presence of gender bias in the classroom. Make students aware of gender bias, and provide students with a classroom environment where gender bias does not exist.**

In an essay written for a group of New York State educators, frame your response by identifying a grade level/subject area for which you are prepared to teach, then:

- explain the importance of minimizing instances of gender bias in the classroom and of making students aware of the presence of gender bias;

- describe two strategies you would use to achieve this educational goal; and

- explain why the strategies you describe would be effective in achieving this educational goal.

Be sure to specify a grade level/subject area in your essay, and frame your ideas so that an educator certified at your level (i.e., elementary or secondary) will be able to understand the basis for your response.

There are two common mistakes you will want to be sure to avoid when writing your essay. The first mistake is that test takers do not accept the value of the educational goal provided in the essay assignment. Even if for some you reason believe that gender bias *should* exist in the classroom (e.g., gender bias exists in the real world, so students should be equipped to face these realities), you need to be mindful of your primary goal: passing the ATS-W. So go along with the goal outlined in the essay assignment and explain why you feel the goal is an important one. The second mistake that test takers make is that they forget to specify a grade level and subject area. It is especially important to note that even if you are teaching elementary school and you have the same students all day, you need to indicate in your essay that you are teaching all subjects. While it might seem a commonsense assumption to you that a first grade teacher is teaching all subjects, the people who are grading your essay insist that you make that point clear. So remember the following:

- Agree with the educational goal provided in the essay assignment.

- Indicate both your grade level and subject area, even if it's to say that you are teaching all subjects.

Getting Ready to Write

Assuming you are comfortable with your writing mechanics (if you aren't, spend some time reviewing Chapter 2), the biggest challenge in writing your ATS-W essay will be coming up with two strategies that you will use in pursuit of the educational goal provided in the writing assignment. You will of course want to draw on your own experience in the classroom, but in the event you are short on inspiration, you should consider whether any of the following approaches might be effective in achieving the stated educational goal:

- **Consultation with a professional within the school.** Depending on the nature of the writing assignment, this could be anyone ranging from an experienced colleague to the school's special education professional. If you are going to consult with a third party as one of your strategies, be careful that your strategy isn't simply dumping the problem on somebody else.

- **The types of assignments and assessments you use in the classroom.** Are group projects a more suitable way of achieving the stated goal, or would you be better off assigning individual homework? The type of assessment you utilize could also affect how successful you might be in the pursuit of the educational goal. Would a term project be a better approach than a norm-referenced test?

- **Classroom design and techniques of classroom management.** Depending on what you wish to accomplish, is it a more prudent approach to have desks lined up in rows, or would you be better off if the desks were arranged in a circle?

- **Bringing in outside speakers or taking students on field trips.** Remember, one of the features of a "good" teacher is that the teacher integrates the classroom into the community at large. For many assignments, a "real world" component provides a worthwhile strategy for achieving the stated educational goal.

Regardless of what two strategies you choose, you should be comfortable with the idea that there are many different approaches NES will find acceptable. Because of that, you are not expected to guess which two approaches they think are best. Your primary concern should be to come up with two approaches that could plausibly help achieve the educational goal and to adequately explain how that might happen.

A Typical Essay Outline for the ATS-W

I. Indicate your grade level and subject area.

Using the template from NES's own guidebook, any of the following is acceptable:

Grade level/subject area: tenth grade, Spanish

Grade level/subject area: second grade, all subjects

Grade level/subject area: kindergarten, molecular biology

Okay, maybe that last one would be a bit weird, but something as simple as one of these is a fine way to start.

II. Explain why the educational goal is worthwhile.

You can get a lot of mileage out of this part of the essay if you consider the needs of various types of students. For example, if the educational goal is to create a positive educational environment for students with disabilities in a mainstream classroom, you should also explain why the presence of students with disabilities can be of benefit to students who do not have disabilities (such as the promotion of greater awareness of people who are different). The pursuit of pretty much any educational goal can have benefits for students beyond those who are specifically mentioned in the goal. With a little creativity, you should be able to see and thus explain how all students can benefit.

III. Present and explain your first strategy.

Be as specific as possible when you explain what it is you intend to do to achieve the stated educational goal. Instead of saying, "I would assign group work," get into the details of the assignment and give some idea of how you would assign the members of the groups. Tailor the specifics of your strategy to the goal at hand so it becomes very easy for you to explain why your strategy will be effective. Longer essays seem to garner higher scores than shorter essays, so don't be afraid to elaborate.

IV. Present and explain your second strategy.

Do what you did in item III, but of course elaborate on a second strategy.

V. Conclusion.

Briefly restate your two strategies and state that these two approaches will achieve the laudable goal that has been presented in the assignment.

A Sample Essay

Grade level/subject area: ninth grade/social studies

Gender bias should be removed from the classroom to whatever degree it can be. This is the case because both male and female students are negatively affected by the presence of such bias. Female students may be conditioned to mistakenly believe that certain academic or career paths are unattainable, and male students may be encouraged to think in a manner that prevents them from seeing and appreciating equally valid points of view that would give them a greater understanding of the world and thus greater chances for future success.

These issues are particularly salient in a classroom made up of young teenagers: These students are in the midst of exploring their own identities and are particularly vulnerable to making inappropriate generalizations about gender roles. Additionally, the students are at a point in their cognitive development where they are more likely to identify and question some of the assumptions that are made regarding gender roles. Since it is self-evident that one of the goals of education should be to enable each student to fully realize his/her potential, the classroom teacher should work to remove any obstacles. In my ninth grade social studies classroom, I would implement the following strategies to enable both teacher and students to become aware of and work to avoid instances of gender bias.

To help guarantee that I am not introducing gender bias into the classroom, I would establish some basic rules of order for classroom discussion that would curtail at least some of the effect of male students' aggressiveness in discussion groups. Specifically, I would arrange the students in a circular seating arrangement and would work around the circle to give all students a chance to contribute to the conversation. To avoid the situation in which students blurt out statements and interrupt a classmate who is talking, I would make it clear that the student who is speaking "has the floor" until the student indicates that he/she is finished speaking. While it would be a long-term goal for the school year to have less rigid rules of order for discussion as students get used to allowing classmates to communicate ideas without interruption, the option would always be there to implement these rules of order if the situation warranted it. In this manner, I would expect that all students would be treated equally with respect to gender. Additionally, I would keep careful track of which students I call on to answer questions in class when we are not having group discussions. I would later reflect on these results to see if I am introducing any kind of bias (gender or otherwise) into the classroom. It would be important for me to be aware of the fact that some forms of bias can be present at a subconscious level, and to effectively address these biases I would need to objectively analyze my methods.

By managing classroom participation more actively, I would expect that nobody in the classroom would be made to feel as if his/her contribution to classroom discussion is unwelcome or unimportant. I would further reinforce the idea in my students' minds by highlighting meaningful contributions made by some of the more timid students in the class. The important lesson to learn for the long term is that the people who are the loudest or most aggressive are not necessarily the only people with something valuable to say and that something important is lost when a group operates under that assumption.

Another strategy I would implement in addressing the issue of gender bias would be to embed a lesson on gender bias into an examination of current events. With events in the news such as the fall of the Taliban, the reconstruction of the Afghan government, and the presence of such newsworthy people as National Security Advisor Condoleezza Rice, there are some terrific opportunities to have students examine the realities of gender bias on a global scale and to consider some of the myths of gender differences that exist in our own country. The presence of such strong role models as Condoleezza Rice or Senator Hillary Clinton stands as evidence that women can achieve prominent places in our society.

While my discussion of the abuse of women perpetrated by the Taliban would focus on the fact that they were victimized solely because they were women, I would not discuss Condoleezza Rice or Hillary Clinton in terms of their gender but would instead focus on their accomplishments. The reason I would make this distinction in my teaching is that I want to model for my students the idea that bias is only completely gone when it is not present and we stop thinking about the distinction at all. Hillary Clinton isn't a viable presidential candidate in spite of the fact that she's a woman or because of the fact that she's a woman; she's a viable presidential candidate because of her qualities as a person. The topic I would close with in this discussion would be to ask the class why there are so few women serving as United States senators when it is clear from examples such as Hillary Clinton, Elizabeth Dole, or Barbara Boxer that well-qualified women do exist.

What I would hope to get from this discussion is for students to see that gender bias does not have to be as oppressive as what women experienced under the rule of the Taliban for it to be present: Bias can exist in more subtle ways yet can still have a negative effect. To evaluate whether students are understanding the concept I am trying to communicate, I would ask them to work in small groups and do a presentation of one element of gender bias that exists in the school or the community/country as a whole. An interesting point to bring up after the presentations would be to note how many presentations focused on gender bias against females and how many presentations focused on gender bias against males: Does this also represent some form of gender bias?

By managing how classroom discussion is conducted and by utilizing details from current events, my students will learn in an environment where gender bias is reduced to some degree. Additionally, my students will have learned to question the assumptions they make about gender and it is hoped that, as a result, they will have a broader conception about what they and their classmates can accomplish.

5

Math and Science

MATH AND SCIENCE

Let us clear something up for you: The Math and Science section of the LAST does not require complete and thorough knowledge of every scientific fact and mathematical formula you've ever heard. You will not be asked about things like the Krebs Cycle, Avogadro's number, or electron shells. What you will have to do is apply basic knowledge in math and science to real-life situations (such as calculating a 15-percent tip on a restaurant bill). As with other portions of the LAST, some questions will require you to read passages about scientific topics and answer questions based on the given information. Remember, *every* teacher who's been certified to teach in New York has passed this test, so you don't have to dust off your college science textbooks and memorize the contents. If that were the case, no one but the science and math teachers would be able to pass the test!

Take a Deep Breath and Relax

This next section will cover everything you'll need to do well on the LAST math and science questions. We will review the basics you need and, more importantly, we will teach you how to crack the various types of math and science questions you'll see. You will use the global test-taking strategies introduced in the beginning of this book, plus some other math- and science-specific approaches that will help you master the test. So while other test takers are busy trying to memorize the periodic table, you will be working on the real information you need to beat this portion of the LAST.

A LITTLE MATH, A LOT OF COMMON SENSE

To do well on the math questions on the LAST, you will need to review some very basic math such as what an integer is, how to figure out an average, and how to calculate the area of a square. However, more of what you will need to do to solve the math questions is think about how to approach the problem. You'll need to read word problems carefully to figure out what's going on. You'll need to gather and fit together pieces of information to solve problems efficiently and accurately. Our goal is to review all the basic math stuff you'll need, and to teach you how to use the information you have to get to the right answer.

Basic Math Terminology

Digits
Numbers are made up of digits. For example:

In the number 368, 8 is the units digit, 6 is the tens digit, and 3 is the hundreds digit.
In the number .457, 4 is the tenths digit, 5 is the hundredths digit, and 7 is the thousandths digit.

Fractions
Numerator: Top (part)
Denominator: Bottom (whole: the fraction bar means *divide* or *out of*)
To add and subtract: Get a common bottom number (denominator) first.

$$\frac{1}{2} + \frac{2}{3} =$$

$$\frac{3}{6} + \frac{4}{6} = \frac{7}{6}$$

To multiply: Multiply straight across the top and straight across the bottom. If possible, reduce/cancel first.

$$\frac{1}{2} \times \frac{2}{3} = \frac{2}{6} = \frac{1}{3}$$

To divide: Flip the second fraction, and multiply straight across as you did above.

$$\frac{1}{2} \div \frac{2}{3} =$$

$$\frac{1}{2} \times \frac{3}{2} = \frac{3}{4}$$

Decimals

To add and subtract: Make sure you line up the decimal points.

$$\begin{array}{r} 2.58 \\ +3.067 \\ \hline 5.647 \end{array}$$

To multiply: Multiply numbers, count up the number of decimal places to the right of the decimal point in the given numbers, and place the decimal point that many places in from the right in the product.

$$2.5 \times 2.5 = 6.25$$

To divide: Move the decimal point to the right to get rid of it. Move it the same number of places to the right in the number being divided (add zeros if necessary).

$$6.25 \div 1.25 =$$

$$625 \div 125 = 5$$

Turning Complex Fraction Problems into Real-life Examples

Many problems involving fractions and percentages can be turned from problems that evoke unpleasant memories of your high school algebra class into simple exercises that are just like the kinds of things you do every day. The trick is to figure out how to set up the problem. Let's look at the problem below:

6. On Friday, Jane does one-third of her homework. On Saturday, she does one-sixth of the remainder. What fraction of her homework is still left to be done?

(A) $\frac{1}{18}$

(B) $\frac{1}{9}$

(C) $\frac{5}{9}$

(D) $\frac{5}{6}$

Any time you are given a problem with two fractions that you are supposed to apply consecutively, turn the problem into a real-life situation. In this case, let's pretend that Jane's homework assignment is to do 18 problems (to get the real-life number for this problem, multiply the denominators [the bottom numbers] of the two fractions you were given in the problem). On Friday, Jane does one-third of her homework. In our real-life example, that means she did 6 problems on Friday (one-third of 18). On Saturday, Jane does one-sixth of the remainder. First of all, you need to figure out how many problems she has left on Friday. To do this, simply subtract the number of problems she did on Friday (6) from the number of problems in the assignment (18). This means that she had 12 problems left to do on Saturday. Since the problem tells us that Jane did one-sixth of these problems, this means she must have done two more problems on Saturday (don't knock yourself out, Jane). So, in our real-life example, Jane has done 8 problems out of 18. This of course also means that she has 10 problems left to do.

The question asks you to determine what fraction of Jane's homework is still left to be done. Since she has 10 problems left out of 18, the answer should be $\frac{10}{18}$, which of course reduces to $\frac{5}{9}$ (dividing both the numerator and denominator by 2). The answer to this question is therefore answer choice (C).

RATIOS AND PROPORTIONS

While a fraction is a part of a whole, a ratio is a part of a part, like a recipe. If a recipe for four servings calls for four eggs and two cups of milk, the ratio of eggs to milk is 4 to 2, also written 4:2 or 4/2. If the number of servings is increased or decreased, each of the ingredients would increase or decrease accordingly. For example, if you wanted to make only 2 servings of this recipe, you would use half of each ingredient: 2 eggs and 1 cup of milk. Notice that while the actual amount of each ingredient changed, the ratio between the ingredients remained the same. Similarly, if you were to double the number of servings, you would double the amount of each ingredient: 8 eggs and 4 cups of milk.

Try this ratio problem.

7. Team A and Team B play against each other in a series of baseball games. After 24 games, the ratio of wins between Team A and Team B is 5 to 7 with no ties. How many of the 24 games were won by Team A?

(A) 10
(B) 12
(C) 14
(D) 19

Remember that a ratio does not necessarily represent actual numbers. In this problem, the ratio of wins between Team A and Team B is 5 to 7, but these cannot be the actual numbers since the total number of games played was 24, and 5 plus 7 is only 12. If you double the ratio, however, Team A would have won 10 games while Team B won 14 games, bringing the total number of games played to 24. Therefore, answer (A) is the correct number of wins for Team A.

PERCENTAGES

Percentage problems are common on the LAST. You work with percentages in real life all the time—discounts at your favorite stores, and so on. To solve percentage problems easily, turn them into real-life examples just as you did with fraction problem.

8. At Clinton College, 50% of the students have radios. Of the students who have radios, 30% have televisions. What percentage of the students at Clinton College have both a radio and a television?

   (A) 15
   (B) 20
   (C) 40
   (D) 80

For percentage problems, the real-life number you want to use is 100. Why? Because 25 percent of 100 is 25, 50 percent of 100 is 50, 37 percent of 100 is 37, and so on. By using 100 as your real-life number, you get away with not having to do unnecessary computations.

In the problem above, let's suppose that 100 students go to Clinton College. This means that 50 students have radios (50 percent of 100). Thirty percent of those students have televisions as well. So, how do you figure out 30 percent of 50?

Quick Percentages

There are some percents that you don't even need to calculate to figure out.

To get 10% of any number, just divide the number by 10.

$$10\% \text{ of } 300 = 300 \div 10 = 30$$

To get 5% of any number, just find 10% and divide by 2.

$$5\% \text{ of } 300 = 300 \div 10 = 30 \div 2 = 15$$

$$10\% \times \frac{1}{2} = 5\%$$

To get 20% of any number, just find 10% and double it.

$$20\% \text{ of } 300 = 300 \div 10 = 30 \times 2 = 60$$

$$10\% \times 2 = 20\%$$

To find 1% of any number, just divide by 100.

$$1\% \text{ of } 300 = 300 \div 100 = 3$$

To find 2% of any number just find 1% and double it!

$$2\% \text{ of } 300 = 300 \div 100 = 3 \times 2 = 6$$

$$1\% \times 2 = 2\%$$

Back to the Problem

8. At Clinton College, 50% of the students have radios. Of the students who have radios, 30% have televisions. What percentage of the students at Clinton College have both a radio and a television?

   (A) 15
   (B) 20
   (C) 40
   (D) 80

When we left this problem, we needed to figure out 30 percent of 50. Since 30 percent is $3 \times 10\%$, all we really need to do is figure out 10 percent of 50 ($50 \div 10 = 5$). Since $3 \times 10\%$ is 30 percent, then 3 times 5 should give us the correct answer to the question. Go ahead and pick answer choice (A) with confidence.

All percentage problems can be tackled with relative ease if you remember to use 100 as the real-life number and apply the quick percentage techniques mentioned above.

PROBABILITY

Keep in mind that every licensed teacher in New York State has passed this test, so the kinds of probability questions you'll get on the test will be relatively straightforward. All you'll really need to do is follow a couple of simple rules.

1. To figure out the probability of an event, you will need to set up a fraction. The numerator (the number on top) expresses how many outcomes are acceptable. The denominator (the number on the bottom) expresses how many total possibilities exist. For example, the fraction that expresses the probability that a two will come up when a six-sided die is rolled is $\frac{1}{6}$. The top number expresses that only one outcome is acceptable (the number two), and the bottom number expresses that there are six possible outcomes available (one, two, three, four, five, or six). The probability of an even number being rolled, however, would be $\frac{3}{6}$ (expressed in an answer choice as the reduced fraction $\frac{1}{2}$). This is because there are three numbers on the die that are even (two, four, and six) and there are six total numbers on the die.

2. The probability of any individual event is unaffected by what has happened in previous events (i.e., they are independent events). Using the example of a six-sided die, the fact that a two is rolled on five successive rolls does not change the fact that the probability of a two being rolled on the sixth roll is still $\frac{1}{6}$.

Try the following probability question to make sure you've got it.

A two-sided chip is red on one side and black on the other. If you toss the chip into the air 10 times, what is the probability that it will land on red on the tenth toss if it has landed on red six of the preceding nine tosses?

(A) $\frac{1}{10}$

(B) $\frac{1}{5}$

(C) $\frac{1}{4}$

(D) $\frac{1}{2}$

Remember, each toss of the chip is an independent event, so what has happened on the nine preceding tosses doesn't matter. To figure out the answer to this question all you need to do is set up the fraction correctly. Since there is one red side of the chip, your numerator (the top number) should be one. Since there are two sides to the chip, your denominator (the bottom number) should be two. Your answer, therefore, should be answer choice (D), $\frac{1}{2}$.

GEOMETRY AND VISUAL PERCEPTION

Geometry on the LAST is not like most geometry. Rather, you'll have visual questions that can be answered just by looking at a figure or diagram. The most important thing to remember is just to pay attention to what you see and to pick an answer that does what the question is asking you to do. Try the example on the following page.

78. The bakery sells four sizes of cakes, as shown below. Each cake has twice the number of servings as the next smaller cake. If Cake A has 4 servings, which fraction of cake would give you the largest piece?

Cake A   Cake B   Cake C   Cake D

(A) $\dfrac{1}{2}$ of Cake A

(B) $\dfrac{1}{4}$ of Cake B

(C) $\dfrac{1}{8}$ of Cake C

(D) $\dfrac{1}{10}$ of Cake D

The answer is (D). The one that looks the biggest is the biggest! Most questions will be visual, but you will still need to know some geometry facts.

GEOMETRY FACTS

Angles

- There are 180° in a straight line.
- There are 90° in a right angle.

Circles

- There are 360° in a circle.
- The radius is the distance from the center to any point on the edge of the circle.
- The diameter is the longest distance through a circle.
- The radius is half the diameter.
- Circumference = $2\pi r$
- Area = πr^2

Rectangles

- Opposite sides are equal.
- All four angles are each 90°.
- The perimeter is the sum of all sides.
- Area = $l \times w$

Squares

- All sides are equal.
- All four angles are each 90°.
- Perimeter = $4s$
- Area = s^2

Triangles

- The largest side is opposite the largest angle.
- The smallest side is opposite the smallest angle.
- The height must make a 90° angle with the base.
- Area = $\dfrac{1}{2}bh$

Isosceles Triangles

- Two sides are equal.
- The angles opposite the equal sides are equal.

Equilateral Triangles

- All sides are equal.
- All angles are each 60°.

MINI BRAIN TEASERS

Among the math questions on the LAST there will likely be some word problems that test the basics of spatial reasoning. The key to solving these types of problems is to sketch a rough diagram. Let's look at an example:

80. A five-story building has floors numbered 1 through 5. Joe lives two floors above Sam, and one floor below Pat. If Sam does not live on floor 1, what floor does Joe live on?

(A) 1
(B) 2
(C) 3
(D) 4

First of all, you should have a rough sketch of the building. Something as simple as this will be fine:

5
4
3
2
1

Next, you know that Joe lives two floors above Sam and one floor below Pat. This should look a little bit like this:

Pat

Joe

--

Sam

Okay, so now it should be clear that Sam cannot live on floors 3, 4, or 5 because you need to save room for Joe and Pat to occupy higher floors in the building. Also, the question tells you that Sam does not live on the first floor. This of course means that Sam must be living on the second floor. Now you can combine your two diagrams to give you the following:

5	Pat
4	Joe
3	--
2	Sam
1	--

Since the question is asking you what floor Joe lives on, the diagram above should be enough to convince you that Joe lives on the fourth floor and that the credited response to the question is (D).

Is the Math Giving You Trouble? Use POE

Process of Elimination is as critical on math questions as it is on all of the LAST questions. POE increases your accuracy by getting rid of trap answers. It also increases your speed—eliminating wrong answers reduces the amount of calculating you need to do.

Let's try a problem:

1. A woman made 5 equal payments on a loan. If the total of all 5 payments was $465, how much was the first payment?

   (A) $75
   (B) $85
   (C) $93
   (D) $100

You don't need to set up an equation to solve this or, for that matter, most of the math questions on the LAST. Instead, use the information given to find the answer quickly and accurately. In this case, you know that one of the four numbers given has to be the right answer. By trying an answer in the middle—let's try (B)—you can make a lot of progress toward finding an answer. Since 5 payments of $85 would equal $425, you know that answer choice (B) is too small and can eliminate it. Further, if $85 is too small, then $75 is also going to be too small. So now you're down to two choices. (D) is pretty easy to eliminate since 5 × $100 is $500, and you are looking for an answer that gets you to $465. So, the answer has to be (C) since it's the only one left.

FINAL WORDS OF WISDOM FOR MATH QUESTIONS

As you know, the LAST questions are not arranged in order of difficulty. It's up to you to assess each question to decide if it's a "do it now" or "save it for later." Be careful not to burn up all your time on one or two really tough questions, and be sure to use good test-taking strategies such as POE to knock out obviously wrong answers and leave only good choices. Finally, remember to not leave any questions blank no matter how impossible the question seems.

SCIENCE—EEEEK!

If you've been contemplating a different profession because you can't face the science portion of the LAST, relax. The majority of the "science" problems on the test are nothing more than paragraphs *about* science that essentially contain the answer to the question asked. In other words, they are glorified reading comprehension questions about scientific topics.

Try the following example:

It has been observed that plants exhibit phototropism (bending toward light) when placed in the presence of a light source. The actual part of the plant that bends toward the light source is not the tip of the plant but rather a region farther down the stem. Four flowering plants were exposed to sunlight to determine the site of light detection and the plants' responses.

Experiment 1

When light struck Plant 1 from the side, a region a few millimeters down from the tip bent as it grew until the tip pointed directly toward the light source.

Experiment 2

Plant 2 was also placed in the presence of sunlight, but the tip of the plant was covered with a dark cap. The plant failed to bend toward the light source.

Experiment 3

Plant 3 was exposed to the same conditions as Plant 2 except that a clear cap replaced the dark cap. This plant bent toward the light source.

Experiment 4

> When a flexible dark collar was placed around
> the bending region of Plant 4, the plant bent
> toward the light source.

Before we even look at what the test writers might want to ask, we'll want to answer a very basic question: *What's going on here?*

Answering science questions on the LAST will sometimes require you to have a basic understanding of scientific method and how experiments work. Everything you'll need to know is covered in the following pages.

SCIENTIFIC METHOD FOR NONSCIENTISTS

If you're reading this section, then we'll assume that you did not major in one of the sciences in college. If you did major in science, you most likely know this stuff at a much greater level of detail than the LAST would ever presume to measure. Whether you majored in biochemistry or are just a fan of *ER*, the following is all you really need to know about the scientific method to do well on the test.

What Do Scientists Do, Anyway?

When you get right down to it, science is about answering questions by conducting experiments. To learn something useful from an experiment, scientists need to make sure things are done in the "right" way. That "right" way of doing an experiment can be thought of as the scientific method. We'll use the plant experiment from the previous page as an example to discuss the various steps in a well-designed experiment.

Step 1: **What scientific question are you trying to answer?**
Scientists want to know things like, "What happens if…?" "What causes the thing I'm seeing?" or "How are two things similar (or different)?" Many times, scientists will make a prediction of what answer they will find at the end of their experiment. This predicted outcome is known as the **hypothesis.** In the plant experiment, the scientist is trying to figure out what makes a plant bend toward a light source.

Step 2: **Testing the hypothesis.**
In an experiment, the scientist will run a series of tests that have slight differences from one another. The scientist does this to determine whether relationships exist between something that the scientist is deciding to change (the independent variable) and any other changes that occur along with the change the scientist has introduced (the dependent variable). In plant experiments 2, 3, and 4 from the previous pages, the scientist is placing items (a dark cap, a clear cap, and a dark collar) on different parts of a plant. Why is the scientist doing this? To see if the presence of these items will make the plant not bend.

What about experiment 1?

So what's the deal with the first experiment? The scientist doesn't seem to be doing anything except for putting a plant next to a light source. Experiment 1 is actually done to demonstrate what would "normally" happen had the scientist not introduced any independent variables. Why does the scientist do this? Because you have to compare your experimental results with a normal situation. Otherwise, how would you know if you were seeing any kind of results at all from the introduction of the independent variables? The plant in experiment 1, and in fact any experiment that introduces no outside variables, is known as the **control group.** It's something that you include in an experiment for the sake of comparison.

Let's say we wanted to examine the impact of Internet access on student learning. If we were to look at a class made up only of students who had Internet access and observed that they were doing well, we would have no way of knowing whether the students' Internet access had anything to do with their success. Why? Because we have nothing that we can compare with our observed results.

So in this example with the plants, the first experiment is done just to demonstrate that a plant will bend toward a light source if nothing is put on it.

Step 3: Evaluating the results.

Let's start by looking at the results of experiments 1 and 2. In experiment 1 (the control group), the plant bent toward the light source. In experiment 2 (a dark cap was placed over the tip of the plant), the plant did not bend toward the light source. So, the introduction of the independent variable (the dark cap) resulted in the plant not bending toward the light (the dependent variable). Given certain other assumptions that we will discuss shortly, we can conclude that the two sets of differences are somehow related to each other.

Here's a question you might see on the LAST about this difference:

27. The results of Experiments 1 and 2 indicate that

(A) the plant requires both sunlight and nutrition to bend.
(B) the tip of the plant detects the light source.
(C) the light-proof cap assists the plant in its bending action.
(D) it is the amount of sunlight that causes the bending of the plant.

What we know is that when a dark cap was put on the tip of the plant, the plant did not bend. We should look for an answer that summarizes this relationship. Now let's discuss the answer choices in turn:

(A) Since there is nothing in the experiment that alters the nutrition that the plant gets, you really can't defend this answer choice. Remember, you aren't expected to be an expert in science to answer these questions, so you should focus on the things you are told in the passage.

(B) This is a great answer. When the tip of the plant was uncovered, the plant bent toward the light. When the tip of the plant was covered with a dark cap, the plant did not bend. Also notice how experiment 3 helps you determine that it is the darkness and not the weight of the cap that is creating the observed effect.

(C) This would be a really weird answer to pick. The plant with the light-proof cap did not bend, so it would be a bit odd to say that the light-proof cap *assists* the plant in its bending action.

(D) This is a close second choice, but the experiment never really tests relative *amounts* of light that the various plants receive. Instead, it's more accurate to say that one plant gets light and the other plant gets no light.

Using this same type of reasoning, you can compare any pair of the four experiments to answer two questions:

1. What differences are there in the independent variables (the things that the scientist did)? In this case, the scientist introduced a dark cap, a clear cap, and a dark collar.

2. What changes do you see that might have resulted from the changes that the scientist introduced? In this case, the scientist noticed that one plant (the one with the dark cap) did not bend toward the light source while the other two (the one with the clear cap and the one with the dark collar) did bend toward the light.

So, the results of the experiment seem to indicate that a plant will not bend toward a light source unless the tip of the plant is receiving light.

THE APPROACH TO LAST SCIENCE QUESTIONS

To crack the science questions on the LAST, you must work methodically. Here's the approach:

Step 1: **Read it.** Read the given information with a critical eye. Don't get bogged down in too much detail, but be on the lookout for what the scientist is changing (the independent variable) and what happens as a result (the dependent variable).

Step 2: **What's the deal?** Summarize in your own words what you think is going on. Keep it short and simple. Remember, the real work doesn't start until you read the question.

Step 3: **Answer before you answer.** Once you read the question, use the info you know to "answer" the question in your own words. Your answer may be specific, or it may simply be a summary of what the answer should be like. The point is to get some idea of what you might want to say before reading answer choices designed to confuse and mislead you.

Step 4: **Process of Elimination (POE).** Cross off answers that don't make sense or do not relate to your "answer."

Step 5: **Pick an answer and move on.** If you still have more than one answer choice left, make a guess and move on.

Try the following example:

Step 1: Read It

Dr. Keller, a research scientist, was interested in studying the effects of plant hormones on the growth of particular plants. One of her experiments involved the plant hormone gibberellin and its impact on dwarf tomato plants. The chart below depicts her observations after 180 days of growth.

	Amount of Gibberellins (ml)	Average Height of Tomato Plants (cm)
Sample 1	0	10.0
Sample 2	2	13.5
Sample 3	4	15.7
Sample 4	6	16.0
Sample 5	8	16.0

Step 2: What's the Deal?

Before you go any further, ask yourself, "What's the deal? What's going on in this passage/experiment?" In other words, get a clue of what's going on before you blindly read a bunch of answer choices that are designed to confuse you. What do you see going on in the above experiment? You should notice that when gibberellins are first introduced, the plants have a dramatic growth spurt. However, you don't keep getting the same results if you add greater amounts. Going from 4 milliliters of gibberellins to 6 milliliters of gibberellins doesn't really do that much at all, and going from 6 milliliters of gibberellins to 8 milliliters of gibberellins does nothing.

Step 3: Answer Before You Answer

Now that you've got a good idea of what's going on, let's look at a question:

28. Which of the following graphs would best represent the effect of gibberellins on dwarf tomato plants in the study?

Don't panic because of the graph. We'll review graphs in a minute, but simply use what you know—your answer to "What's the deal?"—to answer the question.

You'll want to look for a graph that shows that at first height increases as gibberellins are added but that height tapers off at 16 centimeters once you've added enough gibberellins. Since the two variables increase together, the line of the graph should slope up from left to right; however, since the effect tapers off as gibberellins are added, the line should level off rather than be perfectly straight. Notice that the steeper the line, the greater the change in height, while a horizontal line indicates little or no change.

Step 4: POE

Now use your answer to eliminate answer choices that are not like yours.

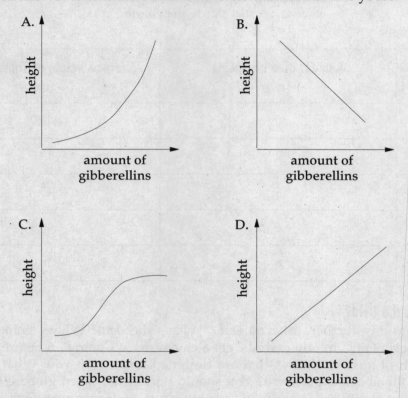

POE made that question simple, even before you've reviewed graphing. You needed an answer that showed "increased, then leveled off." To increase means to go up, so (B) is out. To level off means to go horizontal at the end. (A) and (D) keep going up, so they are out. The answer therefore has to be (C).

To Recap

You can beat any science question on the LAST by working step by step:

Step 1: Read it.

Step 2: What's the deal?

Step 3: Answer before you answer.

Step 4: POE.

Step 5: Pick an answer and move on.

GRAPHS—ALL YOU NEED TO KNOW

Graphs will present the independent variable on the x-axis (the horizontal line) and the dependent variable on the y-axis (the vertical line). You can probably get away with not even knowing that. What you will need to do is answer two simple questions to guide you to an answer:

1. Do the two variables change in the same direction? That is, as one increases does the other increase (or as one decreases does the other decrease)? If so, then the line will slope upward from left to right. If the two variables change in opposite directions, then the line will slope downward from left to right.

2. Do the two variables change at exactly the same rate? For example, is it true that for every two of one you get three of the other? If the two variables change at a directly proportional rate, then the line will be straight. If the two variables change at different rates, then the line will be curved.

YOU CALL THAT SCIENCE?

The science questions on the LAST may require a little more brainpower and maybe some terminology, but they won't require you to read and memorize every biology, chemistry, and physics book you can get from the New York Public Library.

What you will want to become familiar with are some basic types of "scientific" arguments and the assumptions they require to be more convincing. You'll want to know these so you can evaluate the "scientific" arguments you will face on the LAST. Furthermore, learning to see the required assumptions behind certain types of arguments will also be a useful tool in constructing your LAST essay, which of course asks you to evaluate arguments.

ASSUMPTIONS AND POTENTIAL FLAWS IN EXPERIMENTS

When the results of experiments are compared with one another, an important assumption is being made by the scientist: The difference that the scientist introduces (the independent variable) and the observed results (the dependent variable) are the *only* differences that exist. Otherwise, the effects that the scientist attributes to the introduction of the independent variable might be due to poor experimental design.

Suppose we were to look at two groups of farm animals. One group was fed organic feed and showed no negative health effects. The other group was fed chemically processed feed and developed stomach cancer. Can you say for sure whether the chemically processed feed was what caused the stomach cancer?

What if you also knew that the farm animals that were given organic feed lived on a farm in a relatively unpolluted part of the countryside while the farm animals that were given chemically processed feed were kept in a warehouse next to a chemical waste facility? Would this cause you to question whether the difference in food was what was causing the observed differences in health between the two groups? What if you were to find out that the group of farm animals that contracted stomach cancer was genetically predisposed to get cancer while the other group was not?

In any well-designed experiment, the groups that are being compared are assumed to be as similar as possible. In this manner, we can be more confident in attributing observed differences to the independent variables that are being introduced by the scientist. However, if you notice that other variables are being introduced that are not being tested for, then you would be wise to question whether the experiment is really saying what the scientist claims the experiment says.

Keeping this fact in mind, try the following question about the "gibberellins" experiment:

32. Which of the following was assumed in the design of the experiment?

   (A) Each plant requires the same amount of water.
   (B) The plants are genetically identical.
   (C) The plants are naturally green all season.
   (D) The plants will be exposed to sunlight.

Remember, when a scientist draws a conclusion from experimental data, the scientist assumes that no differences exist in the two experimental groups other than the independent variables. While (A) is a good second choice because it highlights one similarity between the two plants being studied, it doesn't necessarily mean that the two plants are similar in other relevant ways. Answer choice (B) is much better because it makes a much stronger statement that the two plants are the same in every way except for the difference introduced by the scientist which is the whole purpose of the experiment.

Let's look at another one:

A recent study conducted in California of the effect of yoga on the health of women had shocking results. Three hundred women who ordinarily exercise in a gym approximately five days per week were asked to participate in the study. The women were divided into three groups: Group A, made up of 100 women, attended an ashtanga (intense, exercise-oriented) yoga class on the beach for one hour every Monday through Friday morning for six months. Group B, made up of 100 women, attended a hatha (meditative) yoga class in the yoga studio every Monday through Friday morning for six months. The 100 women of Group C attended the gym of their choice for one hour every Monday through Friday morning for six months. At the end of six months, the women were all subjected to a variety of tests including blood and urine analysis.

While the individuals in Group A showed the most improvement in overall health and fitness, they also demonstrated a remarkably high level of a chemical compound in their systems that is typically a precursor to skin cancer. This chemical compound was not apparent in the women of either Group B or Group C. The researcher concluded that ashtanga yoga, while seemingly the best exercise, is more risk than it is worth.

Whoa! Does the experiment really say that ashtanga yoga can lead to skin cancer? While it is true that Group A (the ashtanga yoga people) had indicators that they might contract skin cancer while the other groups did not, was this the only difference between Group A and the other two groups? Remember, in good experimental design there is only one difference that the scientist/researcher will introduce between groups. In this case, there is at least one other difference that you are told about in the passage. Did you see what it was?

The women in Group A attended a yoga class *on the beach* five days a week, while the other two groups remained indoors. Might there be some relationship between being outdoors on the beach every day and an increased risk of skin cancer? That certainly seems a much more plausible explanation for the observed results of the experiment (one group has an increased risk of skin cancer and the others don't).

Of course it may be true that ashtanga yoga actually *does* have something to do with skin cancer rates; however, from this particular experiment it would be impossible to say if such a relationship exists, due to the poor design of the experiment.

And now here's a test question about the experiment:

33. Which of the following would best weaken the researcher's conclusion?

    (A) The women in Group B showed a greater decrease in percentage of body fat than the women in Group C.
    (B) The women in Group C sustained more injuries than the women in Groups A and B.
    (C) The women in Group A were the only women who exercised outside in the sun, thus exposing them to harmful ultraviolet rays.
    (D) The women in both Groups B and C retained more body fat than the women in Group A, and overall body fat content is a major contributor to certain forms of cancer.

To weaken the researcher's conclusion (ashtanga yoga contributes to skin cancer), you will want to consider whether there was some other potential cause present. In fact, any time you are presented with a claim that one thing causes another, you should be on the lookout for other possible explanations. Now let's consider those answer choices.

In answer choice (A), the concept of body fat is discussed. Not only is this issue not explicitly related to the experiment's conclusion about skin cancer, but it also ignores Group A. You are not going to be able to weaken the conclusion of the experiment without talking about that group.

In answer choice (B), the notion of injuries is brought up. Keep your eye on the ball, and focus on the experiment's conclusion. The experiment states that ashtanga yoga is more risk than it's worth. What the experiment doesn't claim is that ashtanga yoga on the whole is safer or more dangerous in general than either of the other two activities mentioned in the experiment. So, the fact that the women in Group C sustained more injuries really doesn't do much at all to address the researcher's claim regarding the connection between ashtanga yoga and skin cancer.

In answer choice (C), the additional difference between Group A and the other two groups is discussed. It's the credited response because it offers another explanation as to why the members of Group A appear to have a greater risk for skin cancer.

Answer choice (D) contains a classic example of why you need to read answer choices very carefully. Note that answer choice (D) claims that body fat content is a major contributor to certain forms of cancer. Is skin cancer one of them? Since you can't say for sure, you really can't defend this choice. You might be tempted to pick this because you're thinking that the other two groups are going to have an increased risk of contracting other types of cancers, but it's important to remember to focus on the claim that the experiment makes: Ashtanga yoga is more risk than it's worth. Whether the other groups have a greater or lesser chance of getting cancer is not really relevant to the argument, unless you were to establish that ashtanga yoga is the one and only way to reduce body fat to a degree where risk of other types of cancers are prevented. Even then you would need to bring in a lot of evidence about other types of cancers compared with skin cancer so you could weigh relative risks.

Remember—you're not expected to have comprehensive scientific knowledge. All you really need to do is focus on the design and conclusion of the experiment. If the author is claiming that two things in the experiment are associated, you should question whether something else might be responsible for the observed results of the experiment (do additional differences exist besides the independent variable?). If something else might be responsible for the differences you're seeing in the experimental results (the dependent variable), then bringing that issue up will weaken the experiment's conclusion.

LIES, DAMN LIES, AND STATISTICS

You may run into a problem on the LAST that will draw conclusions from a statistical sample. Although the problem might appear to be intimidating because it looks too "mathematical," there are a few simple things to keep in mind that will make these types of questions quite doable. A few terms will be discussed that are not as important as understanding the reasoning behind this particular type of experimental design. So, if you're faced with understanding either the terms or the process, focus on the process.

In a very real way, the experiments discussed earlier (the plants bending toward light and the groups of women doing yoga) were both examples of drawing a conclusion from a *sample*. A sample is just a fancy way of saying that you want to find out something about a very large group (known in statistics as a *population*), but you don't want to test every single member of the population.

If you've ever been telephoned at home by someone asking survey questions, you've been a part of a sample. Your answers will be used by researchers to draw conclusions about a huge number of people to whom they will never actually talk. Other examples of researchers drawing conclusions from samples include television news networks predicting the outcome of an election based on exit polls or the infamous Nielsen television ratings that determine which television shows are most popular. In either case, information is gathered from a small percentage of people, and those answers are taken to be similar enough to the population at large that meaningful conclusions can be drawn. With respect to political exit polls, this worked really well until the 2000 presidential election, when there were some problems with news networks incorrectly predicting the winner of the state of Florida. You might have heard something about it…

When claims are made about a population on the basis of information gathered from a sample, researchers make some fundamental assumptions to support those claims. Not only do researchers assume that the people responding to the survey questions are telling the truth (or in the case of the 2000 elections, that voters actually marked the spot on their ballots that corresponded to the candidate they intended to vote for), but the researchers also make an assumption that the sample (the people they talked to) is *representative* of the population (the people who we're trying to learn about).

What the word "representative" means in this case is that the sample is enough like the population as a whole that you can actually draw some reasonable conclusions from the data that you've gathered. If I were to conclude that the student body of Jerry Garcia High School overwhelmingly approved of the school's new dress code (black T-shirt and black jeans) because the members of the school's drama club liked the changes, I would probably be making a mistake. Why? Because it's probably not reasonable to think that the attitudes of the school's drama club are representative of the attitudes of the student population as a whole.

The single most important thing to remember about all of this is to question whether a sample is representative of a population. If the sample is not representative, then you shouldn't be drawing any conclusions from the data you collect.

In another example, if you were to find out that 4 out of 5 lawyers surveyed believed they were underpaid, what would you need to know to conclude that 4 out of 5 lawyers in general believe they are underpaid? You would need to know that the lawyers surveyed are enough like lawyers in general that the conclusion makes sense. If you found out that the survey was conducted at the seventeenth annual "Underpaid Lawyers Convention," then you would have reason to suspect the conclusions drawn from the survey (although you could still reasonably conclude that 4 out of 5 lawyers *attending the convention* believe they are underpaid).

PERCENTAGES AND ACTUAL NUMBERS AREN'T THE SAME THING

Some of the science questions might rely on your ability to see the difference between percentages and numbers. Consider the following statements:

30 percent of the students at West Kennison High School are honors students.
45 percent of the students at East Kennison High School are honors students.

So, which school has more honors students?

While it might seem obvious to you that East Kennison High School has more honors students (45 percent is bigger than 30 percent), that is not a conclusion that you can properly draw from the two statements. Why? Because you don't know how many students attend each school. If 1,000 students go to West Kennison and 200 students go to East Kennison, then it would actually be true that more honors students attend West Kennison (300) than attend East Kennison (90).

In summary, comparing the percentages of two different groups will not tell you anything about the relative sizes of two different groups. You would need more information to be able to figure that out.

I/II/III/IV QUESTIONS

Some of the science questions you will see will give you Roman numeral choices with which to work. A less savvy test taker might panic due to the fact that it appears that one needs to be able to answer multiple science questions to arrive at the credited response. Remember, however, that you can apply a few basic principles underlying Roman numeral questions that will allow you to avoid some of the difficulties other people will be facing. Those principles are:

1. If you understand one of the Roman numeral statements and you know it is right, eliminate all answer choices that do not contain that particular Roman numeral.

2. If you understand one of the Roman numeral statements and you know it is wrong, eliminate all answer choices that do contain that particular Roman numeral.

3. If all remaining answer choices have one of the Roman numerals in common, then that particular statement has to be right.

Here's an example of how you might apply this on test day:

Of the following statements about complex scientific reasoning, which of the following MUST be true?

I. This choice is pretty easy to understand, and you know that it must be true.
II. Here's a really complicated idea. You have no idea what it's trying to say.
III. Here's a statement you understand and know to be false.

(A) I only
(B) I and II
(C) I and III
(D) II and III

Okay, since you know Roman numeral I is correct, you can eliminate answer choice (D). Also, since you know that Roman numeral III is wrong, you can eliminate answer choice (C) as well. So at this point you are down to choices (A) and (B). What do you do now? Pick one of the two choices right away and keep moving (that's right, you might just have to guess once in a while). You should see, however, that you now have a fifty-fifty shot at getting the correct answer to a question containing a statement that you didn't even understand. Even more important is that you didn't burn up a lot of time that you will need to answer other questions and to write your essay.

Science Questions in Summary

The science questions on the LAST are designed so that the questions can be answered by people who took no math or science in college. Much of what you will be asked can be answered by referring to accompanying paragraphs of text or simple charts or diagrams. By approaching the problems according to the five steps, remembering the basic ideas behind the scientific method, and by knowing how to spot fallacies in scientific arguments concerning the use of statistics and samples, you should be armed with enough knowledge to pass this part of the test. You might not know enough to win a Nobel Prize, but you can use what you do know to clear this hurdle on your way to becoming a licensed teacher.

6

History and Social Sciences

HISTORY AND SOCIAL SCIENCES

While we are going to review some history and social sciences concepts in this chapter, much of what you will be asked on this section of the LAST will be tested in the form of reading comprehension questions. That is, the information that you will need to answer the questions will be provided to you in a passage, not based on your memory. Remember, as with the other sections of the LAST, the questions are designed so that someone who didn't major in some aspect of the topic being measured should be able to answer the questions correctly: Your ability to get right answers on this section will rely much more on your test-taking and reading comprehension skills than on your knowledge of dates and historical events. The contents of this chapter are presented with this reality in mind.

HISTORY PASSAGES

You can use the basic reading comprehension approach, which we will discuss in more detail in Chapter 8, to answer most history and social sciences questions.

1. Read and translate the question into your own words.

2. Look for the answers in the passage. Use key words in the question to help you zero in on what you are looking for.

3. Answer the question in your own words before moving on to the answer choices. Your chances of being distracted by trap answers will be greatly diminished if you know roughly what you want to say before considering the choices.

4. Use POE (Process of Elimination) to get rid of answer choices that don't match yours, then pick one of the remaining choices and move on to the next question.

Try this one. Read the selection below, adapted from a speech given by Jean Baptiste Amar before the National Assembly in France in 1793. Don't forget to read the question first so you know what you're supposed to be doing with the passage.

> In general, women are hardly capable of lofty conceptions and serious cogitations. And if, among ancient peoples, their natural timidity and modesty did not permit them to appear outside their family, do you want in the French Republic to see them coming up to the bar [to practice law], to the speaker's box, to political assemblies like men, abandoning both the discretion that is the source of all the virtues of this sex and the care of their family?

Which of the following statements most closely summarizes the speaker's arguments?

(A) Women in France should be extended the rights given to all men.

(B) Political clubs play an influential role in French society and therefore should be exempt from government sanctions.

(C) Women in France are not qualified to participate in political clubs.

(D) Women in France should be prohibited from forming women-only political clubs, although they should be permitted to join men's clubs already in existence.

So, what is this guy saying? He doesn't seem to have a lot of regard for women's abilities and is arguing that they should not be participating in legal and political discourse. Your goal should be to find an answer choice that best captures this idea.

Answer choices (A) and (D) don't look so good. Both of them, to different degrees, talk about increasing women's participation in law and politics. The passage is opposed to such participation. Answer choice (B) doesn't look that good either because the passage never discusses government sanctions. Therefore, there's really no way to justify that answer choice. Answer choice (C), however, is a pretty close paraphrase to the idea we wanted to find. The passage claims that women are not qualified ("women are hardly capable of lofty conceptions and serious cogitations") and should therefore not participate in political or legal groups.

Here is another one. Remember, read the question first.

The United States pulled out all the stops in preparing for its entry into World War II. Remember, the United States had been attempting to stay neutral in the period after World War I. In order to fight World War II, munitions had to be manufactured, planes had to be put together, and boats had to be built quickly. The government imposed rationing, sold war bonds, instituted a draft, and stepped up production to meet the challenges of fighting a war overseas. The war effort was one of the most effective mobilizations of industrial forces in history. Less than a year after Pearl Harbor, the United States had produced more than forty-seven billion dollars worth of war materials: 32,000 tanks, 49,000 airplanes, and eight million tons of ships.

7. Which of the following actions was NOT taken by the U.S. government to ensure victory in World War II?

(A) Nationalizing the railroads
(B) The institution of a draft
(C) The sale of war bonds
(D) Rationing

The fourth sentence of the passage is key. The passage mentions that the United States "imposed rationing," answer choice (D); "sold war bonds," answer choice (C); and "instituted a draft," answer choice (B). Since the question asks you what action was NOT taken by the United States, you should be comfortable choosing answer choice (A).

Not/Least/Except

Notice that the question asked, "Which...action was NOT taken?" Not/least/except questions are common on the LAST. Not only can these questions be time-consuming, but they are also confusing. Be sure to read all the test questions carefully so you don't make careless mistakes. In the event that you are facing a not/least/except question, apply the following procedure to make sure you don't fall into a trap.

Answering not/least/except questions:

- Cross off the word NOT/LEAST/EXCEPT if it appears in the question.

- Check each answer choice to see whether it's right or wrong according to the passage.

- If the answer choice is mentioned in the passage, put a "Y" next to it; if it's not mentioned in the passage, put an "N" next to it.

- Pick the one answer that stands out. For example, if you have three "Y"'s and one "N," then the answer to the question is the one with the "N" next to it.

Try one more:

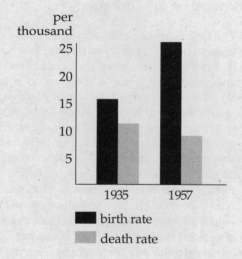

All of the following could account for part of the changes documented in the chart EXCEPT

(A) a proliferation of automobiles and new highway construction.
(B) the discovery of penicillin.
(C) the introduction of the polio vaccine.
(D) better surgical techniques.

For this question, you are looking for something that will either explain an increase in the birth rate or a decrease in the death rate. Answer choice (A) doesn't seem to explain either. If anything, a proliferation of automobiles might cause an increase in the death rate due to the increase in traffic fatalities. Answer choices (B), (C), and (D), however, do explain a decrease in the death rate, because these three answer choices describe advances in medical science that save people's lives. If people who, in the past, would have died are now surviving, that would cause a decrease in the death rate. Since the question is an EXCEPT question, you should pick the oddball answer. In this case, that would be answer choice (A).

Translation Questions

You might find passage excerpts within other types of questions. In this case, you'll need to read everything they give you. The best way to handle these is to translate them. When you read a portion of a passage, make a quick summary of it in your own words—that way you won't get tripped up by complicated language.

Try this one. After each answer choice, write a few words that summarize the quote. Then use your own words to answer the question.

Which of the following excerpts from the Gettysburg Address refers to the democratic nature of the nation?

(A) "Now we are engaged in a great civil war, testing whether that nation or any nation so conceived and so dedicated can long endure."

(B) "The brave men, living and dead, who have struggled here have consecrated it far above our poor power to add or detract."

(C) "It is for us the living rather to be dedicated here to the unfinished work which they who fought here have thus far so nobly advanced."

(D) "…and that government of the people, by the people, and for the people shall not perish from the earth."

You want to make sure you understand what the question is asking. In this case, the question is asking you to identify the quote that most closely refers to the democratic nature of the nation. Answer choice (A) talks about the Civil War and highlights the question of whether the nation will survive. It doesn't really talk about democracy, however. Answer choice (B) honors those who have fought and died in the Civil War and wars that preceded it. Does it talk about the democratic nature of the nation? Not really. Answer choice (C) says that those who are living need to finish the work begun by those who sacrificed their lives. It doesn't really touch on the democratic nature of the nation. Answer choice (D), however, is a great answer choice. "Of the people, by the people, and for the people" is a direct reference to democratic values.

By breaking down the answer choices and approaching the question in small steps, even answer choices with a lot of complex-looking language can be tackled with relative ease.

I/II/III/IV Questions

Another type of history question that you might see is the Roman numeral question. A passage or a question will be followed with three to five statements, and you need to decide which of those statements are true. These questions are designed to take you a long time, but you can efficiently arrive at the right answer by using the following approach:

- As soon as you come to a statement that is false, eliminate any answer choice that contains it.

- As soon as you know that a statement is true, eliminate any answer choice that doesn't contain it.

- If a statement is included in all the remaining answer choices, then you don't need to check that statement since it has to be true.

- Only check statements that appear in answer choices you haven't eliminated.

Don't forget to read the question first before jumping into the passage.

> "...All merchants shall have safe and secure exit from England, and entry to England, with the right to tarry there and to move about as well by land as by water, for buying and selling by the ancient and right customs, quit from all evil tolls, except (in time of war) such merchants as are of the land at war with us. And if such are found in our land at the beginning of the war, they shall be detained, without injury to their bodies or goods, until information be received by us, or by our chief justiciar, how the merchants of our land found in the land at war with us are treated; and if our men are safe there, the others shall be safe in our land..."

34. The previous excerpt from the Magna Carta outlines which of the following ideas?

   I. Merchants engaged in trade are free to travel throughout England at will.

  II. Englishmen engaged in trade in another country during wartimes will be made prisoners and released only after the war has ended.

 III. Merchants engaged in trade are allowed to leave and enter England freely.

(A) I only
(B) I and III only
(C) I, II, and III
(D) None of the above

Statement I is supported by the second half of the first sentence ("…with the right to tarry there and to move about as well by land as by water, for buying and selling…"). Since statement I is part of the answer you want to pick, you can now eliminate answer choice (D). The passage makes no statement about what might happen to Englishmen engaged in trade in *another country*, so there's not enough evidence available to support including statement II in your answer. You may therefore eliminate answer choice (C). Finally, the first half of the first sentence supports the inclusion of statement III in your answer ("All merchants shall have safe and secure exit from England, and entry to England…"). The answer, therefore, is answer choice (B).

Charts, Pictures, and Cartoons

History and social sciences questions on the LAST can come in other forms as well. For example, you might find some questions that ask you to look at a political cartoon or a historically relevant piece of art and draw some conclusions about it.

For questions that are based on charts and graphs, your first step should be to get a general orientation as to what's going on (very much like what you would do on a similar type of question from the Science section of the test). Can you state in your own words what the chart or graph is trying to show? Once you have an idea of what the chart or graph is all about, move on to the question.

Try the example below:

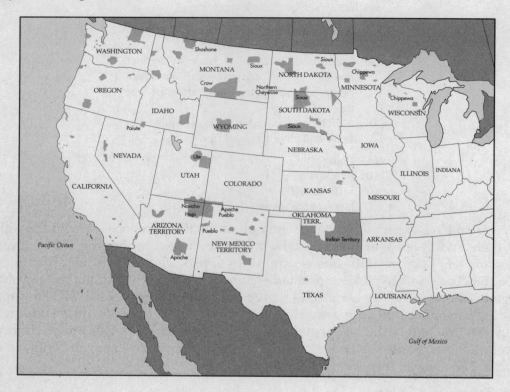

15. The creation of the reservations for Native American tribes shown in the map above can best be explained by which of the following statements?

(A) The United States government was making every effort to provide Native Americans with ample land to make up for their historical displacement.

(B) Native Americans had always been concentrated in desert areas.

(C) Native American tribes won more land during the period from 1875 to 1900 through both violent conflict and negotiation with the government.

(D) Mining interests and the expansion of the population westward led the federal government to forcibly restrict Native Americans to lands chosen by the government.

The shaded areas on the map represent established reservations for Native American tribes. Notice how the reservations are a relatively small portion of the map and that the reservations seem to be placed in relatively unpopulated areas. Is there an answer choice that matches up with what you see?

Answer choice (A) looks suspicious because of the presence of the word *every*. The map doesn't seem to go with the idea that the government is making *every* effort to provide Native Americans with *ample* land to make up for their historical displacement. Answer choice (B) is going to be hard to defend for a couple of reasons. First of all, there's nothing on the map that tells you where Native Americans lived prior to the establishment of reservations. Next, it flies in the face of common sense that all Native Americans would choose to live in the desert when other locations would have more abundant sources of food and water. You can eliminate answer choice (C) because there's nothing on the map that would communicate how it is that Native Americans won more land (or if they even did). Answer choice (D) looks very strong. The relatively small size of the reservations compared with the map as a whole supports the phrase "forcibly restrict," and the locations of the reservations are on parts of the map that are relatively unpopulated by descendants of those who came to the continent. Your most appropriate answer choice is therefore answer choice (D).

Questions that are based on political cartoons can be approached in much the same way. You need to be mindful of the fact that political cartoonists will sometimes make exaggerations in a political cartoon to make a point. So, as with poetry, you have to be aware of the fact that not everything you see can be taken literally.

Let's look at an example:

The cartoon most clearly implies that since its decision in *Roe v. Wade* the Supreme Court has

(A) ignored public opinion on the issue.
(B) experienced serious conflict between female and male justices over the issue.
(C) refused to deal with the issue again.
(D) struggled to accommodate conflicting viewpoints on the issue.

So what's going on in this cartoon? The question itself is helpful because it identifies the people in the boat as the Supreme Court (in case you didn't recognize the artist's portrayal). The cartoon portrays the justices as trying to navigate a boat around two obstacles (they are actually explosive mines, but knowing exactly what the obstacles are is not that important as long as you see that they are trying not to hit them). The obstacles are labeled "pro-choice" and "pro-life." So, the cartoon is clearly not literally about the justices of the Supreme Court going on a boating trip but instead is meant to represent something else (it's a visual metaphor). So what could this mean? Let's look at the answer choices.

The justices don't seem to be ignoring anything in the cartoon. Instead they are actively trying to steer the boat so they don't hit the obstacles. Therefore, you can safely eliminate answer choice (A). Next, the cartoon doesn't clearly indicate that there is a male versus female split over the issue. The cartoonist is going to try to make the main message very clear so all readers can figure out what's going on. So if you don't see what the answer choice is saying clearly presented in the cartoon, you can go ahead and eliminate the choice. This is exactly what you are going to do with answer choice (B). Now you're down to the last two choices. Does the picture look like they are refusing to deal with an issue or does it look like they are struggling? It looks like they're struggling, and what they are struggling to do is to avoid the two obstacles. The two obstacles, labeled "pro-choice" and "pro-life," represent the conflicting viewpoints that are mentioned in answer choice (D). Therefore, answer choice (D) is the most appropriate choice.

In summary, you should look for things that the cartoonist makes prominent in the cartoon by exaggeration or by creating an unusual situation. Then find an answer choice that gives a clear meaning to what that exaggeration or unusual situation might mean.

You might also need to interpret a graph or two, so it's important to have a handle on how to read them.

A Review of Basic Graph and Chart Skills

- The x-axis is the horizontal line; the y-axis is the vertical line.

- A point on the graph (whether it is on a line or standing alone) can be indicated with a pair of coordinates.

- Coordinates describe the location in reference to the x- and y-axes.

- Be sure to note how the two axes are labeled, and see if a key accompanies the graph. That information will be critical for you to be able to make sense of the graph.

Here's an example of how graphs might be tested on this part of the exam:

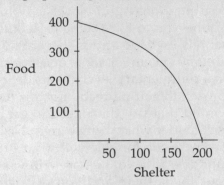

The production possibility curve for society X, illustrated above, indicates that

(A) society X cannot produce adequate amounts of both food and shelter.
(B) society X would be best served by producing 150 units of shelter and 150 units of food.
(C) to produce 200 units of shelter, society X would have to forego the production of food.
(D) to produce 350 units of food, society X would have to forego the production of shelter.

Here are a couple of questions for you. How many people live in society X? How much food and shelter do the people of society X need? If you can't answer these questions, don't worry. You weren't given enough information to answer these questions. Why bring this up? Because answer choices (A) and (B) both rely on your being able to answer those questions. For answer choice (A), how can we know whether society X can produce adequate amounts of both food and shelter if we don't know how much it needs? For answer choice (B), how can we know what's best for society X if we don't know how much it needs? Because both of these answer choices rely on information you weren't given, there's no way that these choices can be right. Moving on to answer choice (C), if you look at the graph you should see that if society X produces 200 units of shelter, then it would produce no food at all (follow the line that is written on the graph). So, answer choice (C) is supported by the graph (to forego means to produce none). With respect to answer choice (D), the graph indicates that society X would be able to produce 40–50 units of shelter if it were to produce 350 units of food. So, that means that society X would NOT have to forego the production of shelter to produce this much food. You can therefore eliminate answer choice (D) because it is inconsistent with the information you are given on the graph.

In summary, for questions that rely on charts, graphs, or political cartoons, you will be able to focus on the answer that the test writers are going to credit if you stick to what you can defend by reference to the information you are provided. For the most part, you will not have to rely on any knowledge that you brought with you to the exam on test day: The answers are there to be found. All you need to do is find them.

Does this mean that you don't need to have *any* knowledge of history or social sciences to get every one of these questions right? Not exactly. Just as it's true that the Math and Science section will require you to have some basic knowledge (for example, you may be asked questions that rely on basic arithmetic, or you may be asked to calculate the area of a rectangle), you may encounter some questions on the History and Social Sciences section that rely on a rudimentary level of outside information.

So what is the best approach to getting ready for this (or any other) section of the LAST? First of all, keep in mind that you don't need to get a perfect score on the test. As long as you pass, it doesn't matter what your score is. Next, you also need to be concerned about making sure you are comfortable with your prospects for writing a passing essay. If you're not comfortable with your essay-writing skills, our recommendation is that you put most of your focus there and you restrict your preparation for the multiple-choice sections to learning to apply the techniques described in these chapters.

If your test is still a number of weeks away, and if you feel pretty good about your essay skills, then you may want to brush up on real knowledge in one portion of the LAST or another. How do you know what sections of the test you might need to study? Take the practice exams included in this book and get your hands on the preparation materials provided by NES. The combination of these two resources should give you an idea of where you might need to put in more study time.

The History and Social Sciences section of the LAST can be an especially tricky part of the test to study for. The scope of U.S. and world history and the possible questions you might get on other topics in social sciences could have you studying until your head explodes. The most frustrating part is that it's possible that you could study for dozens of hours and still see a question on something you didn't review. Or you could not study at all and find out that you already knew the material you were asked on the test. If we had to guess, we'd say the second situation is much more common than the first.

Given what the test measures and how the test goes about measuring it, the strategy we advocate is to focus on your essay writing and on becoming a smarter test taker. However, if you have the time and inclination to review concrete knowledge, we want to give you some degree of guidance as to what you might need to know. One way of thinking about what you might need to know is to consider what someone who took an introductory-level course on the subject in college might remember five years after graduation. To illustrate what we think is an appropriate level of knowledge for history and social sciences, here are a couple of lessons for your review.

ECONOMICS—THE LAW OF SUPPLY AND DEMAND

How do things get their prices? Economic theory says that the price of an item is dictated by two things: supply and demand. *Supply* means how much of something is available, and *demand* means how much people want that thing. The price of an item is originally determined by the interplay between these two things.

As an example, let's talk about gold. Gold is something that people all over the world covet. It's also something that you don't just see lying around in the street. In fact, there's not enough gold to go around for everyone who wants it. So it can be said that the demand for gold is high and the supply of gold is low. When an item is in high demand and in low supply, this will typically cause the price of the item to go up. Why? Because the way our society decides who gets the items that are in short supply is to make them available to the highest bidder.

So, what do you think would happen to the price of gold if a gigantic amount of gold were discovered? Now it would be much easier for the people who wanted gold to acquire it, and as a result, the price of gold would come down. Why? Because the people who want to sell gold are now facing more competition from other people who sell gold. So if you don't drop your price, then your customers will go somewhere else. What this means is the following:

- **As the supply of an item increases, its price will decrease.**
  Alternatively, what do you think would happen to the price of gold if half of the world's gold disappeared? Assuming that gold remained as popular as it ever was before (demand is unchanged), you would expect that the price of gold would go up. Why? Because people are now competing just as much for a significantly smaller amount of gold. If you had gold to sell, you would notice that you had a bunch of people interested in buying your gold. In fact, you wouldn't have enough gold to sell to everyone who wanted to buy. So what would you do? You would raise the price of gold until you had just enough people left to sell the gold you wanted to sell. What this means is the following:

- **As the supply of an item decreases, its price will increase.**
  Using a more everyday example, let's say you were eating pizza and your friend asked you for a piece. If you had a large pizza all to yourself, you would most likely give your friend a piece without even thinking about it. Why? Because the supply of pizza is high. What if you had only one slice? Then you might not want to give your friend a piece of pizza since you would be left with none (and you're hungry). So, the value of something depends on how much there is.

Of course, changes in demand will also affect the price of something. Think of what happens to the price of the most popular toys during the holiday season. In the mid-1990s, Furbys were selling for ridiculous amounts of money. Why? Because they were really hard to find (supply was low) and every kid wanted one (demand was high). A couple of years later, the price was much lower because of a combination of the increase in supply and the drop in demand. This is an example of the following:

- **As demand for an item increases, its price will increase.**

- **As demand for an item decreases, its price will decrease.**

  What kind of price do you think you could get for a bucket of rotting fish? Zero sounds like a pretty good guess. Why? Because demand for buckets of rotting fish is zero.

So, in summary, the price of an item depends on how difficult it is to get and how badly people want it. Principles of economics that are any more complicated than this are not going to show up on the LAST. They may show up in economics textbooks, but you shouldn't be concerned about learning them for this particular exam.

HIGHLIGHTS OF AMERICAN HISTORY

Early seventeenth century—The first English settlers arrive in North America in Jamestown, Virginia, and in Plymouth Rock, Massachusetts. This is not good news for the native inhabitants of the continent.

July 4, 1776—The Declaration of Independence is signed in Philadelphia. Although fighting between the colonists and British troops had been going on since April of 1775, this is generally regarded as the birthday of the United States and the beginning of the American Revolution.

Late eighteenth century—The Articles of Confederation and the United States Constitution are written. The Constitution formalizes the Bill of Rights. Among these rights are freedom of speech, religion, assembly, and the right to bear arms.

Nineteenth century—Westward expansion. Growth of the railroads and growing conflicts over slavery.

1860s—The Civil War. Southern states attempt to secede from the Union. Abraham Lincoln signs the Emancipation Proclamation, granting freedom to enslaved Americans. It will be another 100 years before civil rights legislation is finally passed.

1914–1918—World War I. Known as "The Great War" or "The War to End All Wars." The United States doesn't join the war until 1917. The United States, France, Great Britain, and Russia defeat Germany and Austria-Hungary. This extremely bloody war is best known for trench warfare and the use of poisonous gas.

1920—Passage of the Nineteenth Amendment. Women are given the right to vote (known as "women's suffrage").

Late 1920s–1930s—The Great Depression. The United States is in a ton of trouble economically. The stock market crashes and unemployment is rampant.

1939–1945—World War II. The United States stays out of the fighting until it is attacked by the Japanese at Pearl Harbor on December 7, 1941. President Franklin Roosevelt refers to the day as "a date which will live in infamy." The Allies (United States, Great Britain, France, Soviet Union) defeat the Axis Powers (Germany, Japan, Italy). The war comes to an end with the United States dropping atomic bombs on Hiroshima and Nagasaki, Japan, in August of 1945. The United States emerges as a world power.

1946–1980s—The Cold War. The post–World War II era sees much of the world divided into two camps of conflicting political ideologies led by the United States ("capitalist" nations, NATO) and the Soviet Union ("communist" nations, Warsaw

Pact). Each side develops and stockpiles a huge arsenal of nuclear weapons, and a number of armed conflicts arise around the world as a result of this struggle for power. Most notable among these conflicts is the Korean War in the 1950s and the Vietnam War in the 1960s and 1970s. The Cold War ends in the late 1980s. The Berlin Wall is torn down and a new era of Soviet leadership emerges in the person of Mikhail Gorbachev. The Soviet Union eventually breaks up into independent nations.

1974—Watergate. President Richard Nixon's men are caught circumventing the democratic process by attempting to place listening devices in the Democratic National Committee's headquarters at the Watergate Hotel. Rather than face certain impeachment over one of the worst scandals in American political history, President Nixon resigns.

1993–1997—The Clinton Presidency. President Bill Clinton undergoes an impeachment trial but is found not guilty and completes his term in office. Dot-coms lead to an economic boom and then a recession. Ethnic conflicts flare in Eastern Europe and Africa.

Precise dates have been left out of much of this because we want to make clear that the level of knowledge you will need to exhibit is most certainly not that detailed. In fact, the specifics of what is provided above are likely more than you would need to know for the LAST.

In closing, it's important for you to remember two things about the content review at the end of this chapter. While this content review is meant to give you a rough idea of the kinds of things that the test might ask, it is not intended to be a comprehensive coverage of all the possible things that you might see on the test. Instead, it is intended to give you an idea of how carefully you might need to study things in the course of your preparation.

CLOSING THOUGHTS

The key to success on the history and social sciences questions is to make sure you read the questions carefully and use the information provided to eliminate bad answer choices and focus on the most appropriate answer. Especially when faced with information that looks unfamiliar and intimidating, keep in mind that the questions are designed so they can be answered by people who don't have extensive knowledge in these subjects. It is our ardent belief that if you don't panic and focus on what you are told in the corresponding reading passage, chart, graph, or political cartoon, you shouldn't have any major trouble.

7

Arts and Humanities

ARTS AND HUMANITIES

The questions in the Arts and Humanities section are drawn from a variety of sources. Among those sources are:

- images of artworks;

- poems and excerpts from fiction or essays; and

- short reading comprehension passages about visual art, performing arts, religion, or cultural traditions.

The arts and humanities questions are very similar to the rest of the test in that you need little more than what you are told in the test itself to answer the questions correctly. As opposed to the kind of thinking a literature or art history major might do about the passages or reproductions that you will encounter on the LAST, the trick to answering these questions is not to delve too deeply into a work of art or excerpt of literature. Since these questions are designed to be answerable whether your major was art or archaeology, you can approach these questions with the following maxim in mind: *What you see is what you get.*

ART GLOSSARY

While it's our impression that you will never be asked to describe in detail the differences between a Manet and a Monet, you should be familiar with some basic art vocabulary.

abstract:	This is a style of painting that doesn't attempt pictorial representation (in other words, you can't tell exactly what you're looking at). One kind of abstract style is also referred to as **surreal.**
asymmetrical:	This is when the two sides of a painting (right versus left; top versus bottom) are not balanced in their composition. This approach can be used to introduce a certain type of contrast.
composition:	This is the arrangement of elements in an artwork; for example, a composition might be based on a triangle, with two objects at the bottom and one at the top.
contrast:	This is putting things next to one another in a composition in a way that emphasizes their difference; for example, dark areas in a photograph might contrast with light areas.
facade:	This is the front of a building (or any side that has particular architectural interest).
foreground:	This is the part of a painting or photograph that appears to be nearest to the viewer.

foreshortening:	When you draw or paint an object so that it has the illusion of depth, so that it seems to go back into space. "Foreshortening is squishing a shape to make one part of it look closer to your eye than the other."—Mark Kistler, TV artist/instructor.
geometrical:	Anything that has a geometric shape; look for squares, triangles, circles, lines.
horizontal:	A line that goes from side to side (such as the horizon), and that is the opposite of vertical.
juxtaposition:	When you put two dissimilar things close to each other to draw attention to their differences.
ornate:	Something that is highly decorated.
perspective:	This is an artistic technique that makes something one-dimensional appear three-dimensional. Perspective creates a sense of depth—of receding space. Examples of techniques are making figures smaller and higher in the composition to make them seem further away; having the lines of an image become closer to create depth in a sketch or painting.
repetition:	Closely related to harmony, this refers to a way of combining elements of art so that the same elements are used over and over again.
representational:	This is when you depict or portray subjects in a realistic way. Representation can be thought of as the opposite of abstraction (a style that does not attempt to portray things as they appear in the "real world").
stylized:	Something that is characterized by a particular style rather than being simply representational.
symmetrical:	This is when two sides are balanced; two sides are mirror images of each other.
vertical:	A line that goes up and down (such as a pine tree), and that is the opposite of horizontal.

QUESTIONS ABOUT IMAGES (OR PAINT-BY-NUMBERS)

Whether the question is about a photograph, a painting, a sketch, or stage design for a drama, you need to remember that nobody is expecting you to rely on any kind of academic training to be able to answer the questions. Instead you should be thinking about comparing what you see with the available answer choices. Think of these questions as being absolutely straightforward and don't overthink yourself into picking a wrong answer. In other words, if you can't find evidence to support a choice, it's not your answer.

Steps for Image-Based Questions

1. Read the question, and circle key words.

2. Restate the question in your own words. Be sure you understand exactly what you are being asked.

3. Go straight to the answer choices. For each one, look for evidence in the image to support or undermine each word in that choice.

4. Eliminate everything for which you cannot provide evidence.

5. Don't cross out answer choices because they look "too obvious." Remember, things that look easy in this section often look that way because they are easy.

Use the reproduction below of the painting *Lewis and Clark* by Alfred Russell to answer the questions that follow.

1. The artist focuses the viewer's attention on the woman in the painting by doing all of the following EXCEPT

    (A) creating a strong contrast between light and dark.
    (B) creating diagonal lines in the picture.
    (C) creating perspective.
    (D) creating a feeling of tension among the figures.

Certainly answer choice (A) is something the artist does by dressing the woman in light clothing in contrast to the dark clothing worn by the surrounding figures. All the human figures in the painting are emphasized by the use of contrast with a background, but the woman stands out more because of the contrast in color between her clothing and the clothing of the other figures in the painting. The diagonal lines in the picture mentioned in answer choice (B) also draw the eye to the woman in the painting by extending the diagonal line of the river in the background through the woman's outstretched arms. Even if you're unsure at this point, the fact that diagonal lines exist in the painting means that you should consider that they are being used for the purpose described in the question. The artist also uses perspective—answer choice (C)—to draw attention to the woman by putting her in the foreground of the painting. For answer choice (D), however, there isn't really much support. The expression on the woman's face and the fact that the men don't have their rifles in any kind of threatening position seem to indicate that the people in the painting are getting along okay. So it would be safe to say that the artist does not create a feeling of tension in the painting. (D) is therefore the credited response, since you are asked to pick the answer that describes something the artist *doesn't* do.

ART TERMINOLOGY

Some questions will ask you to use art terms specifically. This is why you were given a glossary of basic art terminology earlier in the chapter.

Refer back to the *Lewis and Clark* painting to answer this question.

2. The term that best describes this work is

(A) surreal.
(B) representational.
(C) decorative.
(D) contemporary.

Although you might have been wishing that "completely boring" was one of the answer choices, you're going to have to pick from these four. Remember, *surreal* means that the painting doesn't look realistic. This particular painting is about as realistic as a photograph in the way the subject is presented; so, while answer choice (A) looks very bad for this reason, this is exactly why answer choice (B) looks so good. *Representational* means that the painting looks realistic. *Decorative* is much too subjective a term to be credited on an objective test. Some people might think this painting would look good hanging in their home and other people wouldn't. Since we're looking for an answer that is "objectively" true, answer choice (C) is the kind of answer you'll want to avoid. With respect to the last answer choice, *contemporary* just means that it looks like it comes from the present time. This painting does not look like it comes from the present time, so (D) is a good answer choice to eliminate. So, the answer to this question is undoubtedly answer choice (B).

Even when it seems that the question requires art-related knowledge, you will be able to eliminate answer choices because you cannot match them to anything in the image or because they require too much of a subjective interpretation.

Let's try a few more:

Use the photograph below of the Crystal
Cathedral in Garden Grove, California, designed
by architect Philip Johnson, to answer the
question that follows.

3. The architect uses which of the following to
create the soaring effect of the building?

(A) Natural forms
(B) Ornamentation
(C) Repetition
(D) Symmetry

Natural forms? Nope. It looks like a manmade structure to us. Additionally, there's
not a great deal of ornamentation going on here. There is a giant cross on top of the
building, but the soaring effect comes more from the repeating vertical lines in the
building's design—which is why (C) looks so good. Finally, there is actually an element
of asymmetry to the building due to the shorter portion of the building on the right side
of the photograph juxtaposed against the taller portion of the building on the left side of
the photograph. The credited response to this question is therefore (C).

Use the reproduction below of the painting
The Persistence of Memory by Salvador Dali
to answer the question that follows.

4. The artist was most likely interested in
    achieving which of the following?

    (A) Drawing the viewer's eye to the sky in the
        painting
    (B) Recreating a specific natural landscape
    (C) Evoking a feeling of discomfort in the
        viewer
    (D) Showing keen observation of detail

What's the first thing you noticed when you looked at this painting? The sky, or the melting clocks? If I want to draw your attention to something, then I need to make it the most prominent part of the painting. The sky doesn't fit that bill, so you should go ahead and eliminate that first answer choice. (B) is easily eliminated because the painting doesn't resemble a specific natural anything (it is, of course, an abstract painting). (C) seems a bit weird and hard to understand, but that's not reason enough to eliminate it as an answer choice. Finally, (D) can be eliminated because the painting is not overly detailed. So, while (C) is weird, it's not blatantly wrong. Additionally, one can imagine how a painting that is so surreal might evoke feelings of discomfort in the viewer. So, (C) is the answer that the test writers are looking for.

Use the reproduction below of a painting by Raffaello Sanzio (Raphael) to answer the questions that follow.

5. The mood created by the position of the figure's head and direction of the gaze can best be described as

    (A) thoughtfulness.
    (B) servitude.
    (C) vengeance.
    (D) surprise.

For this question, it's much easier to see how the figure should *not* be described. *Surprise* and *servitude* just seem way off base. The figure does not look surprised, and the figure is portrayed as having some degree of strength that would not normally be associated with servitude. Finally, the figure doesn't look angry, so *vengeance* seems a bit odd as well. The fact that the figure is looking back over his shoulder seems to communicate that the figure might be reflecting on things from the past. *Thoughtfulness*—answer choice (A)—would therefore be the best choice of the bunch.

6. The lifelike nature of the figure is achieved through which of the following?

    (A) Contrasting lighting effects
    (B) Abstract forms
    (C) Intricate brushwork
    (D) Caricature

The figure seems to be presented in more or less a representational style, so (B) would not be a good choice to pick. For the same reason, (D) should be eliminated (caricatures look very cartoonish, since they exaggerate prominent features in the figure). There isn't good evidence of contrasting lighting effects, while there is sufficient evidence of intricate brushwork. The best answer to this question is therefore (C).

ART IN SUMMARY

To prepare to answer questions from visual arts, review the list of basic art terminology from the beginning of the chapter and remember that what you see is what you get.

LITERATURE

As with the visual arts questions, questions that cover literature (poetry and excerpts from novels and short stories) do not depend on the kind of knowledge that is unique to a college literature major. Instead, this section is going to rely for the most part on your ability to eliminate answer choices that don't go with the passage and to apply some basic terminology to assist you in narrowing down the answer choices.

LITERATURE GLOSSARY

allusion: A reference to something or someone, usually literary.

figurative: Figurative language is language that is not literal: It does not mean exactly what it says. ("He's a string bean" means that the man is very thin, but it does not mean that the man is literally a vegetable.)

irony: The use of words to convey the opposite of the literal meaning (A story can be ironic as well. O. Henry's classic story "The Gift of the Magi" is a great example of irony. The husband sells his watch to buy his wife an ornate hair comb for Christmas, only to find that his wife has sold her hair to buy him a watch chain.)

metaphor: A comparison that does not use the words *like* or *as*.

- She was a breath of fresh air in the classroom.
- My love life is a desert.

onomatopoeia: A word intended to simulate the actual sound of the thing or action it describes (for example, sizzle, hiss, pop).

point of view:	The standpoint from which a story is written. First-person narrative means the story is written from one character's point of view, using *I*. Third-person stories are written from an outside point of view.
rhyme scheme:	A pattern of end rhymes, such as ABAB (meaning that the first and third lines rhyme and the second and fourth lines rhyme).
satire:	Ridicule of a subject.
simile:	A comparison that uses the words *like* or *as*.

- Your eyes are like mud puddles.

- Trying to teach Jimmy calculus was like trying to eat Jell-O with chopsticks.

symbolism:	The use of an object to represent an abstract idea (for example, a dove is used to represent peace).

QUESTIONS ABOUT LITERATURE

The questions will ask you about theme, mood, the effects of literary devices (metaphor, irony, etc.), figurative language, characters, or author's point of view. The questions may also ask about the cultural context of the work.

Steps for Literature-based Questions

Unlike science or history passages, literary excerpts generally do not have topic sentences for you to read. Instead, particularly if it's a poem, you may need to skim the whole thing to answer general questions. If there are several questions attached to an excerpt, do the specific questions first and the general questions second. We'll discuss this strategy more in the next chapter.

1. Read the questions, and circle key words. Have an idea of what you are looking for before you attack the passage.

2. Skim the passage or poem, reading for a general impression.

3. Forage for answers in the passage.

4. Answer the question in your own words before consulting the answer choices.

5. POE: Match answer choices to evidence in the passage/poem. Eliminate any choice that is not supported by direct evidence in the passage/poem.

Read the excerpt on the next page by Nigerian author Chinua Achebe, then answer the questions that follow.

For eight years, Okeke would have nothing to do with his son, Nnaemeka. He always displayed so much temper whenever his son's name was mentioned that everyone avoided it in his presence. By a tremendous effort of will he had succeeded in pushing his son to the back of his mind. The strain had nearly killed him but he had persevered, and won. Then one day he received a letter from Nene, his son's wife.

...Our two sons, from the day they learnt that they have a grandfather, have insisted on being taken to him. I find it impossible to tell them that you will not see them. I implore you to allow Nnaemeka to bring them home for a short time during his leave next month.

The old man at once felt the resolution he had built up over so many years falling in. He was telling himself that he must not give in. He tried to steel his heart against all emotional appeals. He leaned against a window and looked out. The sky was overcast with heavy black clouds and a high wind began to blow, filling the air with dust and dry leaves. It was one of those rare occasions when even Nature takes a hand in a human fight. Very soon it began to rain, the first rain in the year. It came down in large sharp drops and was accompanied by the lightning and thunder which mark a change of season. Okeke was trying hard not to think of his two grandsons. But he knew he was now fighting a losing battle. He tried to hum a favourite hymn but the pattering of large raindrops on the roof broke up the tune. His mind immediately returned to the children. How could he shut his door against them? He imagined them standing, sad and forsaken, under the harsh angry weather—shut out from his house. That night he hardly slept, from remorse—and a vague fear that he might die without making it up to them.

7. The mood of the passage is enhanced by its

(A) first-person narration.
(B) nature imagery.
(C) classical allusions.
(D) complex sentence structure.

Answer choice (A) can be eliminated because the point of view in the story is from a third-person narrator. It isn't one of the characters who is telling the story. (B) looks really good because of how the author uses the thunderstorm to reflect the turmoil going on in Okeke's mind. Classical allusions aren't present in such an obvious way that non-literature majors would be expected to see them. There also doesn't seem to be anything about sentence structure that is driving the mood of the story. The best answer choice is the one that goes with the most obvious element of the story (the storm), and that would be answer choice (B).

8. The reference to Okeke shutting his door against his grandsons is intended to be understood as both

    (A) figurative and literal.
    (B) a superstition and a fear.
    (C) mythical and sentimental.
    (D) a memory and a hope.

Answer choice (A) looks like a really good answer. Okeke shutting his door against his grandsons can be seen figuratively from the perspective that Okeke has excluded them from his life. It can also be taken literally within the context of Okeke imagining his grandchildren standing outside his door during a rainstorm. Neither *superstition* nor *fear* seems to really go with this story, so (B) is out. The use of the word *mythical* doesn't seem supported, so you can bypass answer choice (C). Finally, it would be wrong to see the story as saying that Okeke *hopes* to shut his door against his grandsons, so (D) isn't a good answer choice either.

9. The reader can infer from the first paragraph that Okeke probably

    (A) was financially dependent on his son.
    (B) was sensitive to the community's opinions.
    (C) had been a leader in the community.
    (D) cared deeply about his son.

Answer choice (A) doesn't look so good because the financial relationship between the father and son was never mentioned. As for answer choice (B), while the passage does indicate that members of the community stopped mentioning the name of the son in front of Okeke, there's nothing in the excerpt that reveals how Okeke felt about the community's opinions. (C) is a close second choice because you might infer that the reason that others stopped mentioning Okeke's son is that they didn't want to anger their leader. However, it's also plausible that others stopped mentioning Okeke's son because of Okeke's temper. (D) is the credited response, and this answer choice is supported by the story referring to how difficult it was for Okeke to push his son to the back of his mind ("the strain had nearly killed him").

POEMS

Poetry questions can be tricky because they often engage in figurative language. What that means is that things aren't meant to be taken literally in the poem. What the poet writes might be representing an idea quite different from the literal translation. On the bright side, you still have the opportunity to compare answer choices to the passage so you can eliminate answer choices that don't make sense.

Let's look at an example.

> Sweet rose, fair flower, untimely plucked, soon faded,
> Plucked in the bud, and faded in the spring!
> Bright orient pearl, alack too timely shaded!
> Fair creature, killed too soon by death's sharp sting!
> Like a green plum that hangs upon a tree,
> And falls through wind before the fall should be.

11. The poet's central theme is

    (A) the fading of beauty in old age.
    (B) the cruelty of nature.
    (C) the inevitability of death.
    (D) the sorrow caused by an early death.

The theme of a poem is akin to the main idea of a reading passage. What is it that the poet is trying to say in his or her fancy poetic way? Notice how in the above poem themes like "untimely," "too timely shaded," "too soon," and "falls . . . before the fall should be" permeate the work. Given the prevalence of this theme, answer choice (A) doesn't make much sense. Answer choice (B) doesn't really match up either. The poem does, in a way, touch on the cruelty *to* nature if you really stretch, but whether you see it this way you can be sure that answer choice (B) isn't going to be the credited response. While answer choice (C) does correctly identify the theme of death, the concept of "inevitability" doesn't work as well as the concept of "early death" discussed in answer choice (D). So you can be relatively comfortable picking answer choice (D).

Read the poem below then answer the questions that follow.

> There stands death, a bluish distillate
> in a cup without a saucer. Such a strange
> place to find a cup: standing on the back of a hand. One recognizes clearly the
> line along the glazed curve, where the handle snapped. Covered with dust. And
> *HOPE* is written across the side, in faded Gothic letters.

21. Which of the following can be inferred from
    the poet's choice of metaphor?

    (A) The death was unexpected.
    (B) The fact that death exists does not mean
        there is no hope.
    (C) The poet is not afraid of his own death.
    (D) Death is concrete and even mundane.

So death is in an old, dusty, broken cup with faded letters spelling out *hope*. Doesn't sound very hopeful, does it? While it's clear that death is a central theme (it's mentioned in all four answer choices), the trick is to figure out what the poet is saying about death. Answer choice (A) doesn't seem to work that well because the imagery in the poem is reminiscent of something decaying over time and not of a sudden end. (B) can be tricky because although the word *hope* does appear on the cup, it is faded and written in a font that suggests obsolescence. The poem is not a statement about hope as much as it is a statement about the futility of hope. As far as answer choice (C) is concerned, it's impossible to say for sure whether the author is or isn't afraid of his own death since the idea of fear isn't addressed. (D) is very interesting because the imagery of the dusty and cracked cup fits really well with the answer choice's use of the words *concrete* and *mundane*. (D) is in fact the credited response in this case.

22. The poet employs the image in the last sentence most probably to

   (A) assert that death does not affect him.
   (B) produce an ironic effect.
   (C) show that the cup was old.
   (D) end the poem on an optimistic note.

In the last sentence, you have the word *hope* written in faded Gothic letters. The juxtaposition of the word *hope* with the way the word is presented is intended for ironic effect, therefore (B) is the answer. This question is an excellent reminder for you to be on the lookout for contrasts that are presented in both visual arts and literature. These kinds of contrasts are used to communicate specific ideas. Both answer choices (A) and (C) are relatively easy to eliminate because for (A) the author really doesn't speak about effects of death and (C) indicates a much too literal reading of the poem. For poetry especially, you need to consider how the author is communicating ideas figuratively. Answer choice (D) is tempting if you don't catch the juxtaposition between the word and how it is presented and instead focus specifically on the word itself. However, by considering the theme of the poem as a whole, you are steered away from (D) quite easily.

Read the poem below, "My Mother Is Not Watching" by Leslie Ullman, then answer the questions that follow.

My Mother Is Not Watching

from the door as I start my first
walk to school. I am not afraid
though this crisp eyelet
dress feels like someone else's skin
and these houses
tall faces turning
away. This morning
my mother gets to stay
where she chooses, raising
one shoulder, cradling the phone
so her hands are free to coat each
nail to a shield over each
pale finger. Smoke from her cigarette
curls across the table like the breath
of a visitor, the glamorous

woman she secretly loves.
In this dress I'm her dream
and no one's daughter.
School is a story whose ending
she tells me she doesn't know.
Now she opens the paper to follow
a war far away, while I march
into autumn, beneath the fences
and high windows which in time
I won't see, just
the blackboard worn thin
with words that vanish
each night. I will find my way
through their sounds, a song
unwinding, and one day
I will open a book and not
notice I'm reading.

23. Which of the following statements best
expresses one theme of the poem?

   (A) Learning can occur unobserved.
   (B) Childhood is harder than adulthood.
   (C) Education restricts imagination.
   (D) Parental neglect damages children.

Answer choice (A) is certainly good enough to not eliminate it right away. This choice is especially attractive because of the use of the word *can*. Using soft language like *can* and *sometimes* makes an answer choice much easier to defend than if the answer choice uses absolute terms such as *must* or *always*. Answer choice (B) can be eliminated because childhood is never directly compared with adulthood in the poem; therefore, it's impossible to say whether the poet thinks one is harder than the other. (C) is a very interesting answer choice from the perspective of test design. Do you think that a teacher certification examination is going to say something so negative about education? Hardly. As far as answer choice (D) is concerned, it would be wrong to see this poem as a story about parental neglect. The story instead is about a child's first day of school and perhaps her mother's first time to herself in a number of years. All things considered, answer choice (A) is the best answer choice. Certainly the daughter is learning without being observed by the mother.

24. The child compares reading with

   (A) following a path.
   (B) unraveling a thread.
   (C) hearing a melody.
   (D) dreaming a dream.

The poet discusses learning to read at the very end of the poem. In reference to words on a blackboard, she states, "I will find my way/through their sounds, a song/unwinding..." This imagery matches up perfectly with answer choice (C).

SHORT PASSAGES

A few questions may be based on short—probably one-paragraph—passages. Treat these just as you would any reading comprehension passage. Keep in mind that your goal is not perfect comprehension but instead to find answers to the questions that you are asked. You can best accomplish this by following a few simple steps.

Steps for Passage-based Questions

Because these passages will probably be only one paragraph long, there's no need to read topic sentences only. Instead, as with literary excerpts, you will skim the whole passage before going back in to search for answers. Here are the steps printed for you again.

1. Read the questions, and circle key words.

2. Skim the passage, reading for a general impression.

3. Forage for answers in the passage.

4. Answer the question in your own words.

5. POE: Match answer choices to evidence in the passage. Eliminate any choice that is not supported by direct evidence in the passage.

Read the passage below, in which a mime relates an experience of a performance, then answer the question that follows.

> I remember once when an audience seemed perplexed at what I was doing. At first, I tried to gain a more immediate response by using slight exaggerations. I soon realized that these actions had nothing to do with the audience's understanding of the character. What I had believed to be a failure of the audience to respond in the manner I expected was, in fact, only their concentration on what I was doing; they were enjoying a gradual awakening—a slow transference of their understanding from their own time and place to one that appeared so unexpectedly before their eyes. This was evidenced by their growing response to succeeding numbers.

48. Which of the following ideas did the author most likely intend to suggest?

(A) The audience's lack of response simply reflected their captivated interest in the performance.
(B) The author was forced to resort to stereotypes to reach an audience that was otherwise unattainable.
(C) Exaggeration is an essential part of mime because it allows the forums used to be fully expressed.
(D) The audience, although not initially appearing knowledgeable, had a good understanding of the subtlety of mime.

Answer choice (A) looks good enough to keep for now. It seems to parallel the story well in that the audience looked disinterested but it turned out that they were actually paying close attention to the mime's performance. Since *stereotypes* were never mentioned or alluded to in the excerpt, you don't have enough evidence to support choice (B). With respect to answer choice (C), while *exaggeration* is mentioned early in the passage, it is not mentioned as a specific element of mime as an art form. Whether the audience "had a good understanding of the subtlety of mime" is never revealed in the short passage, so answer choice (D) isn't really something that you can defend. All things considered, the best choice of the bunch is answer choice (A).

LITERATURE IN SUMMARY

Because you aren't expected to have a thorough academic background in literary theory, the key to doing well on literature questions is actually very similar to the key to doing well on visual arts questions: Use the accompanying passage to eliminate answer choices that don't match up. Additionally, for questions that accompany poetry, you will want to consider that poems often communicate ideas figuratively. Look for main themes in the poem and consider how the language is being used to communicate broader ideas than what is literally said.

8

Communication Skills

READING COMPREHENSION

Although we call it Reading Comprehension, this section is less about reading and more about looking stuff up.

HUNT AND GATHER

If a three-paragraph passage is followed by two questions, how much of the passage could those two questions really cover? And what parts of the passage are you most interested in understanding? You won't need to absorb everything that a reading comprehension passage contains; after all, you're not reading for your own edification—you're just reading to find answers to questions. Because you don't have an unlimited amount of time to take the LAST, your time is better spent hunting for specific information rather than reading the entire passage from beginning to end.

Remember that you don't get points for reading, you get points for answering questions correctly.

READ WHAT YOU NEED

1. Read the questions first to figure out what you need to know.

2. Forage for answers in the passage.

3. Answer the question in your own words before looking at answer choices. This helps you to avoid choosing trap answers or thinking too much about answer choices that have nothing to do with what you read.

4. Use POE to get rid of answers that don't match yours, then pick an answer choice and move on. Don't get hung up on a question until you've had a chance to answer all other questions on the test and have completed your essay.

Let's apply these steps to a sample passage.

1. Read the Questions First

In almost every case, you don't need to read the entire passage to answer the questions about it. The way to figure out what you do need to read is to look at the questions first. As you read each question, decide whether it is general or specific. General questions ask you for the main idea of the passage, the author's primary purpose, the author's attitude, and so on. As you read these questions, circle what the question is asking you, for example, "main idea," "primary purpose," and "tone." Specific questions ask you about pieces of information from the passage. Each of these will contain a lead word—a word or phrase in the question that is easy to spot in the passage. Circle these lead words as you read the questions so that you know what you're going to be hunting for.

For the following passage, read the questions first and decide if they are general or specific.

The United States is currently home to an unprecedented 4,000 nonnative plant species and 2,300 alien animal species. These plants and animals arrive by air and by sea from other continents, often in the bilge water of tankers and as stowaways on aircraft. Previously, very little was done to stop this transport of alien plants and animals. But now, some aliens are so out of control that they are threatening the very existence of America's native species.

Of the 1,900 imperiled American species, 49 percent are being endangered by aliens. Aliens are currently the leading threat to species populations, next to habitat destruction. In some locations, the influence of aliens is already as bad as it can be. In Hawaii, more than 95 percent of the 282 imperiled plants and birds are threatened by aliens.

A crucial preventative measure is to outlaw the release of ballast water in ports. Some ports, like the port in the San Francisco Bay, are populated by almost 99 percent alien species. Yet, limiting the inclusion of alien species will not be easy. Many new species enter undetected.

However, some alien species provide great help to our environment. America's economy thrives on many of our immigrants— soybeans, wheat, cotton, rye, and fruiting trees all originated on other continents and were brought over by colonists. Without any data or observations, it is difficult to predict if an alien species will be beneficial or harmful to our environment.

31. Which of the following is the best summary of the passage?

(A) The United States is home to over 6,000 alien plant and animal species.
(B) Alien species cause a number of devastating problems in our ecosystems, which do not have solutions.
(C) Alien animals and plants can help our environment.
(D) It is difficult to predict the effects of an alien species on our environment.

32. The author specifically mentions the state of Hawaii in the passage because it has

    (A) benefited the most from alien species.
    (B) been greatly hurt by alien species.
    (C) been largely unharmed by alien plants or animals.
    (D) a port that contains 99 percent alien species.

33. What can be inferred from the author's suggestion to outlaw the release of ballast water in ports?

    (A) Ballast water pollutes the ocean.
    (B) Ballast filters are costly to port operators.
    (C) Alien species often enter our environment through ballast water.
    (D) The San Francisco Bay port does not want any more alien species.

Okay, so this passage wants you to give a summary (general question), and wants you to comment specifically on Hawaii and on proposed laws against the release of ballast water (specific questions). Everything else in the passage is completely irrelevant as far as taking the test is concerned.

2. Forage for Answers in the Passage

Do the specific questions first and the general questions second. You should do the questions in this order because you can use the information you have read while answering the specific questions to help answer the general questions.

When answering specific questions, find the lead word or phrase in the passage. You should read one sentence before it and one sentence after it to put the information in context.

3. Answer the Question in Your Own Words

If you know what the answer is before you look at the answer choices, you won't be fooled by tricky wrong answers.

In question 32, you're asked to figure out why the author mentions the state of Hawaii. The author mentions that a large percentage of endangered species in Hawaii are directly threatened by alien species. So, an answer that says something like "alien species can be bad" would be a good thing to say. Looking at the answer choices, you can eliminate (A) and (C) because it's clear from the passage that Hawaii hasn't benefited or been unharmed by the presence of alien species. Answer choice (D) is actually talking about San Francisco rather than Hawaii. The credited response is therefore answer choice (B), which also goes very well with the paraphrase we had in mind before looking at the choices.

In question 33, you're asked to infer something about the suggestion that the release of ballast water in ports be outlawed. By *infer*, the test writers simply mean you should pick an answer choice that can be defended by direct reference to the reading passage. Since this part of the passage is about minimizing negative impact of alien species, and since the only port mentioned in the passage is in the San Francisco Bay (which is said to contain 99 percent alien species), your answer should parallel this theme. So, something that relates release of ballast water to introduction of alien species would be a good answer to choose. Answer choice (A) is a tempting choice if you don't restrict your thinking to the passage in front of you. It might be true that ballast water contains pollutants, but this particular reading passage never discusses that point. Answer choice (B) is wrong for a similar reason: Ballast filters and their cost are never mentioned. Answer choice (C) should be jumping off the page at you as the answer you want to pick. It sticks directly to the main theme of the passage and relates directly to the information given in the part of the passage you've been asked to consider. Answer choice (D) looks suspicious because of the use of the word *any*, which we will discuss in greater detail shortly.

Question 31 is the main idea question. We've already seen from our reading to answer the other two questions that there is some lengthy discussion of alien species and their negative impact. Answer choice (A) fails to capture this element of the passage, and answer choice (C) just looks plain wrong given what we've read so far. Answer choice (B) is very tempting, but is wrong for two reasons. First, the passage never discusses whether the problems that stem from the introduction of alien species have solutions. Second, it ignores the presence of the final paragraph that discusses some beneficial alien species. This last paragraph sets up the conclusion of the passage, which is directly paraphrased in answer choice (D).

In summary, to answer questions based on reading passages, you should focus entirely on what you are told in the passage and pick answers that best match up with the information you are given.

4. Use POE
Here are two great tips to help you eliminate wrong answers.

Tip #1: Eliminate extremes
The presence of extreme language usually indicates that an answer is wrong. Why? Because things are rarely always true or always false. If we were to tell you that everybody likes William Shakespeare, how many people do you have to find to make us wrong? Just one person who doesn't like Shakespeare! On this test, you'll generally want to pick answer choices that are safe, not ones that make extreme claims.

Try this on the question below:

> 34. Why do scientists fear aliens entering our ecosystem?
>
> (A) Alien species will always harm our ecosystem.
> (B) The cost of damage done by aliens is in the billions of dollars per year.
> (C) Alien species have never been beneficial to our environment.
> (D) Alien species have the potential to disrupt our ecosystem.

Answer choices (A) and (C) are directly contradicted by the last paragraph of the reading passage. Of the two remaining choices, (D) is a much safer choice. The billions of dollars per year mentioned in answer choice (B) is a huge number and is not necessarily supported by the passage. Answer choice (D), however, says so little that it's almost impossible for it to be an incorrect statement. Notice how the word *potential* is used to suggest that something might happen or might not happen. Also, notice how the answer choice doesn't say *dramatically disrupt* or *seriously disrupt*. It just says *disrupt*. Could alien species possibly cause some small disruption in our ecosystem? The example of Hawaii would seem to confirm that this answer choice is true. Remember, be suspicious of answer choices that seem to say more than can be safely said.

Tip #2: Answers to main idea questions: Not too big; not too small

A common mistake that people make when answering main idea questions is to pick an answer that doesn't match well with the scope of what's said in the passage. When considering answer choices for main idea questions, you should ask yourself the following questions:

1. "Is it all there?"

   The test writers will write wrong answers to main idea questions by including one piece of the main idea but not the whole thing. Most frequently, the test writers will include an answer choice that is the main idea to only one of the paragraphs. However, your answer needs to address the main idea of the *entire* passage, not just a part of the passage.

2. "Could the author have done this in three paragraphs?"

   On questions that ask for the author's main idea or purpose, the test writers will also create wrong answer choices by writing something the author could never have accomplished in a few paragraphs.

Consider the following passage. Remember to read the questions first (there are a few questions in the coming pages that accompany this passage) so you know what you're looking for.

Imagine going to a fast food restaurant a few years from now. You order a burger, and before you receive your order, the burger is placed through gamma ray treatment. Order some fish, and you'll have to wait for the fish to be placed under a pressure three times higher than the pressure found in the deepest part of the ocean. Why would restaurants go to such lengths? Simply, to make sure your food is safe.

The threat of bacteria entering into our food is at an all-time high. New bacteria such as *Escherichia coli* and *Vibrio vulnificus* have alarmed many food handlers, as well as caused an increasing number of food poisoning deaths over the last five years. As a result, food processors are adopting rigorous standards of cleanliness.

Food scientists are helping. Many scientists are proposing radical alternatives to common food treatment, such as some of the examples described above. While the new techniques are more costly, they are not as costly as the potential lawsuits, bad publicity, and human loss that one outbreak could cause.

The real price to this new technology may not be in dollars, but in overall taste. Scientists admit that tastes may vary in certain foods depending on their processing treatment. As a layman, it seems that placing an oyster under 90,000 pounds of pressure sure seems likely to have some effect on the taste. I just hope that when the gamma rays are removing any bacteria, they'll leave me with the wonderful joy of eating a delicious burger.

14. The writer's main purpose in writing this passage is to

   (A) predict popular foods in the twenty-first century.
   (B) explain why some food-processing techniques will change in the future.
   (C) perform a comprehensive cost analysis of the food-processing industry.
   (D) demonstrate recent scientific advancements.

So what is the author trying to do? The author is explaining that changes to the way food is processed are coming and further explains why those changes are necessary. The author closes the passage by wondering how these processing techniques might affect the taste of food.

Answer choice (A) can be eliminated because the passage never mentions the popularity of different kinds of foods in the future. Instead, the author discusses the future in terms of how food treatment might change. Answer choice (B) looks pretty good. It talks about two important elements of the passage as a whole. First, it discusses things in terms of what will happen in the future. Second, it specifically mentions food-processing techniques. These are both major themes in the passage. Answer choice (C) is much too broad for a three-paragraph essay. A comprehensive analysis of an entire industry sounds like a book-length project, not something that would be found on a passage in a timed exam. Answer choice (D) doesn't look good because the techniques (*advancements*) being discussed in the passage are things that the author predicts will happen soon, not things that have already happened. Further, the advancements are not really demonstrated but instead mentioned in passing as examples.

VOCABULARY-IN-CONTEXT QUESTIONS

To answer a vocabulary-in-context question:

1. Go back to the passage and read the sentence containing the word, as well as one sentence before and one sentence after.

2. Fill in your own word in place of the word you are asked to define.

3. Eliminate answer choices that don't match the word you provided.

15. Which of the following best defines the word "layman" as it is used in the fourth paragraph of the passage?

    (A) Common person
    (B) Expert
    (C) Private citizen
    (D) Clergyman

The author uses the word *layman* more or less to mean "not an expert." You can eliminate answer choices (B) and (D) because they bear no relationship to the definition that you provided. Choosing between (A) and (C) can be a little trickier. The author is trying to draw a distinction between scientists who are developing these food-processing techniques and people who will be going to restaurants and eating the food. The answer choice that more appropriately conveys the meaning of lack of expertise is (A). If the passage were instead comparing public servants with people who were not public servants, then (C) would be more appropriate.

TONE/ATTITUDE QUESTIONS

For questions asking about the author's tone or attitude, be careful about picking answer choices that convey extreme emotions or that indicate the author doesn't care about the topic. It's okay to say that the author is neutral on a topic, but if the author took the time to write about something you can be sure that he or she has some degree of interest.

16. Which of the following best describes the author's attitude toward the new food-processing techniques?

    (A) Flabbergasted
    (B) Concerned
    (C) Disgusted
    (D) Frustrated

Answer choices (A) and (C) are much too extreme to be good answers to this question. (D) isn't as strong as (A) and (C), but it doesn't really match up with the author's tone. The author is, for the most part, neutral in the presentation, but does express some concern about how these new food-processing techniques might impact the taste of food. Answer choice (B) is an excellent answer given what was stated in the passage.

Remember, avoid extreme or overly emotional language when answering tone/attitude questions.

Let's look at one more passage:

The following passage is from a book written by a zoologist and published in 1986.

The domestic cat is a contradiction. No other animal has developed such an intimate relationship with humanity, while at the same time demanding and getting such independent movement and action.

The cat manages to remain a tame animal because of the sequence of its upbringing. By living both with other cats (its mother and littermates) and with humans (the family that has adopted it) during its infancy and kittenhood, it becomes attached to and considers that it belongs to both species. Like a child that grows up in a foreign country and as a consequence becomes bilingual, the young cat becomes bimental. It may be a cat physically, but mentally it is both feline and human. Once it is fully adult, however, most of its responses are feline ones, and it has only one major reaction to its human owners. It treats them as pseudoparents. The reason is that they took over for the real mother at a sensitive stage of the kitten's development and went on giving it milk, solid food, and comfort as it grew up.

1. The primary purpose of the passage is to

   (A) show the enmity that exists between cats and dogs.
   (B) advocate cats as making good pets.
   (C) distinguish the different characteristics of domestic and wild cats.
   (D) explain the contradictory nature of domestic cats.

Answer choice (A) would be a weird answer to pick because dogs are never mentioned in the passage. Answer choice (B) is closer than (A), but still not quite there. The author really doesn't say whether cats would make good pets. Instead, the author is focusing on the mental development of domestic cats. Answer choice (C) doesn't look that great because wild cats are never mentioned in the passage. If the author were interested in distinguishing differences, then one would expect to see at least some discussion on wild cats. Finally, answer choice (D) looks pretty good. The passage begins by stating that "the domestic cat is a contradiction" and then goes on to explain how that happens. As a consequence, (D) would be the one you should pick.

2. According to the passage, which of the following are true statements about the domestic cat?

   I. The domestic cat is tame because of its upbringing.
   II. A young cat considers itself part feline, part human.
   III. Wild cats can easily be tamed if they live with humans.
   IV. The reaction of a domestic cat to its owners is the same as all other domesticated animals.

   (A) I, II, III, and IV
   (B) III and IV only
   (C) I and II only
   (D) I, III, and IV

Roman numeral I is consistent with the beginning of the second paragraph. Therefore, you'll want to eliminate answer choice (B). Assuming for a moment that you don't remember whether Roman numeral II is true, look at Roman numeral IV. Do you know that the reaction of a domestic cat to its owners is the same as *all* other domestic animals? There's certainly not enough in the passage to support this, and common sense would cause us to suspect that this statement is false. Does a goldfish or a turtle react to its owners the same way a cat does? Probably not. So now you can eliminate answer choices (A) and (D) and are left with just one choice, (C), which is in fact the credited response.

RESEARCH AND WRITING

When conducting research, the information you find can be categorized as **primary** or **secondary** sources. A primary source is something that is written and/or created (i.e., a photograph or sound recording) by an individual at the time an event occurs. Diaries and letters are common examples of primary sources. Similarly, a newspaper article from 1851 about an earthquake that took place in 1851 is also considered a primary source.

Secondary sources are written and/or created after an event has occurred, often by individuals who were not directly involved in the event. For example, books and articles about the signing of the Declaration of Independence in 1776 that were written in 1976 (or at any time after the American Revolution) would be secondary sources of information.

Whenever you use information from a primary or secondary source for your own writing, you must give proper credit for using that information. Failure to do so is considered plagiarism. Sources can be properly cited in a body of text through the use of footnotes (bibliographic information appearing at the bottom of the page) or endnotes (bibliographic information appearing at the end of the written piece). Footnotes and endnotes can also be used to further clarify a point or add information without detracting from the main body of writing.

More Flavors—Grammar and Usage Questions

Communication skills questions can come in a few more flavors. Try the next two questions to see how these work.

Read the passage below then answer the questions that follow.

(1) "Translate," as defined in the dictionary, is to change from one state or form to another. (2) For example, we associate translation with international political events where interpreters are needed. (3) Most often, we use the word in terms of language. (4) Or we commonly think of translation in the context of literature, a text being translated from one language into another. (5) Both cases show how translation has given us many benefits.

(7) Yet can those barriers truly be broken? (8) Are there not obstacles to translation?

(9) The expression "good-bye," which in French is translated as "au revoir." (10) Regarded as equivalents, the literal translation of "au revoir" is "until I see you again." (11) Thus, there is a difference in meaning, and this difference, although negligible, points to the fact that the simplest of expressions has the potential to be misunderstood. (12) And if there are difficulties with simple expressions; the difficulties are even greater with more complex ones.

75. Which of the following sentences would best introduce the second paragraph as sentence (6)?

(A) We accept the idea that translation can successfully cross linguistic barriers, that a perfect translation is possible.
(B) Linguistic barriers exist so that each language remains true to its origins.
(C) Translation is a lost art, one that will never live up to the barrier-breaking potential that existed hundreds of years ago.
(D) Translation can be thought of as building barriers between two linguistic entities.

For a question that asks you to provide a transition, you should look for an answer that contains a little bit of the ideas from the preceding sentences and a little bit of the ideas from the following sentences. In this case, you need to find a bridge between the idea of what translation is and the idea of breaking barriers. Answer choice (A) looks good, because it contains the ideas you want the answer to contain, and if you insert the sentence where it's supposed to go, it looks good. You can eliminate answer choice (B) because the origins of language are not discussed in the passage. You should be suspicious of answer choice (C) because of the presence of absolute language (*never*). Finally, answer choice (D) should be eliminated because it says that translation is a means of building barriers rather than building connections. The most appropriate choice is therefore (A).

76. Sentence 12 should be revised to fix which of the following errors?

   (A) An error in parallel structure
   (B) An error in subject-verb agreement
   (C) An error in semicolon use
   (D) It is a run-on sentence

The verb construction in the passage is the same, so (A) is not the answer you want to pick. Subjects and verbs agree (*there are, the difficulties are*), so answer choice (B) is not what you're looking for. Answer choice (C) appears to be a good answer because the semicolon in the sentence is where a comma should be. Finally, the sentence does not appear to be a run-on sentence. You can therefore eliminate answer choice (D) and pick (C) as your response.

COMMUNICATION SKILLS QUESTIONS IN SUMMARY

Here are the main issues that you'll want to remember and apply when approaching reading comprehension:

1. Read the questions first. Remember, you don't have to know everything the passage says. Instead you need to focus on answering the questions.

2. Be suspicious of extreme wording and of answer choices that say more than you could reasonably expect the passage to say. This is true for main idea questions, specific questions, and attitude/tone questions.

3. For vocabulary-in-context questions, cross out the word you are being asked to translate and provide your own word. To determine what word you should use, read one sentence before and one sentence after the word you are asked to define.

4. You will be asked questions on grammar and usage. Review the grammar section of the essay-writing chapters found earlier in this book to become familiar with the most commonly measured grammar rules.

9

Knowledge of the Learner

KNOWLEDGE OF THE LEARNER

The people who make this test want to be sure that you know what makes kids tick. The test writers' reason is that the more you know about how children learn, the better you'll be able to teach them. The Knowledge of the Learner section of the ATS-W covers developmental topics such as theorists and their theories, gender and academic diversity, and students with special needs.

Since this test measures your ability to *apply* the knowledge of the learner, you should focus your preparation accordingly. Rather than memorizing the names of the different stages of development according to Piaget, it's more important to understand what kids are like at different ages. Accordingly, the focus of the following pages will not be a comprehensive review of the ideas of prominent theorists in the field, but instead will present information in a way that applies more directly to how questions will be posed on the ATS-W.

Let's take a look.

WHAT KIND OF STUFF DO YOU NEED TO KNOW ABOUT YOUR STUDENTS?

Cognitive Development

"Cognitive Development" is a fancy-sounding term that is intended to describe how students' minds work with respect to approaching academically related tasks. Knowing at what stage students are in their cognitive development is important because it will guide you toward developmentally appropriate teaching practices. For example, a kindergarten teacher would not be successful using an approach that required students to have abstract reasoning skills.

Moral development

As children develop cognitively, their perception of right and wrong will evolve in their minds. Understanding how your students perceive their relationships with others, and rules in general, is important because it will suggest appropriate solutions to problems involving student disputes with one another and with authority figures.

Social development

Another aspect of development that you will need to be mindful of is social development. The most prominent theorist associated with this field is Erik Erikson, who posited that people go through a series of stages in which certain issues need to be resolved. While these stages progress from birth through old age, we will focus specifically on the stages that are relevant to school-age children, since that's what you will need to know for the test.

FEATURES OF DEVELOPMENT ORGANIZED BY GRADE LEVEL

Pre-K Through Second Grade

- **Cognitive development**

  Students at these grade levels are still developing cognitively and will make mistakes in perception because their brains are still developing. At this stage, children are unable to consider more than one aspect of a problem at a time (called *perceptual centration* by Piaget) and will make errors because of this. In one experiment, Piaget demonstrated that children of this age will mistakenly think that when a colored liquid is poured from a tall, thin glass into a short, wide glass, the amount of liquid has changed. The child makes this error because the child can focus on only one element at a time. In this case, the child focuses solely on the height of the liquid in the glass. Since these kinds of errors are normal for children of this age, they should not be seen as an indication that something is wrong with the child cognitively.

  Additionally, children of this age are not able to consider points of view or perspectives other than their own. This is not due to a child's being self-centered in any kind of malicious or intentional way; it's just a function of cognitive development at this stage in a child's life. This "egocentric" thinking bears a direct relationship to children's moral development.

- **Moral development**

  Students at these grade levels see rules as coming from those in authority and that they should be obeyed for them to stay out of trouble. While children at this age will not question the rules, they will sometimes break rules because they don't completely understand them. Guilt is determined by the consequences of an action, and the intent of the actor is not considered at all. This seems to be related in some way to Piaget's claim that children at this stage cannot consider multiple aspects of a problem and instead focus solely on a single element (the consequences of the action).

- **Social development**

  In the pre-K through early elementary years, students move from one Eriksonian stage to another. Since the second of these two stages lasts through the end of elementary school, it is discussed in detail later in this chapter.

  Pre-K and kindergarten children are in Erikson's stage of initiative versus guilt. While it's not important to memorize the name of the stage, what you will want to remember is that students of this age need to be given the freedom to explore and experiment, and parents and teachers need to be ready for lots of questions from children at this stage. A successful teacher will patiently answer questions and be aware that making a child feel like a nuisance at this age will inhibit the development of initiative.

Third Grade Through Sixth Grade

- **Cognitive development**

   Students can begin to understand logic-based tasks provided that they are working with objects that are actually present or with concepts with which they are familiar through their own experience. While they are not able to think in fully abstract terms, they have moved beyond the perceptual centration that was a prominent feature of the previous stage of development. For example, if presented with a series of pictures, students at this stage can classify them into groups based on a number of themes.

   A good way to distinguish between the cognitive skills of students in elementary school and students in middle school and beyond is that while the younger students are able to learn by observation, they are not yet fully able to extrapolate what they've learned to hypothetical experiments involving items that are not immediately in front of them.

- **Moral development**

   An interesting change takes place between the middle and last couple of years in elementary school. While children in third and fourth grade are very similar to younger schoolmates in that they see rules as handed down by authority figures to be obeyed, children in fifth and sixth grade begin to see beyond the existence of rules and instead begin to understand why rules are necessary. Further, because these older students are more able to consider multiple points of view, they can play a much greater role in establishing rules for behavior among themselves.

   Older children in elementary school begin to see rules as flexible and give due consideration to the intent of the actor in evaluating guilt. Finally, children at this stage have changed their perspective on why rules ought to be followed. While younger children believe that rules should be followed because they have been put there by authority figures, older children begin to see rules as necessary to protect rights. That is, morally wrong acts violate an implicit agreement to respect one another.

- **Social development**

   From first grade through the end of elementary school, children are in the Eriksonian stage of industry versus inferiority. Children at this stage need to be encouraged to try different things to see what they do well. While teachers and parents should be available to assist children, adults need to be careful not to do too much for the child. By facilitating children's work rather than taking it over, children are encouraged to see tasks through to completion rather than simply giving up when things get difficult. To help students make it through this stage successfully, teachers need to recognize that effort on the part of the student is what merits praise: Withholding praise in the event that something isn't done well will tend to inhibit the student's development in the long run by causing the student to shy away from challenges in the future.

Middle School Through High School

- **Cognitive development**

  During this time period, children enter the final stage of cognitive development. They will grow into being able to think in fully abstract terms, as is evidenced by the fact that they can conduct experiments "in their heads." While this skill is developing in the middle school or high school student, one might observe that the student becomes preoccupied with abstract and theoretical matters and may articulate these preoccupations with rather involved metaphysical or political theories.

- **Moral development**

  Moral development of students in middle school and high school is more or less a continuation of the development that began in the later years of elementary school. Rules are seen as representing agreements among parties to protect mutual interests. Students who choose to accept rules (adolescent rebellion will be discussed under the heading of social development) do so either because they are seeking approval or because they understand the importance of rules in maintaining social order.

- **Social development**

  The middle school and high school student is moving through a stage in which the primary issue is the definition of self. Because much of what is appropriate in the mind of the adolescent is driven by the reactions of others, the peer group becomes a major motivating factor. The name of the Eriksonian stage, identity versus role confusion, paints a pretty clear picture of the issue that students in these grades face. Students experiencing role confusion are especially vulnerable to being influenced by fringe groups or gangs.

  Accompanying this stage of social development is the adolescents' perception that parents and teachers don't understand them and that "everyone is watching them." Students who fail to gain peer acceptance can be especially vulnerable to depression, and teachers need to pay attention because of the risk of suicide.

How This Material Might Be Measured on the Test

1. Which of the following statements is/are true?

   I. Sixth graders can group concrete items into categories and can consider viewpoints other than their own.
   II. Tenth graders can engage in both deductive and inductive reasoning.
   III. First graders can understand abstract mathematical concepts.

   (A) I only
   (B) II only
   (C) III only
   (D) I and II only

The cognitive and moral development of sixth graders is such that one would expect them to be able to accomplish the tasks mentioned in statement I. Because (A) and (D) are the only answer choices that contain statement I, you can move ahead to statement II and see if it works. For the purposes of the ATS-W, tenth graders are in the final stage of cognitive development and therefore could engage in the cognitive tasks mentioned in the answer choice. The credited response is therefore answer choice (D).

2. Erikson believes that during childhood, people strive to answer the question, "Who am I?" They need to discover what they value and what their goals are. Approximately when do children usually begin this developmental task?

   (A) When they enter kindergarten
   (B) When they enter third grade
   (C) When they enter junior high
   (D) When they enter eleventh grade

According to Erikson's theory of social development, the stage of identity versus role confusion begins in middle school. Based on this statement, the credited response is answer choice (C).

Test Technique

When you read a question, pay attention to the specified age group. Eliminate answer choices that have students engaging in behavior or activities that are not typical of or appropriate for that age group. Also look out for answers that describe a developmental level, but not the one that is asked about in the question.

3. Julie Trimble teaches third grade. In math, she is teaching students place value, as well as a related topic—money. She lets students work with play money and manipulatives such as Cuisenaire rods. Also, her students have set up a store. Which of the following statements about development are true about Ms. Trimble's class?

   I. The use of physical manipulatives will enhance students' learning.
   II. Because their play involves real-life scenarios, the lessons will be more meaningful.
   III. Because the lesson involves money, the students will be able to successfully run the store without any adult assistance.
   IV. The social opportunities that the store provides should foster students' growth.

   (A) II and III only
   (B) I, II, and III only
   (C) I, II, and IV only
   (D) I, II, III, and IV

The first thing you should notice about any ATS-W question is what grade the question is talking about. The reason you need to pay attention to this is that you should be picking the answer that is most appropriate for the students in the class. In this case, you are working with third graders. Statement I looks good because students of this age are helped in learning by the presence of concrete aids. You can now eliminate answer choice (A). Before moving on to the next statement, consider the remaining answer choices. Notice how all the remaining answer choices contain statement II; because of this you don't need to check statement II—it has to be right, otherwise, there would be no correct answer. Let's move on to statement III now. This one looks bad because it presumes that the students would be able to apply the lesson they received in class to a new situation. By eliminating answer choices that include statement III, you are now left with only one choice. You should therefore select answer choice (C).

Roman Numeral Questions: Review
Although we've discussed Roman numeral questions in the book, here's a review of the approach you should be taking.

1. Read the first Roman numeral statement. If it is correct, circle it; if it is incorrect, cross it out.

2. Look at the answer choices, and eliminate any choice that does not contain a correct statement.

3. Eliminate any choice that contains an incorrect statement.

4. If all the remaining answer choices have a statement in common, there's no need to check that statement because it has to be right.

5. Repeat steps 1 and 2, but only check statements that still remain in the answer choices.

You'll see more of this type of question as we go along.

Teacher Do's and Don'ts

Recall that in the introduction we talked about the idea of a "good" teacher. Rather than imply any kind of judgment of you or any other teacher, we use the word "good" here to remind you that the folks who write and grade the test have some very definite ideas about how teachers should handle a variety of situations. Just as surely as you will want to be sure you have a clear understanding of what students at different grade levels are like, you should also have a very good idea of what kinds of answers will typically be "right" and what types of answers are typically "wrong."

Obviously there is some level of subjectivity behind the claims of what differentiates a "good" teacher from a "bad" teacher; however, for someone with the more immediate goal of passing the ATS-W, providing the answer that the test writers want to see is a more fruitful approach than engaging in an act of political resistance.

Let's take a look at our first set of criteria for what makes a "good" teacher versus what makes a "bad" teacher.

According to NES:

- A good teacher uses developmentally appropriate practices. That is, a good teacher is mindful of students' grade levels and focuses instruction accordingly.

- A good teacher helps students feel good about their successes. This is especially important in elementary grades as students move through stages of social development related to building self-esteem.

- A bad teacher is insincere in her praise.

- A bad teacher uses the same methods with all of her students regardless of their developmental levels.

Here's a sample question to illustrate how you can use the test writers' assumptions of "good" and "bad" teaching to your advantage.

4. Ms. Trimble knows that, according to Maslow, students who feel good about themselves do better in school. Which of the following would be the best method for Ms. Trimble to help her students feel good about themselves?

(A) Posting students' best class work on a bulletin board titled "Look what I did in school!"

(B) Choosing a different student each week to be student of the week, going through her roll-book alphabetically so no one gets forgotten

(C) Noticing which students usually have the right answer in class and mostly calling on those students, making them feel good, and thereby preventing embarrassment in those students who are likely to answer incorrectly

(D) Saying "good job!" every time any student attempts anything, even if unsuccessful

Answer choice (A) looks pretty decent. It recognizes the good work of all students in the classroom and contains a positive message. It's not such a great answer that you wouldn't want to check the others, but it's good enough to keep for now. Answer choice (B) is a bad answer. Although it does attempt to give students some degree of self-esteem, it does so in an insincere way that may very well be noticed by the students. Remember, good teachers are sincere in their praise. Answer choice (C) is also a bad answer, because it leaves students who are not as adept out of the group. Good teachers are going to include all students in classroom discussions and will make students who don't usually get right answers feel better by asking them questions that are more appropriate for their knowledge level (Vygotsky—"zone of proximal developments"). Answer choice (D) is very similar to answer choice (B) in that it is positive yet completely insincere. Praise is positive only if it is given in a way that doesn't seem contrived or automatic. All things considered, answer choice (A) is the best answer because it highlights each student's best work.

MORE "BOOK KNOWLEDGE" THAT YOU MIGHT NEED FOR THE TEST

Bloom's Taxonomy of Learning

Bloom describes six levels of thinking. Teachers should strive to base their instruction methods on the higher levels of Bloom's taxonomy.

1. **Knowledge**—remembering specifics, recalling terms and theories
   - "What is the capital of Tasmania?"

2. **Comprehension**—understanding or using an idea but not relating it to other ideas
   - "Why did Europeans first settle in Tasmania?"

3. **Application**—using concepts or abstractions in actual situations
   - "Draw a map of where Tasmania is in relation to Australia, and shade the most populous regions in blue."

4. **Analysis**—breaking down a statement to relate ideas in the statement
   - "What were the benefits and consequences of using Tasmania as a prison colony?"

5. **Synthesis**—bringing or putting together parts to make a whole or find a pattern
   - "Predict what would happen if the entire U.S. prison population were exiled to one already inhabited state."

6. **Evaluation**—judging value, comparing work with or product to a criterion
   - "What is your opinion on the current methods of punishing criminals in our country? Why?"

Teacher Do's and Don'ts
According to NES:

- A good teacher teaches to a variety of critical thinking levels.

- A bad teacher uses only the first few levels of Bloom's taxonomy.

5. Mrs. Pilkey wants to teach her seventh graders a unit on community service. Her goal is to encourage her students to participate in volunteer activities and to be able to evaluate current community service organizations in the country. Which of the following activities would help Mrs. Pilkey achieve this goal?

   (A) Have students make a list of community service opportunities in the area and share the list with the rest of the school.
   (B) Ask pairs of students to write letters to people who volunteer, asking them about their experiences.
   (C) Have each student research one volunteer organization and write a two-minute presentation on the value of the organization. Students will then choose an organization that they would like to volunteer for and explain why.
   (D) Have the class write a song about volunteering.

The first things you'll want to consider are the students' grade levels and the teacher's educational goals. Remember, the kind of answer you pick should reflect your understanding of your audience and what it is you are trying to accomplish.

In this case, we are trying to encourage seventh graders to participate in volunteer activities and to be able to evaluate current community service organizations in the country. In Bloom's terminology, we are looking to address the highest level of the taxonomy of learning—evaluation.

Answer choice (A) accomplishes neither of the two stated goals. It isn't at all clear how this activity might encourage students to participate in community service nor does it make clear how students are going to be applying skills of evaluation. Instead it seems to be asking students simply to make a list. Answer choice (B) is a little better than (A), but it doesn't seem to be accomplishing the goal of encouraging students to participate in volunteer services. Additionally, instead of relying on their own ability to evaluate something, it relies on other people to do the job for them. Answer choice (C) looks pretty good. It is going to require students to do some form of evaluation in preparation for their individual presentations, and it compels students to select an organization for which they would like to volunteer. Finally, explaining why they have selected the organization for which they have chosen to volunteer is also an exercise in evaluation. Answer choice (D) doesn't seem to be related at all to the stated goals of the project. You can therefore choose answer choice (C) with confidence.

MORE STUFF THAT MIGHT COME UP ON THE TEST

Nature Versus Nurture

This principle balances the effects of heredity (nature) against the effects of environment and experience (nurture). You should understand that both of these might be playing a role in any given situation.

Teacher Do's and Don'ts

According to NES:

- A good teacher makes no prior assumptions about students and their families, yet at the same time is aware that a variety of factors can influence student performance.

- A bad teacher stereotypes her students and is quick to draw unfair conclusions based on their home lives.

What this means, for example, is that it would be wrong to presume that all kids from single-parent homes are a certain way, but it would also be wrong not to consider the impact of coming from a single-parent home when faced with a problem involving a student.

6. The teachers at Overbrook High know that more factors than the environment affect students' development and educational outcomes. All of the following are factors that are strongly related to student performance EXCEPT

   (A) student's expectations.
   (B) teacher's expectations.
   (C) student's socioeconomic status.
   (D) the size of the school library.

Notice first of all that this question ends in the word *EXCEPT*. So what this question is saying is that three of these four things are strongly related to student performance. Also notice that the question itself is discounting environmental factors. Both student and teacher expectations can affect student performance. Research indicates that if a teacher expects a student to perform at a certain level (either poorly or well), the student will meet that expectation for better or worse. Certainly a student's perception of his or her own ability will also affect performance. Next, a number of socioeconomic factors (such as the education level of the student's parents or whether the student is from a two-parent, one-parent, or zero-parent household) could have a strong relation to student performance.

Answer choice (D), however, stands out for a couple of reasons. The question sets you up in a way to anticipate this choice because the question tells you that you should not be considering environmental factors. Additionally, what feature of a library would you suppose is most directly related to student performance? Is it the size of the building? Or is it the number and quality of books in the library or whether the library has good computers with Internet access? Since (D) is the odd one out, it is a great answer choice for an EXCEPT question.

MORE STUFF THAT YOU MIGHT NEED TO KNOW

Learning Styles and Multiple Intelligences

Students exhibit a variety of different learning styles: auditory (listening), visual (through pictures and reading), and kinesthetic/tactile (hands-on experience).

In addition, according to Howard Gardner, students can show intelligence in a variety of ways:

visual/spatial verbal/linguistic musical/rhythmic logical/mathematical	bodily/kinesthetic interpersonal intrapersonal naturalist auditory

These learning styles and intelligences play a large role in the Instructional Planning, Assessment, and Delivery section as well. Teachers need to take them into account when planning lessons and assessments. Why? Because a "good" teacher considers the cognitive level, learning style, and individual needs of each student. Can this really be done in a "real world" classroom with 35 students? In the world of the ATS-W, that's an irrelevant question. Instead, you should focus on what it is you think that the test writers want you to say.

7. Linda Quiring teaches biology at Overbrook High School. She uses a variety of instructional methods to ensure that students with different perceptual modalities benefit from the lessons. Linda's student Ross is a kinesthetic learner. From which of the following assignments would Ross most likely learn the most?

(A) An experiment in which students place plants in different lighting situations to learn about photosynthesis
(B) A chapter about photosynthesis in the textbook
(C) A video about photosynthesis
(D) A lecture in which Linda tells the students to take notes about photosynthesis

Ross is a high school student, so we can be pretty sure that cognitively he is ready for pretty much anything that Ms. Quiring might want to teach. We're also told that Ross is a kinesthetic learner, which means he needs to have some kind of activity or motion integrated into the lesson to receive maximum benefit from the lesson. So, which answer choice involves the most moving around?

Answer choice (A) has students physically moving plants around (or physically changing lighting and leaving the plants where they are). In either case, the students are manipulating either the position of the plants or the arrangement of light. Sounds pretty kinesthetic to us. The remaining choices all have Ross participating in a much more passive way. Although turning the pages in a book or taking notes are physical activities, they are common school activities and are therefore not the kinds of things the test writers are thinking of when they want to hear about accommodating a kinesthetic learning style.

Teacher Do's and Don'ts
According to NES:

- A good teacher engages learners with a variety of modalities and learning styles. Remember, a "one size fits all" approach is not their first choice.

- A good teacher acknowledges achievement in all means of intelligence.

- A bad teacher uses a limited number of teaching methods.

- A bad teacher only recognizes success in certain areas.

8. Ross knows that he is a kinesthetic learner because earlier in the year, Linda assessed students' learning styles. After the assessment, she discussed the results of the assessment with each student privately and with the class as a whole. What are the likely reasons for Linda sharing the assessment results with the whole class?

    I. She wanted all of her students to statistically analyze the results using formulas covered in the honors math class that some of her students are currently taking.

    II. She wanted students to learn a lesson about diversity.

    III. She wanted each student to be aware of his or her own learning style to become more efficient learners.

    IV. Teachers are legally required to share the results of every assessment with students.

(A) II and III only
(B) I, III, and IV only
(C) II, III, and IV only
(D) I, II, and III only

Did you notice in this question that every answer choice includes statement III? What this means is that statement III has to be right and that you don't even need to check it. Statement I doesn't look like a good choice because it would require students who are not in honors math to be using formulas that they don't even know. While the strategy indicated in statement I might be a good way of adding some complexity to the project for talented and gifted students, it doesn't seem appropriate for an entire biology class. Therefore, you can eliminate answer choices (B) and (D) from your list of choices. Now that you are left with answer choices (A) and (C), you should notice that both answer choices contain statement II. That means statement II must be correct and you don't have to check it. So the remaining question is whether statement IV is correct. No such legal requirement as the one mentioned in statement IV exists, so you can safely eliminate answer choice (C) and select answer choice (A) as your final answer.

ACADEMIC DIVERSITY

A classroom can have a range of student ability levels and needs. Teachers need to take into consideration the ability levels of all the students in their classes while planning and teaching a lesson, but they must also specifically think about students with special needs and how the lesson must be adapted for those children. Teachers should consider a student's IEP (*Individual Education Program*) when preparing lessons and assessments.

The IEP is a crucial part of the education of a student with special needs. It begins as a meeting between the teacher, parents, any other education professionals who will be involved in supporting the student, and often the student. The purpose of this initial meeting is to outline the educational goals of the student. The IEP takes into consideration many things: the family life of the child, the child's strengths and weaknesses, the child's goals, and the goals of the class.

For an IEP, the teacher plays a vital role in creating the plan as well as implementing it. Some of the teacher's responsibilities include

- researching a child's background and his/her needs so the teacher may be prepared for the initial meeting

- taking into consideration the goals of the class as a whole in the creation of the IEP

- making sure the class lesson plans reflect the IEP's goals and objectives

- making sure a child is able to meet the objectives of the IEP successfully while remaining an active participant in the school and classroom

- frequently checking in with the IEP team to report progress

- maintaining the IEP through yearly meetings

You should be familiar with the following common student special needs and methods to adapt a classroom to meet these particular needs. Not only might you be tested on this information on a multiple-choice question, but you may also be asked about the issue of accommodating students with special needs as your essay question. Further, as students with special needs are incorporated into mainstream classes (inclusion), all teachers need to be familiar with these issues.

1. **Hearing impaired**
   - Speak clearly and slowly.
   - Face the student when speaking.
   - Provide adequate visual instruction.
   - Position the student in the classroom away from other sounds.

2. **Visually impaired**
   - Read out loud.
   - Provide tape-recorded lessons.
   - Ensure appropriate lighting.

3. **Learning disabled** (students who function two years below ability level)
   - Provide adequate structure.
   - Provide brief assignments.
   - Provide many auditory experiences and hands-on opportunities.

4. **Attention deficit/hyperactivity disorder** (ADHD)
   - Reduce distractions.
   - Reduce the length of tasks.
   - Reward on-task behavior.
   - Use progress charts.

5. **Gifted students**
   - Provide a variety of challenging learning experiences.
   - Do not isolate from the rest of students.

6. **Lower SES**—students from a lower socioeconomic status often have problems at home that lead to them acting out and having attention problems in school.
   - Be sensitive to these students.
   - Do not lower your expectations.
   - Provide extra support and motivation.

7. **Fine Motor Disability**—students who have difficulty with handwriting and putting thoughts on paper
   - Allow students to dictate into a tape recorder.
   - Allow students to type assignments.

8. **Bilingual Students**
   - Incorporate these students' cultures and languages into classroom activities.
   - Provide appropriate visuals.
   - Rewrite or explain text materials.
   - Highlight unfamiliar vocabulary before a lesson.
   - Never leave these students (or any student) out of an activity.

In all cases, teachers should know to refer students to a specialist if conditions are undiagnosed but apparent.

Try this question:

9. Which of the following environmental factors affect student learning?

   I. Sound
   II. Light
   III. Temperature
   IV. Room design

   (A) I only
   (B) III only
   (C) I, II, and III only
   (D) I, II, III, and IV

All four of these Roman numeral choices could of course potentially affect student learning. If the classroom is too noisy, too dark, too cold, or arranged inefficiently, there are going to be problems. Therefore, the answer to this question is definitely (D).

Test Technique

As we mentioned earlier in the chapter, you should look for answers that show compassion for all students. If an answer obviously presents a teacher as uncaring and insensitive, eliminate it. In fact, any answer choice that has a teacher doing something to make his or her own life easier is an answer you should view with suspicion. A "good" teacher is completely unconcerned with his or her own well-being but instead is guided by what is best for the students. While this may at times have you picking answers that you think are "unrealistic," you need to remember that your goal is to pass the test.

Teacher Do's and Don'ts
According to NES:

- Good teachers take into account all of the factors that contribute to development and learning.

- Good teachers are sensitive to the varying needs and levels of students in their classes.

- Bad teachers are inflexible in their plans and teaching methods.

10. Calvin Sheppard teaches kindergarten at Overbrook Primary School. Over the summer, he wrote many lesson plans that he expects will help his students learn the alphabet and even begin reading. On the first day of school, however, he discovers that he has a class of 14 students who do not know the alphabet and one student, Erik, who is already reading at a second-grade level. Calvin should

    (A) stick with his planned lessons for everyone, since 14 of the students will benefit academically, and Erik will need to learn patience anyway.
    (B) suggest to his principal that Erik be placed in second grade.
    (C) adjust his reading lessons so that Erik can participate at his level while the other students learn the basics.
    (D) request a gifted support teacher to work with Erik in Calvin's classroom.

Your first step, as always, should be to focus on the grade level and the goal or problem to be addressed. In this case, we have a kindergarten class with one student who is well ahead of his peers when it comes to reading. So, what do you suppose the test writers think Mr. Sheppard should do?

Answer choice (A) is a bad answer because it completely ignores Erik's needs. A "good" teacher is going to find a way to make everyone's classroom experience a pleasant and productive one. Answer choices (B) and (D) are both examples of Mr. Sheppard "passing the buck." Answer choice (B) is bad because we don't know for sure that Erik is at a second-grade level for any activity except for reading. While moving him to second grade addresses Mr. Sheppard's problem in some ways, is it really the best thing for Erik or the other students in second grade? Answer choice (D) is being a bit lazy as far as the test writers are concerned. The test writers prefer answers where you handle the problem yourself while possibly consulting with experts to help you effectively execute a teaching strategy. Answer choice (C) is a classic right answer for this test. The teacher treats Erik as an individual and doesn't pass the problem off to somebody else. In time, these answer choices become very easy to pick as you learn that the possibility of a solution working isn't really all that big an issue. Instead, you are supposed to pick the answer that conforms most closely to the test writers' ideal of what should be done.

GENDER DIVERSITY ISSUES

Studies show that:

- Boys are more likely to have adjustment problems in school than girls are.

- Girls tend to be more successful in the primary grades, while boys are more successful in secondary education.

- Certain standardized tests have been found to be biased against girls.

- Girls tend to do more poorly in math than do boys, probably because of societal influences.

Test Technique

Avoid answers that seem to assume the worst about students, but recognize that there are real differences between boys and girls. This is more or less the same idea we discussed earlier in the chapter: Don't prejudge any students simply because they are a certain gender, race, or SES status, but keep in mind that a number of factors *may* be contributing to the issue you are facing.

Teacher Do's and Don'ts

According to NES:

- Good teachers use their knowledge of development to remain sensitive to students.

- Bad teachers are quick to make negative assumptions about students.

11. James Quilleran (whom the students call "Mr. Q") teaches at Overbrook High School. He teaches ninth-grade students during second period. He notices that in this class, the girls generally get their class work done with little intervention on his part. Many of the boys, however, need Mr. Q's constant attention. Otherwise, they are unfocused and physically active. This is most likely because

(A) girls usually mature earlier than boys.
(B) many of the boys in Mr. Q's class have ADHD.
(C) the types of assignments that Mr. Q assigns are more interesting to girls.
(D) Mr. Q teaches math, a subject in which girls generally outperform boys.

This question is asking you why ninth-grade boys are unfocused and physically active. While it is true that they *may* have ADHD, it isn't seen as all that unusual that ninth-grade boys are as the question describes. What this question is doing is testing your ability to discern a real difference between boys and girls. Answer choice (A) looks very strong because it is a scientific fact that explains what Mr. Q is seeing with his students. Answer choice (B) is a classic wrong answer. It assumes the worst of his students rather than considering other possible explanations. Without knowing anything about the types of assignments that Mr. Q assigns, it's impossible to defend answer choice (C). Finally, answer choice (D) contradicts what is scientifically known about the differences between boys and girls. Therefore, the answer you want to pick here is choice (A).

ADDITIONAL DEVELOPMENTAL AND EDUCATIONAL TERMS

bilingual classrooms:	There is a growing number of non-English speakers in the classroom, and they require special help. The many ways to deal with this include English submersion programs, ESL classes, and supporting the native language within a traditional English classroom. Relevant vocabulary terms include *LEP* (limited English proficiency) and *TESL* (teaching English as a second language).
charter schools:	These are independent public schools created by various people in the community, often with a specialized focus. Some say that it is hard to assess the success and quality of a charter school and that charter schools often have very homogeneous student bodies.
cognitive:	Something that relates to thinking and learning.
high stakes testing:	Many states require students to take tests as a method of assessing schools and allowing students to continue on to the next level of their education. High scores can bring positive rewards to students and schools. Low scores can bring punishments. The hope is that setting a high standard of education will require schools and teachers to work harder and students to achieve more.
mainstreaming/ inclusion:	Something that involves placing many different types of learners (particularly students with special needs) in one classroom. • began in the 1970s by placing students with disabilities in classrooms with students without disabilities • now called inclusion • pros—can have positive effects on all students, both socially and academically, including higher self-esteem, understanding of others, greater compassion • cons—requires extra help in the classroom, curriculum must be adapted more to meet needs of all students, could be stressful for some special needs students

motor skills: Aspects of a child's physical development.
- fine motor skills refer to things such as using a pencil, tying shoelaces, buttoning a coat, and so on
- gross motor skills refer to larger-scale movements, such as jumping, throwing, catching, and climbing
- motor skills develop as children age

12. Overbrook School District offers numerous in-service trainings throughout the year. One seminar offered is titled "Cognition." In this session, teachers learn what is known about cognition, and how they can use that knowledge in the classroom. All of the following statements could be taught in this seminar EXCEPT

(A) "Students can be taught how to think more effectively."
(B) "Metacognition is a higher-level thinking skill that can aid students in learning."
(C) "Students automatically acquire learning strategies."
(D) "Students who are aware of their perceptual strengths often do better in school."

Note first of all that this is an EXCEPT question. Remember, if this type of question gets confusing, you can avoid that confusion by answering "yes" or "no" to each answer choice. Whichever answer choice is the odd one out will be the one you should pick.

Answer choice (A) looks like it's true. One way that students can be taught how to think more effectively is by learning memory skills. Mark this choice as a "yes." Answer choice (B) looks good too. It seems plausible that a higher-level thinking skill can aid students in learning. Mark this choice as a "yes." Answer choice (C) doesn't look very good. If students were to automatically acquire learning strategies, then what's the point of having a teacher? Mark this choice as a "no." Answer choice (D) looks good. If a student is aware of his or her strengths in terms of a cognitive skill, then that student should do better in school. Therefore, (C) is the correct answer.

10

Instructional Planning

INSTRUCTIONAL PLANNING, DELIVERY, AND ASSESSMENT

These topics combine to make up about half of the multiple-choice questions on the ATS-W. NES wants to be sure you know how to create an informative lesson, teach the lesson effectively, and assess how well you taught it. As with the questions that cover the Knowledge of the Learner, questions that cover Instructional Planning, Delivery, and Assessment will require you to recall some of the basics from your education courses. A review of the most important issues is presented in the following pages.

LESSON PLANNING

Planning means outlining clear lesson objectives and goals. All good planning requires clear objectives and both types of goals:

- **long-term goals** (whole units, monthly goals, yearly goals)
- **short-term goals** (specific lesson objectives, usually per subject period)

Objectives should

- meet state standards, national standards, or local school curriculum guidelines.
- be *age and development-level appropriate*. Review the Knowledge of the Learner chapter for more information on different levels of child development.
- be phrased in language that states what the student will gain from the lesson, not what the teacher intends to do. Remember, this test is about thinking in terms of the student, not the teacher.

Lessons should aim to reach many levels of critical thinking. Simply asking the five W's is not sufficient. The following words are useful objective terms related to different levels of Bloom's taxonomy.

1. **Knowledge**—list, tell, name, define, identify, who, what, where, when, how (multiple-choice tests, fact-recalling essays)
2. **Comprehension**—summarize, describe, associate, contrast (oral questioning, asking "what happens next?," comparing and contrasting)
3. **Application**—apply, demonstrate, calculate, relate, classify, change (math word problems, grouping items, testing a theory)
4. **Analysis**—infer, explain, compare, analyze, separate, connect (problem solving, finding errors in logical reasoning)
5. **Synthesis**—combine, modify, rearrange, create, plan, design, invent (revising something to improve it, making a machine to perform a task, taking knowledge from different areas and using it to solve a problem)
6. **Evaluation**—assess, decide, measure, rank, convince, support, summarize (choosing among three possible solutions, justifying your reasoning for something)

Here is how this content might appear on the ATS-W:

1. Sandra Kowalski teaches a high school class in government. She knows that her students are currently reading Harper Lee's novel *To Kill a Mockingbird* in their English class. This novel details a criminal defense attorney's efforts to exonerate a wrongly accused man. Sandra wants her lesson plans for the next 10 days to relate to this novel, so she will include a field trip to the county court, a role-playing exercise in which students act out a trial, conduct research on the U.S. Constitution, and take a written exam in which students compare the criminal justice system of today with that of the novel's time. The most likely objective of the unit Sandra is teaching for the next 10 days is that

    (A) students will further develop their dramatic skills.
    (B) students will do background research to enhance their comprehension of *To Kill a Mockingbird*.
    (C) students will learn the laws of the United States.
    (D) students will analyze the way accused criminals are prosecuted.

The first thing to notice is that it's a high school government class. We can assume the students are cognitively developed enough that the lesson doesn't have to be presented in a way that it might have to be for younger students. In support of her students reading *To Kill a Mockingbird*, Ms. Kowalski schedules activities that focus on the criminal justice system. Why do you think she is doing this?

Answer choice (A) looks bad because it isn't apparent why the government teacher would be concerned with developing students' dramatic skills. Answer choice (B) doesn't look so great for the same reason that (A) doesn't look great. It doesn't explain how the activities are supporting the goals of a government class.

Answer choices (C) and (D) both talk about things that would be covered in a government class. Since most of the activities are related to the proceedings of a criminal trial, and since the activities are being conducted in conjunction with a book that is about a criminal trial, answer choice (D) appears to be a closer fit to the specifics of the lessons. Answer choice (C) seems a bit suspicious because it appears to be too broad a goal for students to learn the entire legal code of the United States in 10 days.

STUDENT-DIRECTED LEARNING

Effective teachers allow and encourage students to set their own academic goals and to participate in the creation of objectives. Research indicates that students are much more interested in lessons if they take part in creating learning objectives.

Test Technique

Eliminate answers that include activities used to free up time or make things easier for the teacher. On this test, good teachers are unselfish saints—*unless* the procedure makes the classroom run more efficiently overall, thus reducing the amount of wasted time for the students. See the difference here? If it's good for the students *and* good for the teacher, then it's a good plan. If it's good for only the teacher, then it's a bad plan.

2. Diana Wall is creating a daily schedule for her second-grade class. She wants to include two 10-minute recess periods for her students during the day—one in the morning, and one around 2:00 P.M. Diana does this because

   (A) the other second-grade teacher has a similar schedule.
   (B) she knows how beneficial small breaks can be for children during a day of learning.
   (C) she wants to make sure she has time to prepare for her mid-morning and afternoon lessons.
   (D) she knows that one of the students in her class has an attention problem and she wants to make sure he has plenty of time to play.

Why does Ms. Wall introduce these breaks? They must be good for the students somehow. Find an answer choice that communicates this simple idea.

Answer choice (A) is bad. Teachers should be making decisions based on what is best for the students. Teachers should not be making decisions just because other teachers do something a certain way. Answer choice (B) looks terrific: The teacher's decision is being driven by what is good for the students. Answer choice (C) is terrible as far as the test writers are concerned. According to the test writers, a "good" teacher *never* does anything simply to make his or her own life easier. Answer choice (D) isn't bad, but it's just not as good as (B). Which answer serves the interests of more students while hurting nobody? Answer choice (B) is therefore your best choice.

Teacher Do's and Don'ts
According to NES:

- Good teachers use lessons that incorporate their students' interests and personal learning objectives.

- Bad teachers use strictly teacher-created lessons.

3. Lynn Scanlon begins each unit by asking her students what they want to learn about the new topic. She does this mainly because

    (A) it will make her own lesson planning easier because she will have to think up fewer ideas herself.
    (B) students who set their own goals are more motivated to learn.
    (C) she will be able to assess their learning more effectively at the end of the unit.
    (D) she wants to determine whether the students have an interest in the intended topic of study.

(A) is another example of an answer choice that is wrong because it is motivated by the teacher wanting to avoid work. Answer choice (B) looks great. It is expressed in terms of what is best for students, and it reflects conventional wisdom regarding the topic. Answer choice (C) isn't expressed in terms of what is best for the students, and it's also not clear how asking students what they want to learn will have an impact on how well the teacher can assess student learning. Answer choice (D) is expressed in terms of what is best for the students, but it doesn't explain how the teacher's educational goals are going to be easier to meet because of this. This difference between answer choices (B) and (D) is what makes (B) the credited response.

COLLABORATIVE LEARNING

Collaborative ("cooperative") learning utilizes student strengths and weaknesses to create a rich academic environment that fosters peer relationships and healthy competition. Students work in heterogeneous groups of varying numbers (usually no more than six) to solve a problem or complete an assignment. When the project is finished, students share in a discussion of the learning process that has just taken place.

Teacher Do's and Don'ts
According to NES:

- Good teachers provide students with opportunities to learn from one another.

- Bad teachers dominate the classroom and control every lesson.

4. Sandra's students frequently work in cooperative groups. Sandra assigns the groups in such a way as to maximize both learning of the subject matter (government) and learning about collaboration. Which of the following are most likely characteristics of the groups in Sandra's class?

    I. The groups are heterogeneous in terms of ability.
    II. The groups are homogeneous in terms of ability.

III. The group members change from day to day.

IV. The students in each group work together for several months.

V. Each group has from three to five members.

(A) I and IV only
(B) II and III only
(C) I, IV, and V only
(D) II, III, and V only

Statement I looks good from the standpoint of what you are supposed to know about collaborative learning. If the members of the group are different, then they learn more than if they were all the same. Since statement I is true, you are left with only two answer choices—(A) and (C). Since they each have statement IV in them, you don't have to check statement IV and because you can assume that it is correct. All that's left for you to do now is check statement V to see if it's true. Since it is, you can now safely select answer choice (C) as your answer.

THEMATIC CURRICULUM

Using a thematic curriculum involves teaching one concept over a variety of different subject areas (i.e., science, art, reading, writing, and technology) and through a variety of different methods. The benefits of thematic units include reaching many different learning styles and making connections for students across a wide curriculum.

5. Which of the following is an example of a thematic curriculum?

(A) Students studying "diversity" in science (biodiversity), social studies (the community), and art (diversity of influences on an artist)

(B) Students in second grade doing three different physics experiments on "force"

(C) Students in the third through sixth grades all simultaneously studying Mexico in social studies, each grade at its own appropriate level

(D) High school students learning about banking first at a simple level ("what banks do"), then an intermediate level ("how they do it"), and finally at a complex level ("why they do it")

Remember, a thematic curriculum is when students study the same thing from the perspective of different subjects. This is best expressed in answer choice (A), since a topic (diversity) is being studied from the perspective of different subjects (science, social studies, and art). While the other answer choices do describe a phenomenon being presented more than once, none of these examples have students in the same grade examining a subject from different perspectives. Answer choice (C) is wrong because the students in each grade are only studying the topic from the perspective of one subject.

In summary, kids in the same grade studying the same topic in different classes is an example of a thematic curriculum. Kids in different grades studying the same topic in one class for each grade is not an example of a thematic curriculum.

More Teaching Strategies and Terms

cooperative: Either deductive or inductive activities that students participate in as part of a group

deductive: Teachers or other students present the material in lecture format (i.e., basic lectures, student presentations, videos).

discussion: Either deductive or inductive activities that focus on talking about a subject and either answering specific questions or sharing ideas

inductive: Students learn by discovery (i.e., free exploration time with a new tool, science experiments, brainstorming).

modeling: The teacher demonstrates the skill or concept being taught.

resources: Materials that aid in teaching. Teachers should use a wide variety when creating a lesson, such as manipulatives, technology, print resources, and visual materials. This helps reach a multitude of learning styles.

Test Technique

Eliminate answers that include very low-level instructional methods or inappropriate uses of resources—unless the question asks for the LEAST appropriate method.

6. Jack Shaeffer teaches physical education. He is interested in using some audiovisuals in his class. Which of the following is the LEAST appropriate use of audiovisuals in Jack's class?

   (A) Posters around the locker room depicting children happily participating in sports
   (B) Charts and graphs displaying performance statistics about intramural teams
   (C) A CD-ROM program in which students simulate playing basketball, used instead of actually playing basketball
   (D) A CD-ROM program that teaches students the rules of football, used before students begin to play football

Although you aren't told what grade the students are in, you do know that the teacher is a physical education teacher. Keep this in mind when evaluating your answer choices. Also, you are looking for the *least* appropriate example. Which one would the teacher *not* do?

Answer choice (A) looks fine because it uses visual aids to promote sports by suggesting that they are fun. Answer choice (B) seems appropriate as well since it is related to the athletic activities of the school's intramural teams. Answer choice (C) looks like something that the teacher should *not* be doing. Would it be appropriate for students to be playing computer games during a physical education course? While answer choice (D) also includes a CD-ROM program, it is used in support of the longer-term goal of having the students actually play football. Since answer choice (C) fails to support physical activity, and since this is a physical education course, this is the answer choice you should select as the thing that Mr. Shaeffer should *not* be doing with his class.

7. Jack wants his students to learn what it takes to make a team function well. All week, at the end of every activity that involves teamwork, he asks each student three questions:

"What worked well for your team today?"

"What did not work so well?"

"What would you do differently next time?"

Jack writes down every answer. At the end of the week, he uses an overhead projector to show students all of their answers for the week. He asks them to develop generalizations about teamwork. This is an example of

(A) a deductive method.
(B) cooperative learning.
(C) a thematic curriculum.
(D) an inductive method.

Remember, a deductive method is a teaching method where the teacher presents information and the students take notes. In this case, the teacher is counting on the students to generate conclusions. Therefore, answer choice (A) is not a good choice. Answer choice (B) is a close second choice. Notice, however, that the students never work in small groups. Instead, each student generates his or her own individual observations and then the class as a whole works on drawing generalizations. Since this exercise is missing a couple of key features of cooperative learning, you should be comfortable not picking (B). Answer choice (C) is relatively easy to eliminate since only one subject is being discussed in the question. A thematic curriculum involves a variety of subjects. Finally, answer choice (D) looks very good. An inductive method relies on the students to use information to arrive at their own conclusions, and this is exactly what is happening in this example.

ASSESSMENT METHODS

Teachers should use more than one assessment method to get a more complete picture of a student's abilities.

1. Testing
   - paper-and-pencil tests (fill-in-the-blank, multiple-choice, true-false, short-answer, essay tests, and so on)
   - standardized tests
   - oral exams

2. Portfolios
   - a collection of student work
   - sometimes examples of a student's "best" work, but sometimes the portfolio demonstrates the different stages of one piece of student work
   - the student, either alone or with the aid of a teacher, determines the contents of the portfolio

3. Projects

4. Observation

5. Anecdotal records (usually used to document behavior)

6. Papers

7. Peer and self-assessment

8. Performance-based assessment (students are required to complete a task and are graded on how well they carry out the task)

Testing is generally considered a less authentic assessment method than are the other methods listed above.

Assessment Terminology

criterion-referenced test:	Students are measured against uniform criteria. They are scored out of 100 percent because there is the possibility that students will master all of the concepts tested.
holistic scoring:	Judging a work by the complete picture it presents.
norm-referenced test:	Students are measured against one another. Scores are reported in percentiles, which indicate the percent of the testing population whose scores were lower than or the same as a particular student's score.
reliability:	The consistency of a test; for example, the test will indicate the same score for the same student if taken more than once.
validity:	How well a test measures what it is supposed to measure; teacher-made tests are usually not extremely valid.

8. Ms. King, a high school English teacher, hands out the following questionnaire at the end of each major assignment:

   "How do you feel now that you are done with this assignment?

   If you had more time to work on the assignment, what would you do?

   What can you do better because of this assignment?

   What is one way you will reward yourself for finishing this project?

   Are you ready to move on to the next assignment? If not, why?"

   The purpose of this questionnaire is

   (A) to assist in Ms. King's future lesson planning.
   (B) to provide students with additional writing practice.
   (C) to encourage student self-assessment.
   (D) to encourage discovery learning.

Notice how every question is asking the student to evaluate elements of his or her own work. Of course, you are also looking for answer choices that explain things in terms of why they are good for the student. The most appropriate answer choice to capture both of these ideas is (C).

Test Technique

Eliminate answer choices in which the assessment method does not support the teacher's desired outcomes.

9. Which of the following assessments can best assess higher-level thinking skills?

   (A) Multiple-choice tests
   (B) Fill-in-the-blank tests
   (C) Oral tests
   (D) Projects

To measure higher-level thinking skills, you should be looking for the most involved task on the list. While answer choice (C) could conceivably assess higher-level thinking skills depending on the type of questions asked, the test writers are going to want you to select the task that seems most open-ended. In this case, answer choice (D) would be the answer you could pick.

10. Which of the following assessments can most efficiently assess student recall of factual information?

    (A) Multiple-choice tests
    (B) Portfolios
    (C) Essay tests
    (D) Projects

In this question, you are looking for a method of assessment that will *efficiently* assess student recall. By focusing on the adjective, you should be looking for an assessment technique that can be administered and scored pretty quickly. Further, since you are measuring recall of factual information, you are not looking to test higher-order thinking skills. So, for this question, you are best served by selecting answer choice (A).

Teacher Do's and Don'ts
According to NES:

- A good teacher uses a wide variety of assessment techniques to get the big picture.

- A bad teacher uses only tests to assess a student's performance. A bad teacher fails to measure higher-order thinking skills by only utilizing assessment tools that target lower-order skills.

Classroom Management

Successful teachers have clear management plans in place in their classrooms. There are many different models of management to choose from but, for all students, consistency is vital. You will notice that many of these management techniques are applying behavioral theories. In short, behaviorists claim that students' behaviors can be shaped. Behaviors that teachers want to cultivate can be encouraged through the use of positive reinforcements (praise, good grades, or prizes), while behaviors that teachers want to eliminate can be discouraged through the use of negative reinforcements (punishments or withholding rewards). Some of the various styles and techniques are:

assertive discipline:	This is a method devised by Lee Canter. The basis of the program involves catching students behaving appropriately and rewarding that good behavior. Conversely, they are punished for poor behavior. Critics of the system assert that students should behave because it is the right thing to do, not because of the punishments and rewards associated with an action.
consistency:	Whatever the system, the rules, guidelines, or rewards, they must remain the same or else students will have no true system to follow.
cueing:	Alerting students that a transition is about to happen. This is in fact an example of a conditioned response.
extinction:	In some cases, the best way to stop a negative behavior is to ignore the behavior rather than to provide a negative reinforcement. Why? In some cases, the negative attention from the teacher is exactly what the student is looking for. So, the best way to stop the negative behavior is to withhold the attention that the student is seeking.

Glasser's reality therapy:	Glasser maintains that students are more motivated to behave well when given choices and taught the real world consequences of choices they make.
organization and structure:	If there is a clear structure in place for a certain event or activity, management issues will remain at a minimum.
punishment:	Punishments are meant to improve a particular behavior. They should be logical and deliberate as well as reasonable. It should "fit the crime" and be paired with modeling (the teacher's own actions serve as an example of acceptable behavior) or discussion of the correct way to behave.
reinforcement:	Students are very receptive to praise, recognition, good grades, rewards, or, for that matter, any type of attention that will reinforce a particular behavior. Negative reinforcement allows teachers to show students how to avoid unwanted consequences.
student contracts:	Student contracts are used to address a specific problem behavior or to prevent such a behavior. The student and teacher generally write the contract together, agreeing on the guidelines, and then both sign it. Sometimes, if students uphold their part of the contract, they are given some type of reward.
time on task:	All classroom management is designed to help the students learn more effectively and spend the most amount of time on learning endeavors. Therefore, when in doubt, the classroom management system allowing for that to happen is the most effective choice.
transitions:	Transitions tend to be a time when classroom management becomes most challenging. Students need constant structure and direction and often those are lacking in times of transition. It is essential to be aware of the need for and to implement smooth transitions.

11. Which of the following is the most effective
way for a teacher to begin class?

(A) The teacher writes several math problems
on the board for students to attempt as
soon as they enter the room.
(B) The teacher has students check off their
names on the teacher's attendance list,
and then read quietly in their seats for five
minutes.
(C) The teacher does not interact with the
class until all students have stopped
talking and are in their seats.
(D) Beginning the moment the students walk
through the doorway into the classroom,
the teacher does not allow them to
speak at all until they have been directly
addressed by the teacher.

Answer choice (A) is the most suitable choice of the bunch. This kind of answer is also known as a "Do Now." It's a good choice because it gets the students on task right away. Answer choice (B) is not appropriate because it gives students direct access to the teacher's attendance list. This could pose problems since students might mark absent classmates as present. Answer choice (C) is a poor strategy since it could result in the students wasting the entire class period talking to one another. Finally, answer choice (D) displays behavior that isn't consistent with a teacher who is concerned with establishing a good working relationship with the students in the classroom.

Teacher Do's and Don'ts
According to NES:

- A good teacher has a well-managed classroom where the majority of time is spent on-task.

- A good teacher has solid, consistent transitions and structure for younger students.

- A good teacher provides a nurturing, safe, diverse, cooperative, and bias-free environment.

- A bad teacher creates lists of many specific rules and forces children to memorize them.

- A bad teacher loses control of classroom situations and does not have appropriate systems in place before something happens.

12. Teacher Melissa Kolbert allows her students to place their desks anywhere in the room while they do seat work. She programmed a computer to play a brief melody every period five minutes before the bell rings. When the students hear the melody, they know to finish what they are doing and to put all desks back in rows. Melissa does this because she wants

(A) to use technology in the classroom.
(B) a smooth transition.
(C) students to be seated when the bell rings.
(D) to reinforce the idea of student-selected seating assignments.

What's going on here? The teacher utilizes a stimulus (bell) to elicit a specific behavior (straightening up desks). While this is a use of technology in the classroom, the use of technology is not an end in itself. Answer choice (B) looks very strong, since what the teacher is doing is building in a transition between seat work and the end of class. Answer choice (C) doesn't seem to make too much sense. All the students were seated before the melody played on the computer. The melody in fact got students to get up and move around. Since seating assignments are never discussed in the problem, there's really no way you can justify answer choice (D). So, (B) turns out to be the best choice for this question.

MAINTAINING ATTENTION

There are a few key tricks to keeping motivation and attention in a classroom high.

- Appropriate classroom layout: Set up the classroom so all the students can see you and you can see them.

- Establish yourself as the authority of the classroom, but not an authoritarian.

- Establish a few clear, adaptable rules that outline acceptable and unacceptable behavior.

- Involve all students in questions and answers.

- Maintain momentum of a lesson and avoid side comments and unrelated side discussions.

- Begin each lesson with a *motivation*—something that is interesting to students—that ties their real world into the academic subject and explains the reason for studying the topic.

Teacher Do's and Don'ts

According to NES:

- A good teacher never reprimands or humiliates students in front of their peers.

- A bad teacher uses sarcasm to interact with students.

Here is an example of how this might be measured on the test:

13. Kim Levin is a tenured teacher who is sharing her classroom with Joan, a student teacher. Joan is engaging students in a teacher-led question-and-answer discussion. Joan poses a question and then calls on student Desiree by saying, "Desiree, I don't suppose you know the answer, do you?" When Joan asks Kim for feedback on her discussion-leading skills, Kim most likely tells her,

(A) "That was a good way to motivate Desiree."
(B) "Sarcasm is a useful tool for a teacher, especially when students are not responding in the expected manner."
(C) "Desiree will be less likely to participate in class after today."
(D) "The rest of the class probably likes you more because of what you said to Desiree."

What do you think of what Joan says? She's probably made a mistake because she communicated to Desiree that she thinks Desiree doesn't know the answer to the question. Exhibiting this kind of low expectation for your students is something you will want to work to avoid. Given the error that Joan made, what will be Kim's response to Joan's question? Answer choice (A) is about as wrong as an answer can be. Showing a lack of confidence in your students is no way to motivate them. Answer choice (B) is about as wrong as answer choice (A), since it indicates that sarcasm is a useful teaching tool. Answer choice (C) is exactly what the test writers are looking for. The student will be less likely to participate because the student now believes that the teacher has low expectations of her. Answer choice (D) is also off base because the teacher's primary goal should be the education and development of the students rather than to be popular with students.

14. Joan is already thinking ahead to the time when she has her own classroom. She wants to create a classroom characterized by trust, warmth, and teacher-facilitated teamwork. She wants Kim's advice on seating arrangements. When Joan asks Kim where the teacher's desk should be, Kim says that it should be

(A) in the front and center of the classroom, between the students' desks and the chalkboard.

(B) in the front of the classroom but off to one side so that it does not block the chalkboard.

(C) in the back of the room, with all of the students' desks facing the teacher's desk instead of the chalkboard.

(D) in the back corner of the room, with all of the students' desks facing the front of the room and the chalkboard, and the teacher's desk facing the back.

The teacher should place her desk where she can command the attention of the students yet not interfere with the learning experience. Answer choices (C) and (D) are the easiest ones to eliminate because both of them exhibit significant errors in classroom design. Answer choice (C) has all the student desks facing away from the chalkboard, and (D) has the classroom arranged in a way where the teacher cannot see the students. Answer choices (A) and (B) are very similar to each other, with the difference being that in (B), the teacher's desk doesn't block the chalkboard. The arrangement that is most conducive to the teacher maintaining control of the classroom while not interfering with student learning is described in answer choice (B).

11

The Professional Environment

THE PROFESSIONAL ENVIRONMENT

Part of being a successful teacher is interacting with parents, other teachers, school administration, and the community. NES wants to make sure that you know how to "play nice." Additionally, the test writers want to make sure that you are aware of laws pertaining to teachers and schools.

IMPORTANT TRAITS OF A TEACHER

- A teacher is an authority figure in the classroom.

- You must be caring and nurturing, but at the same time, set clear limits and expectations.

- The teacher is not only a role model, but also a monitor of student development and achievement.

- Personal characteristics that make a successful teacher include confidence, high energy level, organization, creativity, and understanding.

A good teacher must be able to respect and appropriately utilize the chain-of-command.

1. Gert Prevost is a teacher who is currently without an assistant. Gert's principal asks for her input in the process of hiring a new assistant. Gert tells the principal that she wants someone with all of the following personal traits EXCEPT someone who

   (A) is patient with the students.
   (B) fills all silences with talking.
   (C) feels good about himself.
   (D) has a sense of humor.

This particular question is a great reminder of a couple of important test-taking techniques. First of all, notice that this is an EXCEPT question. The "right" answer is going to be the characteristic that you would *not* want in a teacher. By examining the credited response to this question—answer choice (B)—you should also be reminded of a second test-taking technique. Notice that answer choice (B) includes the word *all*. Would it really be the mark of a good teacher to fill *all* silences with talking? That seems a bit extreme, and at least for times when students are taking tests, you would want to make sure you have a teacher who knows how to be quiet.

Test Technique

Remember, "good" teachers put their students and professional commitments ahead of their own needs. Don't evaluate questions in terms of what you think you would do, but in terms of what you think the test writers want you to say. Of course there will be plenty of times when what you would do in the situation will match what the test writers want you to say, and that's fine too.

2. John Loxterman is the former social studies department chairperson and the former track coach of Lawndale High School. He moved to Bayview to take on the same two positions at Bayview High. He is contractually obligated to coach the track team, but he is dismayed to find that Bayview's team this year is made up solely of girls. His team at Lawndale had boys and girls on it. John does not feel comfortable coaching an all-female team. He recognizes that this is a bias in himself, but he doesn't think he can overcome it before school starts in two weeks. Which of the following would be the most appropriate course of action for John to take?

   (A) He should resign from his position at Bayview High.
   (B) He should refuse to coach until the school changes the makeup of the team so that it is half girls and half boys.
   (C) While coaching the girl's team, John should attempt to recruit boys to the team, all the while making sure that his behavior does not reveal any bias.
   (D) He should tell the principal that he wants to coach some other activity.

School starts in two weeks. What do the test writers think Mr. Loxterman should do? First of all, he is going to have to meet his obligation to work for the school. It's much too late to be leaving the school short a department chairperson, and you can eliminate answer choice (A) on those grounds. Next, notice that Mr. Loxterman is contractually obligated to coach the track team. You can be sure that the test writers will fully expect you to live up to any contract that you sign. This point is a good enough reason to eliminate answer choice (B). The final two answer choices pose one of those "real world" versus "test world" issues. You might be reasonable in thinking that you could at least tell the principal what's bothering you and accept that the principal might say no. But in the "test world" you should sacrifice any concerns regarding your own wishes and go with the professional commitment that you have made. So in this case you can safely pick answer choice (C).

TEAMWORK

Working with a team is becoming a common practice in schools. These experiences require cooperation, organization, and a sense of humor. It is critical that a group of teachers utilize their individual strengths and weaknesses for the good of the group.

Some common uses for team teaching:

classroom instruction:	Two teachers work together to teach a larger-than-normal class of students.
curriculum groups:	Teachers often work together to create curricula across grade levels. Sometimes this group can function as a textbook selection committee or as a place to test new ideas or lessons.
other:	Teachers work in groups or teams for a variety of other reasons as well, such as event committees, school spirit groups, and sports teams groups.
special needs adaptations:	A teacher's aide or a special education teacher works in a regular classroom with the primary teacher.

3. Gert has a learning-disabled student, Jamie, in her class. Jamie often is unable to understand the directions for assignments that Gert assigns. Because Gert is currently working without an assistant, she does not have time in class to spend one-on-one time with Jamie. Gert should

   (A) not worry about it since soon she will have an assistant and then will have time to spend with Jamie.
   (B) collaborate with a specialist to come up with ways to make Jamie's class time productive.
   (C) suggest to her principal that Jamie be placed in a special education class until Gert's new assistant starts.
   (D) demand that her principal hire a substitute assistant teacher until the new person starts.

The test writers are looking for an answer that does three things. First, the teacher should take immediate action. Second, the teacher should put the needs of the students first. Third, the teacher should not react to the problem by passing it off to someone else. Let's see what those answer choices say. (A) isn't appropriate because Jamie is falling farther behind every day. Answer choice (B) looks very strong. Gert is taking primary responsibility for addressing Jamie's problem and, further, is consulting with an expert to make sure the student is getting as much out of class as possible. Answer choice (C) is a classic wrong answer on this test, since it is an example of passing the buck rather than thinking about the needs of the student. (D) is another classic wrong answer. An answer choice that involves a teacher storming into the principal's office and making demands is not going to work.

Here's another example of how your professional skills might be measured on the test:

4. The entire student body at Bayview High School is creating a time capsule. The time capsule will be opened in five years. Which of the following statements about the teachers at Bayview High School is true?

    (A) The teachers who are able to work well collaboratively are likely to have the most success with this project.
    (B) Only teachers who plan on teaching at Bayview for five more years should participate in the project.
    (C) The teachers will have to attend an in-service training to learn how to create a time capsule.
    (D) The teachers at every grade level should have the same educational outcomes planned for their students.

Answer choice (A) is a classic example of a right answer. Not only does it exhibit behavior that the test writers are looking to credit (collaborative work), but it also includes the words *are likely* in the answer choice. How can you argue with that? Answer choice (B) isn't really justified as there doesn't seem to be any good reason why teachers who won't be at Bayview when the time capsule is opened shouldn't participate in the project. Similarly, there doesn't seem to be compelling evidence to support answer choice (C). Is attending an in-service really necessary? (D) stands in opposition to one of the principles you should be looking to exhibit in your answer choices. Different students are treated differently according to their specific needs.

Teacher Do's and Don'ts
According to NES:

- Good teachers are not islands unto themselves; they work cooperatively and effectively with other teachers in a team-teaching situation.

- Good teachers are not too controlling in team projects.

- Bad teachers are bossy.

- Bad teachers don't share their ideas.

5. David Fitch, the art teacher at Bayview, has been assigned the role of project facilitator. He is very excited because he has ideas about what every class and every student should contribute to the time capsule. When he leads an introductory staff meeting about the time capsule, he should

(A) tell everyone how he thinks it should be done and send them off with their assignments.

(B) have an open-ended, unfocused discussion so that the staff members with the strongest personalities can assume leadership roles in the project, therefore giving David less work.

(C) in an organized manner, let everyone have a turn giving ideas, and then mention any of his ideas that no one suggested.

(D) tell the staff members that they need to submit every lesson plan relating to the time capsule project to him for pre-approval.

Remember, in questions that deal with group projects, *group leader* is not the same thing as *group dictator*. A good leader keeps the members of the team involved in and supportive of the goals of the project. Keeping this in mind, you can eliminate answer choices (A), (B), and (D). Both (A) and (D) are too dictatorial, and answer choice (B) shows weak leadership and is yet another example of a teacher making a decision to avoid doing work. In answer choice (C), however, Mr. Fitch keeps the meeting organized yet doesn't usurp the decision-making process.

PROFESSIONAL GROWTH

Part of a teacher's responsibility is constantly maintaining and updating his or her skills through professional development seminars and trainings.

PUBLIC SCHOOL HIERARCHY

New York State is so diverse that there are many different hierarchal situations that exist within the school system. You won't need to know any specifics, but you should know that in general the hierarchy works like this:

State

City/District

Superintendent/Local School Board

Principal

Teacher

Some policies are made at the state level, others are made at the district level, and some are made at the school level. The best way to tackle questions relating to responsibility is to find the answers indicating that a teacher

- shows respect for the hierarchy as well as the concerns of the parents and students; and

- refers parents to proper higher administration whenever required, without shifting responsibility unnecessarily.

Teacher Do's and Don'ts
According to NES:

- Good teachers are open-minded and always trying to improve themselves.

- Bad teachers are lazy and too selfishly motivated.

6. Gayle Simons has been teaching first grade for 30 years. She subscribes to and thoroughly reads three professional journals. She is considering attending an annual conference for primary school teachers. Which of the following should be important considerations in her decision whether to attend?

I. She probably knows more than anyone who will be presenting at the conference, so she should avoid the conference, especially since it might make her tired.
II. Even though she is very experienced, she may learn new methods that can benefit her students.
III. The conference may provide her with new opportunities for collaboration.
IV. Because her principal will be impressed by her motivation and the extra effort she is putting forth, Gayle may receive the department chairperson promotion instead of her colleague, Emily Stewart.

(A) I only
(B) II only
(C) II and III only
(D) II, III, and IV only

Statement I looks bad because it's an example of a teacher making a decision based on a desire to avoid work. It also makes the incorrect assumption that a teacher can get to a point where she has learned everything there is to know. You can go ahead and eliminate answer choice (A). Since all remaining answer choices contain statement II, you can go ahead and assume it's true without having to check. Statement III looks very good, especially given that it contains the word *may*. You can now eliminate answer choice (B). Finally, statement IV can be eliminated because it is motivated by self-interest. Therefore, the credited response must be answer choice (C).

POSITIVE RELATIONSHIPS WITH PARENTS

Because of the many changes in the American family, parents often play a different role in the education of their children from that of prior times. Therefore, it is often necessary for teachers to make an extra effort to involve the parents in education.

Some examples of excellent parent/teacher communication are:

- holding regular conferences;

- devising weekly parent newsletters or journals;

- conducting small group parent meetings (not to discuss an individual child's performance, but rather the class goings-on as a whole);

- sending home student work for parents to see;

- sending notes home to those parents who have been nonresponsive to requests for a conference; and

- beginning and ending every conference on a positive note about the student.

7. Bayview Elementary School is also creating a time capsule. Talia Burke, a teacher at Bayview Elementary, wants to involve her students' families in the project. Some of her students' families are poor and do not speak English well, although all of her students speak English fluently. Ms. Burke decides that each family should contribute one quote about the current year. What would be the best way to elicit this information from families?

(A) Send a note home with each student.
(B) Call each student's parents.
(C) Have each student make a drawing of the time capsule, and assign them the task of collecting family quotes and writing them on the picture for homework.
(D) Ask each student to give a quote on behalf of the family instead of getting the family involved since time, money, and language barriers are issues.

This question contains an interesting problem: How does a teacher effectively communicate with parents who do not speak English well? Answer choices (A) and (B) are going to pose problems for Ms. Burke because some of the parents aren't going to understand her phone calls or notes. The difference between your remaining two answer choices is that answer choice (C) cleverly gets parents involved while answer choice (D) does not. The best answer is therefore (C).

Teacher Do's and Don'ts

According to NES:

- A good teacher starts parent-teacher conferences on a positive note even if the conference is about a serious problem.

- A good teacher shares responsibility with a family for a child.

- A bad teacher is confrontational and overly negative during conferences.

Test Technique

Avoid answers that portray teachers blaming parents for a child's behavior.

8. Talia's student Jared Frobnitz has recently become argumentative in class. Talia has been unable to get him to return to his usual cooperative ways, so she has invited Jared's mother, Mrs. Frobnitz, to a conference. Which of the following statements would be Talia's best opening when the conference begins?

    (A) "Mrs. Frobnitz, what has changed at home to make Jared so argumentative all of a sudden?"
    (B) "I am at my wits' end with him, Mrs. Frobnitz!"
    (C) "Jared is usually a joy to teach, Mrs. Frobnitz. I can see that something has changed in him, and I thought that together we could figure out what it is."
    (D) "Mrs. Frobnitz, I'm worried that something is desperately wrong with Jared."

Talia is going to have a very hard time in a parent-teacher conference if the parent is made to feel defensive about the student. Talia should instead be looking to establish a sense of partnership between herself and Mrs. Frobnitz. Answer choices (A), (B), and (D) are all approaches that the test writers want teachers to avoid. Notice how answer choice (C) begins by saying something positive about the student and then works to build a partnership with the parent to seek a solution to the child's problem.

9. Which of the following would be the most helpful material that Talia could bring to the conference with Mrs. Frobnitz?

    (A) An anecdotal record of Jared's behavior
    (B) Jared's recent homework and exams
    (C) A book on good parenting
    (D) Letters from other teachers who have complaints about Jared

To answer this question, it's important to recall what the nature of Talia's problem with Jared is—that he has become argumentative in class. Answer choice (B) will reveal nothing about Jared's problem, and answer choices (C) and (D) are likely to make Mrs. Frobnitz very defensive. Answer choice (A) is the most appropriate answer choice because the most likely source of evidence regarding Jared's recent behavior change would be stories from Jared's teacher.

CONNECTIONS TO THE COMMUNITY

A school is a microcosm of its community. It can be extremely beneficial for a teacher to maintain strong ties to the community where he or she teaches. Community groups can provide financial and volunteer support for a school, and individual community members can function as special guests and information resources for students and teachers. Teachers should make an effort to get to know members of the community and the businesses that exist there.

LEGAL ISSUES

On the test, you may see questions about the following laws, acts, and guiding principles that have affected education:

a. *Brown v. Board of Education*—1954 Supreme Court ruling that ended the "separate but equal" doctrine and forced racial integration in schools.

b. *Education for All Handicapped Children Act (PL 94-142)*—1975 mandate that ensures all disabled children receive free, public, individualized, and appropriate education in the *least restrictive environment*.

c. *Equal Education Opportunity Act*—1974, requires all schools to try to overcome language barriers that impede a student's education.

d. *The safety and welfare of students*—the most important things for teachers to be aware of.

   - Teachers should be aware of a child's appearance to recognize signs of abuse or neglect.
   - Students may never be left alone during the school day.
   - Teachers are responsible for the respect and unbiased treatment of all of their students.
   - Confidentiality is also a serious issue; teachers may never discuss a student's performance or share his/her records with any adult other than the student's parent or guardian and the principal.

TEACHER MUSTS AND NEVERS

   - A teacher upholds the laws related to education in all circumstances.
   - A teacher does not share student records with other people.
   - A teacher does not leave children unsupervised.
   - A *bad* teacher is unfamiliar with legal issues surrounding education.

10. Kris Alutius is a middle-school industrial arts
    teacher. At the beginning of the school year,
    Kris's principal sent the following notice to all
    teachers:

    "Due to budgetary constraints, my office will
    not consider any requests from teachers that
    will cost the school money. Any such request
    will be returned to the teacher unanswered."

    When school started, Kris noticed that many
    of the power tools were in a state of disrepair.
    Kris thinks that they need to be overhauled,
    but he knows that this will be expensive. Kris
    doubts that he is qualified to do the required
    repair work himself. Kris should

    (A) repair the tools to the best of his ability.
    (B) speak to the principal directly about this
        matter.
    (C) pay for the repair work himself and then
        send the school a bill.
    (D) allow the students to use the tools as is,
        since no one got hurt last year.

Nothing says "potential litigation" like power tools in serious need of repair. Answer
choice (D) is grossly irresponsible and would never be a credited response on this test.
Student safety should be based on care and planning, not on a hope that nothing will
go wrong again this year. Answer choice (A) should also be eliminated out of a concern
for student safety. If Kris works on the power tools himself, there is a good chance that
a student could get hurt. In this case, an appropriate response is to refer the issue to
school administration. When you are faced with controversial issues in the classroom,
it's very likely that a school or district policy is in place, and your best bet is to be sure
your administration is aware of the issue and is given an opportunity to weigh in. Addressing controversial issues on your own without school administration involved is a
less desirable behavior as far as the test writers are concerned. For these reasons, your
best choice is answer choice (B).

Test Technique
Always eliminate answers in which a teacher exhibits gross negligence.

11. If Kris were to do nothing about the tools and
    a student got hurt

    (A) the principal would be legally liable since
        he sent the memo.
    (B) Kris could be sued for negligence since
        the tools were his responsibility.
    (C) no individuals would be legally liable, but
        the school district could be sued.
    (D) the injured student and her parents
        would be unable to sue anyone because
        public schools are legally protected from
        lawsuits.

Kris is legally responsible for the condition of the items in his classroom. If Kris has good reason to believe that the tools are dangerous (and he does), then he could be sued for negligence if something were to go wrong. If it were established that the principal should have been aware of the condition of the power tools or actually was aware of the condition of the power tools, then the principal would be legally responsible as well. Since we don't know if this is true, answer choice (A) can be eliminated. Answer choice (B) is the credited response, and since Kris is liable, that would be enough information to allow you to eliminate answer choice (C). Answer choice (D) is just plain wrong. Public schools can and have been sued in the past.

12. A foundation donates some new equipment to the school for use in Kris's industrial arts classroom workshop. The equipment, however, is technologically sophisticated and Kris does not know how to use it. Kris should

(A) inquire whether he could return the equipment and get some that he is familiar with instead.

(B) let the students figure out how to use it first and then have them teach him, since children learn well through inquiry learning and through teaching others.

(C) attend a seminar on how to use the equipment.

(D) put the equipment in storage until he can spend some time figuring out how to use it.

Kris should make this new equipment safely available to his students as soon as possible. Answer choice (A) should be eliminated because it's an example of a teacher doing something to make life easier. Remember, a "good" teacher is motivated by the interests of the students. The likelihood of a serious accident happening while the students are learning how to use the equipment is too high for answer choice (B) to be the correct answer. Answer choice (C) looks great. Kris should engage in opportunities for professional training that relate to his job. Answer choice (D) has the students using the old equipment, and that's not going to be a good idea.

VALUES

Teachers today are faced with many topics which might come up in a classroom that are sensitive to discuss (i.e., sex, drugs, censorship, violence, and current events.). It is important that a teacher be fully aware of the school's policy on values and certain philosophical and belief-based issues, so he or she knows how to deal with such situations.

Test Technique
When faced with a controversial issue, a "good" teacher will defer the decision to the school administration.

13. Julie Trimble is planning a Halloween parade for her students. Jack Flanders is a parent of one of Julie's students. Jack sends Julie a note to inform her that his son, Ned, will not be able to participate in the parade because Halloween is a pagan holiday, and in fact, writes Jack, Julie should not even mention Halloween in school. The other students and parents are already excited about the parade. What should Julie do at this point?

(A) She should write a note back to Jack informing him that the parade will go on as scheduled since no one else has a problem with it.

(B) She should cancel the parade so that Ned is not alienated from his peers.

(C) She should hold the parade as scheduled and assume that Jack will keep his son, Ned, out of school that day.

(D) She should seek counsel from her administration on how the school addresses such situations.

Faith-based issues can be pretty sensitive ones. Rather than risk doing something on your own that might fall outside of your school's policies, it's best to be conservative in these cases and make sure that the problem is referred to the appropriate parties. Answer choice (A) isn't appropriately sensitive to the parent's concerns and could result in some real problems at school. Answer choice (B) is likely to result in Ned being alienated from his peers, since Ned would become known as the kid who ruined the Halloween parade. (C) is one of those answer choices where the teacher is more hoping than guaranteeing that there won't be a problem. Answer choice (D) looks exactly how you would expect the right answer to look on a question like this.

THE ATS-W IN SUMMARY

The depth of knowledge required for the multiple-choice section of the ATS-W is greater than the depth of knowledge required for the LAST. To give yourself the best possible chance of passing the ATS-W, you should make sure you are familiar with the information provided in the previous three chapters. Pay special attention to the information presented in the Knowledge of the Learner section, and consider how much of the other information presented in the chapter would guide the actions of a "good" teacher.

When facing a multiple-choice question on the ATS-W, remember to consider each of the following:

- What grade level is the question talking about? This is important because part of what you need to do is pick an answer that is appropriate for the cognitive, social, and moral development of the students mentioned in the question.

- Are any specific goals mentioned in the question? The best answer to pick is the answer choice that most directly addresses the learning objectives mentioned in the question.

- What would a "good" teacher do? According to the test writers, "good" teachers are selfless, are flexible in their approach, are cooperative with administration and their fellow teachers, are sensitive to the needs of their students, and behave in accordance with professional ethics and all laws governing education.

It's also vital to remember that to pass the ATS-W, you need to pass both the multiple-choice section and the essay section. Don't neglect working on your essay-writing skills unless you are 100 percent confident you are ready to pass that part of the test without any additional practice.

PART ◆ III

Practice Tests and Explanations

12

LAST Practice Test

LAST PRACTICE TEST DIRECTIONS FOR MULTIPLE-CHOICE QUESTIONS

DIRECTIONS

This test contains a multiple-choice section and a section with a single written assignment. You may complete the sections of the test in the order you choose.

Each question in the first section of this test is a multiple-choice question with four answer choices. Read each question CAREFULLY and choose the ONE best answer. Record your answer on the answer sheet in the space that corresponds to the question number. Completely fill in the space that has the same letter as the answer you have chosen. *Use only a No. 2 lead pencil.*

Sample Question:

1. What is the capital of New York?

    A. Buffalo
    B. New York City
    C. Albany
    D. Rochester

The correct answer to this question is C. You would indicate that on the answer sheet as follows:

1.

You should answer all questions. Even if you are unsure of an answer, it is better to guess than not to answer a question at all. You may use the margins of the test for scratch paper, but you will be scored only on the responses on your answer sheet.

The directions for the written assignment appear later in this test.

The words "End of Test" indicate that you have completed the test. You may go back and review your answers.

PART 1: MULTIPLE-CHOICE QUESTIONS

1. Wally weighs 120 pounds and Theo weighs 60 pounds more than Wally. Jack is heavier than Wally but lighter than Theo. How much does Jack weigh?

   (A) 120 pounds
   (B) 140 pounds
   (C) 180 pounds
   (D) 200 pounds

2. In a group of 100 people, 25 have brown eyes, 25 have blue eyes, 20 have green eyes, and 30 have hazel eyes. If one person is chosen at random from this group, what is the probability that the person chosen will have either brown or green eyes?

   (A) .75
   (B) .60
   (C) .55
   (D) .45

3. There is a large group of runners at the beginning of a race. After the first ten laps, half of the runners drop out. After ten more laps, a third of the remaining runners drop out. By the end of the race, there are 24 runners left. Which of the following represents the number of runners at the beginning of the race?

   (A) 40
   (B) 64
   (C) 72
   (D) 81

4. Nina can accessorize her outfits by wearing a hat, a scarf, and a belt. If she can wear one accessory or more at the same time, how many different ways can she wear these accessories?

   (A) 7
   (B) 6
   (C) 5
   (D) 3

5. Pythagoras is best known today for determining the relationship between the sides of right triangles. However, this ancient mathematician also determined that the sound made by a taut string changes proportionally to the length of the string. Thus, he developed the subdivisions of the musical scale that are still used today. Pythagoras and his followers applied similar laws to astronomy and created a philosophy of "Cosmic Music" that explained how the universe functioned using harmonious rhythms. Over the centuries, other thinkers were greatly influenced by this notion of a natural order based on numbers.

   Which of the following is illustrated by the passage?

   (A) The Pythagorean laws of the universe went undiscovered for centuries.
   (B) Mathematical laws can only be applied to astronomy.
   (C) Pythagoras limited his ideology to finding relationships between objects.
   (D) The Laws of Proportions can be applied to mathematics, science, and philosophy.

GO ON TO THE NEXT PAGE

6. Using a device that emits a high-pitched sound, a biologist determined the frequency of sound that triggers the soldier termite's danger mechanisms. These devices were placed at different distances from the colony. Data were collected to compare the rate of a soldier termite's convulsions with the distance of the danger from the colony. All experiments were performed on calm days, and the sound devices were placed on flat land in a straight line from the colony. Different soldiers reacting to a sound source at an equal distance exhibited significant variation in convulsion rates. Furthermore, each soldier seemed to exhibit a uniform number of convulsions, regardless of the distance the sound source was placed from the colony.

Which of the following explanations for this behavior was NOT investigated in this study?

I. Wind may affect a soldier termite's perception of the distance of a danger source.
II. The convulsion rate does not convey information about the distance of a danger source.
III. Experienced soldiers can more accurately determine the distance of a danger source than can novice soldiers.

(A) I only
(B) II only
(C) I and II only
(D) I and III only

7. In Galileo's famous experiment, a cannonball and a pebble hit the ground at the same time after being dropped simultaneously from the same height. Which of the following did the experiment prove?

(A) Some objects resist downward movement because of increased air resistance.
(B) Objects of different masses have different rates of acceleration.
(C) Gravity causes the same rate of acceleration for all objects.
(D) If air resistance and gravitational force are equal, the velocity of the falling object is limited.

8. An inverse relationship is one in which as one variable changes, the other variable changes in the opposite direction. Which of the following scenarios represents an inverse relationship between two variables?

(A) A two-liter bottle of soda sells for $0.99, while a one-liter bottle of the same soda sells for $1.89.
(B) One dress sells for $750 and another dress sells for $499 at the same store, though both cost $145 to manufacture.
(C) As a $5,000 extension is added to a house, the amount of taxes the homeowner pays doubles.
(D) A car that originally sold for $23,000 will go down in price as demand for the car decreases.

GO ON TO THE NEXT PAGE

Use the information below to answer the two questions that follow.

An experiment tested the effects of using organic compost as fertilizer. The plants of each type were raised identically from the same seed source. The first group of plants received no application of fertilizer, while the second group received an application of compost when the plants were eight weeks old.

Average Number of Fruits or Vegetables Per Plant

	Control group	Compost group
Tomatoes	9.4	14.8
Eggplants	2.1	2.3
Peppers	2.3	4.1
Corn	.9	1.8
Potatoes	8.0	12.4

9. Based on the data recorded above, which of the following statements is true?

   (A) Compost is the best fertilizer available.
   (B) Commercial chemical fertilizers may produce high yields, but they deplete rather than enrich the soil.
   (C) Compost is a useful fertilizer for all fruit and vegetable plants.
   (D) For most of the plants in the experiment, compost was effective in raising yields.

10. Which of the following, if overlooked by the conductor of the experiment, would have led to flawed data?

   (A) Temperatures dropped below 40 degrees after some of the tomatoes had flowered, which caused the flowers to drop.
   (B) Because most of the tomatoes in the control group were planted close to a fence, they did not receive as much rain as the other tomatoes.
   (C) Eggplants typically do not produce fruit if the average temperatures are not hot enough.
   (D) Since corn requires a lot of nutrients to grow, it should be planted in fertile soil.

Read the passage below. Then answer the question that follows.

Insulin is a critical hormone that allows individuals to absorb simple sugars (such as glucose and fructose) from their food as it is digested. Most individuals produce the right amount of insulin. In fact, most individuals are not aware of the presence of insulin in the bloodstream. Recently, nutritionists have discovered that foods known as complex carbohydrates—potatoes, carrots, and pasta among them—break down into simple sugars. Sometimes, this breakdown into sugars occurs so rapidly that the sugars may trigger a strong insulin response. This can be a problem, since a high level of insulin will inhibit the breakdown of fatty deposits. Therefore, eating too many carbohydrates leads to too much insulin, which in turn promotes the accumulation of fat. If you want to watch your weight, be sure to watch the number of complex carbohydrates you consume.

11. Which of the following statements, if true, would weaken the argument in the author's last sentence?

   (A) Certain foods, such as whole grains and cereals, can counteract the tendency of other complex carbohydrates to raise insulin levels.
   (B) Decreased insulin levels are associated with certain forms of liver disease.
   (C) Stress is also a factor in the body's ability to break down fatty deposits.
   (D) Complex carbohydrates such as carrots do not contain many calories.

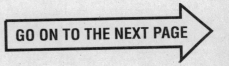
GO ON TO THE NEXT PAGE

12. Four monkeys, Buddy, Curley, Frank, and Martha, are sitting on a fence. Buddy and Frank cannot sit next to each other, and Frank and Martha must sit next to each other. Which of the following is a possible order for them to be sitting in?

(A) Buddy, Frank, Martha, Curly
(B) Buddy, Curly, Martha, Frank
(C) Frank, Curly, Martha, Buddy
(D) Martha, Curly, Buddy, Frank

13. Scientists are studying the effects of friction, a force that is exerted when two objects rub against each other. To test this concept, a scientist records the speed at which a wooden block slides down a series of five-foot diagonal ramps each made of a different material. Which of the following is the dependent variable in the experiment?

(A) The wooden block
(B) The speed at which the block moves
(C) The length of the ramps
(D) The ramp material

14. A certain lemonade mix requires 3 cups lemon juice to make 4 quarts of lemonade. How many cups of lemon juice would be required to make 10 quarts of lemonade?

(A) $4\frac{1}{2}$

(B) 6

(C) $7\frac{1}{2}$

(D) $8\frac{3}{4}$

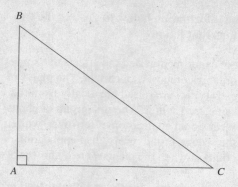

15. Given the right triangle above, which of the following must be true?

(A) $AB = AC$
(B) $BC > AC$
(C) $AB > AC$
(D) $AB \neq AC$

RED > PURPLE
BLUE < ORANGE
ORANGE = TEAL
TEAL > RED

16. Which of the following must be true?

(A) RED > BLUE
(B) ORANGE > PURPLE
(C) TEAL = BLUE
(D) BLUE < PURPLE

GO ON TO THE NEXT PAGE

17. Environmental noise produced by cars, planes, heavy machinery, and small appliances has been shown to cause frustration, stress, and permanent hearing loss. A government health agency has recommended that people limit their exposure to noise to 8 hours of 90-decibel noise or 4 hours of 95-decibel noise. Many health care professionals, however, feel that even these limits do not adequately protect the public from the ill effects of noise pollution.

Which of the following, if true, would most support the health care professionals' view as described above?

(A) Many manufacturers are capable of producing products that run more quietly, but public demand for these products is low.
(B) White-noise machines produce sound that covers or filters disruptive noises.
(C) The government has neglected efforts to mandate more stringent standards for environmental noise.
(D) Noise of less than 90 decibels can disrupt sleep patterns and increase hypertension, while brief exposure to noise above 100 decibels can cause permanent hearing trauma.

18. On a hot summer day, Tim and Andrea Klima decide to spend the day poolside. Their son Ronan wishes to remain indoors in the air conditioning. Tim and Andrea sit in the hot sun for a while, then decide to jump in the pool. "The water is so cold," complains Andrea. "It's only 80 degrees," agrees Tim. Just then, Ronan joins his parents outdoors. After diving into the pool, Ronan comments, "Wow, the pool is so nice and warm—it must be at least 80 degrees."

Which of the following statements best explains the contradiction in the Klima family's perception of the water temperature?

(A) Water has a tendency toward temperature variance, a phenomenon that can be sensed by individuals when they stand at different locations in a pool.
(B) An individual who has been sunbathing outside is able to sense the true temperature of water better than an individual who has been in an artificially controlled environment.
(C) When an individual senses the temperature of water, he is actually sensing the amount of pressure exerted by the water on his skin.
(D) When an individual perceives the temperature of water, he is actually sensing the difference between the temperature of his skin and the temperature of the water.

GO ON TO THE NEXT PAGE

Read the passage below and answer the two questions that follow.

One effect of a moist, warmer-than-usual spring is the increase in the number of ticks. Ticks, no larger than the head of a pin, are reason for concern since they can transmit Lyme disease. Lyme disease is spread by ticks that usually live on mice and deer. However, ticks can also attach themselves to other creatures, including people. If an infected tick bites someone, a large rash will usually appear at the site of the bite within a month. In addition, many will suffer from chills, fever, headache, and mild conditions of arthritis shortly after a rash appears. Untreated, Lyme disease can cause severe arthritis and an irregular heartbeat.

Antibiotics used to be the only treatment for Lyme disease. Now, recent advances have led to the creation of a vaccine. For the vaccine to work, individuals must take three shots over a period of twelve months. Most individuals may find this treatment difficult to administer. A dose of tick-repellent should help the casual outdoor-bound individual avoid the danger of ticks.

19. Which of the following is the best definition for the word *treatment*, used in the first sentence of the second paragraph of the passage?

(A) Management
(B) Remedy
(C) Execution
(D) Strategy

20. According to the passage, the vaccine against Lyme disease is appropriate only for those who

(A) plan on going outside during a warm weather season.
(B) occasionally spend time hiking and traveling outdoors.
(C) are outdoors so often that they must constantly protect themselves against ticks.
(D) live in the northeastern United States.

GO ON TO THE NEXT PAGE

21. Which of the following could be classified as a secondary source when researching the Shirtwaist Strike of 1909?

    (A) *The Diary of a Shirtwaist Striker* published in 1910
    (B) An article in the *New York Times* written in 1984 to commemorate the seventy-fifth anniversary of the strike
    (C) An article in the *New York Sun* written in 1909 detailing the events of the strike
    (D) A pamphlet issued in 1906 advertising positions available in shirtwaist factories

Read the except below, from the 14th Amendment to the Constitution, adopted in 1964; then answer the question that follows.

> The right of citizens of the United States to vote in any primary or other election for President or Vice President, for electors for President or Vice President, or for Senator or Representative in Congress, shall not be denied or abridged by the United States or any State by reason of failure to pay any poll tax or other tax.

The above quotation is part of the 24th Amendment to the United States Constitution, adopted in 1964.

22. Which of the following statements best applies to the Amendment?

    (A) In response to pressure from voters, Congress had been trying numerous means to lower taxes.
    (B) Requiring citizens to pay money before voting had been used as a way to discourage poor people from exercising their right to vote, especially poor minorities.
    (C) The Amendment was strongly supported by Southern states.
    (D) Since the poll tax infringes upon the rights of citizens, Congress believed it should be abolished.

GO ON TO THE NEXT PAGE

Use the map below and the excerpt from the Cork Constitution, written in 1846, to answer the question that follows.

Amid all the talk which we hear about potatoes, we find nothing to guide us to a satisfactory estimate, or even conjecture, as to the actual supply in the country. On one hand we have nothing but fearful forebodings—the stock is exhausted and famine stares us in the face; on the other, we are told of stores that will bring us safely through the season, and that the noise about scarcity is only a political device.

23. Which of the following shows the area discussed in the quote above?

    (A) I
    (B) II
    (C) III
    (D) IV

Read the passage below, then answer the three questions that follow.

Turning and turning in the widening gyre
The falcon cannot hear the falconer;
Things fall apart; the center cannot hold;
Mere anarchy is loosed upon the world,
The blood-dimmed tide is loosed, and everywhere
The ceremony of innocence is drowned;
The best lack all conviction, while the worst
Are full of passionate intensity.

24. The poet's mood can best be described as

    (A) excited and happy.
    (B) melancholy and lethargic.
    (C) apprehensive and pessimistic.
    (D) cold and unfeeling.

25. Which of the following does the poet employ in the first three lines?

    (A) Figurative language that is an intentional overstatement
    (B) Words that resemble their sounds or actions
    (C) The repetition of certain vowel sounds
    (D) A purposeful satirical imitation of another poem

26. The theme of the poem can best be described as

    (A) an expression of the poet's view of the state of the world.
    (B) narrative, since it describes a particular historical event.
    (C) self-referential.
    (D) less important than its striking imagery.

GO ON TO THE NEXT PAGE →

Read the excerpts below, then answer the three questions that follow.

(A) He handed her the letter whose secrets he wanted to carry with him to the grave, but she put the folded sheets in her dressing table without reading them and locked the drawer with a key. She was accustomed to her husband's unfathomable capacity for astonishment, his exaggerated opinions that became more incomprehensible as the years went by, his narrowness of mind that was out of tune with his public image. But this time he had outdone himself.

(B) Mrs. Penniman was a tall, thin, fair, rather faded woman, with a perfectly amiable disposition, a high standard of gentility, a taste for light literature, and a certain foolish indirectness and obliquity of character. She was romantic; she was sentimental; she had a passion for little secrets and mysteries—a very innocent passion, for her secrets had hitherto always been as impractical as addled eggs.

(C) New Orleans is very beautiful and very painful. New York is not that beautiful and not that painful. It is just a normal American town. Whereas New Orleans has a caliber of beauty among the massive oaks, at times a vision of paradise, but there is an unvarnished truth about it, and there are your memories and those held dear.

(D) Had there been an axe handy, or a poker, any weapon that would have gashed a hole in his father's breast and killed him, there and then, James would have seized it. Such were the extremes of emotion that Mr. Ramsay excited in his children's breasts by his mere presence; standing, as now, lean as a knife, narrow as the blade of one, grinning sarcastically, not only with the pleasure of disillusioning his son and casting ridicule upon his wife, who was ten thousand times better in every way than he was (James thought), but also with some secret conceit at his own accuracy of judgment.

(E) The dog was everything a dog should not be. It looked too old to be alive, emaciated, flabby at the same time, and its stringy coat was patched with dried-on mud. I did not understand how Nicholas could get as close as he was to anything that looked the way the creature did. I had seen my brother shield his face in Mexican markets to block out slightly overripe papayas. Ordinarily, he was revolted by men in short-sleeved shirts; he had a horror of clip-on bow ties. Yet there he was, kneeling down beside the creature on the stone.

27. Which makes use of vivid examples to describe a character trait?

    (A) Paragraph A
    (B) Paragraph C
    (C) Paragraph D
    (D) Paragraph E

28. Which describes the effect a man has upon his family?

    (A) Paragraph B
    (B) Paragraph C
    (C) Paragraph D
    (D) Paragraph E

29. In which of the following is the narrator surprised at someone else's behavior?

    (A) A and B
    (B) A and D
    (C) A and E
    (D) B and D

GO ON TO THE NEXT PAGE →

Read the excerpts below, then answer the two questions that follow.

(A) You do not do, you do not do
     Any more, black shoe
     In which I have lived like a foot
     For thirty years, poor and white,
     Barely daring to breathe or Achoo.

(B) Sports and gallantries, the stage, the arts,
     the antics of dancers,
     The exuberant voices of music,
     Have charm for children but lack
     nobility; it is bitter earnestness
     That makes beauty; the mind
     Knows, grown adult.

(C) I've known rivers:
     I've known rivers ancient as the world
     and older than the
     flow of human blood in human veins.
     My soul has grown deep like the rivers.

(D) I placed a jar in Tennessee,
     And round it was, upon a hill.
     It made the slovenly wilderness
     Surround that hill.

(E) In Xanadu did Kubla Khan
     A stately pleasure dome decree:
     Where Alph, the sacred river, ran
     Through caverns measureless to man
     Down to a sunless sea.

30. Which compares the poet with a part of the body?

     (A) Stanza A
     (B) Stanza B
     (C) Stanza D
     (D) Stanza E

31. Which uses repetition to achieve a rhythmic effect?

     (A) Stanza A
     (B) Stanza B
     (C) Stanza D
     (D) Stanza E

Read the passage below, then answer the question that follows.

In the mid-fourteenth century, Europe was hit by one of the most virulent plagues ever experienced by humans. Medieval medical professionals were rendered useless; once black lesions appeared on a person's body, death was inevitable. The streets of European towns were strewn with dead bodies, and anarchy reigned as governmental and religious officials fled to rural areas.

This Bubonic Plague, also known as the Black Death, has been credited for causing dramatic changes in virtually every aspect of European life. The most visible changes occurred in the social, economic, and religious realms, but more subtle changes also took place. The speed and indiscriminate nature of the plague showed the folly and ineffectiveness of European medicine at that time and opened the fields of medicine and biology to scrutiny. This would later result in the scientific revolution in the fifteenth and sixteenth centuries. Perhaps if the plague had not hit Europe so hard, we would not have achieved our current level of medical advancement.

By the time the Bubonic Plague hit Europe in the 1340s, there had been a considerable population increase, as well as several cycles of famines, droughts, and wars. Towns and cities were overcrowded and filthy. The streets were very narrow, running water was scarce, and sewage scattered in the streets attracted scavenging animals such as rodents. Under these conditions—and without the modern luxuries of soap, bathtubs, and electricity—Europe was a prime target for the microscopic bacillus known as *Yersinia pestis*.

GO ON TO THE NEXT PAGE

32. Which of the following best describes the structure of the passage above?

(A) Introduces a topic, describes the background, and draws a conclusion

(B) Provides an anecdotal description of a topic, examines its ramifications, and describes the conditions that contributed to the situation

(C) Describes the background of a topic and provides examples

(D) Examines the historical significance of a situation, describes the reasons why it occurred, and provides examples that illustrate its effects

Use the map below and the excerpt from the National Party's Color Policy, written in 1948, to answer the two questions that follow.

On the one hand there is the policy of equality, which advocates equal rights within the same political structure for all civilized and educated persons, irrespective of race or colour, and the gradual granting of the franchise to non-Europeans as they become qualified to make use of democratic rights. On the other hand there is the policy of separation (apartheid) which has grown from the experience of established European population of the country, and which is based on the Christian principles of Justice and reasonableness.

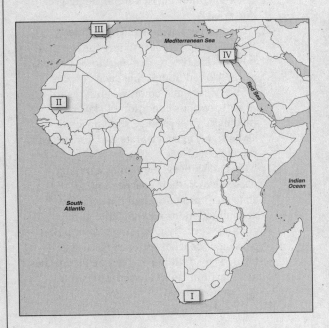

33. Which of the areas on the map indicates the country that created this policy?

(A) I
(B) II
(C) III
(D) IV

GO ON TO THE NEXT PAGE

34. Which of the following text excerpts from American history most closely echoes the ideas in the previous passage?

(A) "That the right of way through the public lands be…granted to said company for the construction of said railroad and telegraph line; and the right…is hereby given to said company to take from the public lands adjacent to the line of said road, earth, stone, timber, and other materials for the construction thereof…."

(B) "…if the colored children are denied the experience in school of associating with white children, who represent 90 percent of our national society in which these colored children must live, then the colored child's curriculum is being greatly curtailed."

(C) "That all persons born in the United States and not subject to any foreign power…are hereby declared to be citizens of the United States; and such citizens, of every race and color, without regard to any previous condition of slavery or involuntary servitude…shall have the same right, in every State and Territory in the United States…."

(D) "That all railway companies carrying passengers in their coaches in this state shall provide equal but separate accommodations for the white and colored races, by providing two or more passenger coaches for each passenger train, or by dividing the passenger coaches by a partition so as to secure separate accommodations…."

Use the graph below to answer the question that follows.

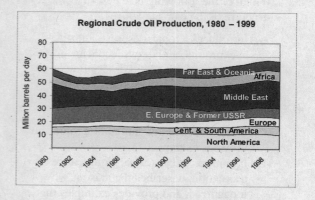

35. The above graph shows the world oil production from 1980–1999. Based on the graph, during which time period would the price of oil have most likely been the highest?

(A) Pre-1980
(B) 1980–1986
(C) 1986–1992
(D) 1992–1998

GO ON TO THE NEXT PAGE

Use the four images below to answer the three questions that follow.

(A)

(B)

(C)

(D)

36. Which of the buildings is the oldest?

    (A) A
    (B) B
    (C) C
    (D) D

37. Practical utility was most important to the architect of which building?

    (A) A
    (B) B
    (C) C
    (D) D

38. Which of the following statements is the most accurate?

    (A) All of the buildings were designed for the same purpose.
    (B) All of the exteriors are ornately decorated.
    (C) All of the buildings have regularly spaced windows.
    (D) At least one of the buildings was intended to be a place of worship.

GO ON TO THE NEXT PAGE

39. It is often not easy for archaeologists to determine wealth and status based solely on material culture, and so they must turn to other sources. Human skeletal remains from ancient burial grounds can offer many clues that elucidate life in the past. At one site, an interesting set of communal graves was discovered: One was very elaborately constructed and contained opulent grave goods, while the other was unadorned and virtually devoid of burial artifacts. Analysis of the dental remains from the multiple individuals found in each grave revealed a greater prevalence of cavities and other dental pathologies among those in the ornate burial. The investigators theorize that the "wealthier" individuals at this site had greater access to food resources that induce such maladies.

According to the passage, it can be inferred that

(A) the quantity of grave goods affects the prevalence of dental pathologies.
(B) analyzing dental remains is the best way to determine socioeconomic status.
(C) dental pathologies are related to economic status.
(D) affluence cannot be determined by studying a set of ancient graves.

40. All organisms are essential parts of the intricate ecological web, from the blue whale to the tiniest mosquito. To humans, mosquitoes are simply vectors that carry diseases and cause general discomfort. However, the very act of transmitting diseases such as malaria and the bubonic plague to humans has helped curb global overpopulation throughout history. Additionally, the threat of mosquito-borne diseases had protected some wilderness areas in Africa from human interference until recent technological advancements. Since various animals eat mosquitoes, more links within the ecosystem are sustained. The complete extermination of mosquitoes, which may seem beneficial to humans, would adversely affect the fragile ecosystem and, consequently, humankind.

It can be determined from the passage that mosquitoes

(A) pose a threat to the world's wilderness areas.
(B) can be both harmful and advantageous.
(C) cause the most discomfort to humans.
(D) form the most important part of the ecosystem.

GO ON TO THE NEXT PAGE

41. In a free market, an increase in the demand for wood will probably lead to

(A) an increase in the demand for wood.
(B) an increase in the price of wood.
(C) a decrease in the demand for wood.
(D) a decrease in the price of wood.

Use the graph below, which depicts the development of railroads in three regions of the United States, to answer the question that follows.

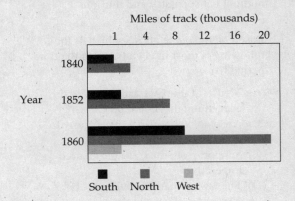

42. It can be inferred from the chart above that southern railroad development

(A) would eventually equal that of the North.
(B) put the South at a distinct disadvantage during the Civil War.
(C) was adequate for the amount of cargo transport needed.
(D) increased faster during the 1840s than during the 1850s.

Use the graph below, which shows the total number of Democratic and Republican representatives in all state legislatures combined, to answer the question that follows.

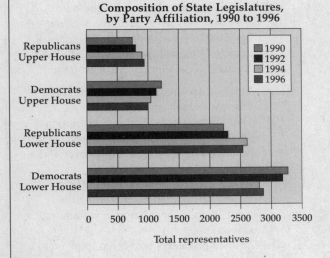

43. The graph above supports which of the following conclusions?

(A) If the trend shown on the chart continues, the Republican Party will soon control most state legislatures.
(B) In most states, registered Democrats outnumber registered Republicans.
(C) Democrats held the majority of seats in state legislatures throughout the early 1990s.
(D) The number of Republican governors increased between 1990 and 1996.

GO ON TO THE NEXT PAGE

44. During the War of 1812, the United States Congress licensed privateers (legalized pirates) who were empowered to plunder enemy ships. These privateers financed their ventures through the sale of the seized cargo. A Florida man has petitioned Congress to license modern privateers to mount a private "war-for-profit" against seagoing smugglers of illegal drugs. Which of the following, if true, is a drawback to the Florida man's proposal?

(A) Modern ships are much faster than those of the nineteenth century.
(B) Although the United States Constitution still authorizes the licensing of privateers, no licenses have been issued for over 150 years.
(C) Modern privateers would be unable to finance their operations by selling the seized cargo without being in violation of the law.
(D) The 1812 privateers plundered ships that belonged to citizens of other countries.

Read the excerpt below written by David Hume, a philosopher who lived during the Age of Enlightenment, and answer the question that follows.

"If we take in our hand any volume; of divinity or school metaphysics, for instance; let us ask, Does it contain any abstract reasoning concerning quantity or number? No. Does it contain any experimental reasoning, concerning matter of fact and existence? No. Commit it then to the flames: for it can contain nothing but sophistry and illusion."

45. Based on the quote above, which of the following is most likely a belief of the time period?

(A) Medieval thinkers had discovered everything that could be known.
(B) An absolute monarchy was a way to improve economic conditions.
(C) Support from the Catholic Church was imperative.
(D) The laws of nature could only be discovered through reason.

GO ON TO THE NEXT PAGE

Use the paintings below to answer the three questions that follow.

(A)

(B)

(C)

(D)

46. In which of the paintings is space created by overlapping layers rather than by foreshortening?

(A) Painting A
(B) Painting B
(C) Painting C
(D) Painting D

47. Which of the following elements do the paintings have in common?

(A) An obsessive attention to small details
(B) The elevation of linear over curved forms
(C) A pessimistic attitude toward society
(D) A highly subjective rendering of reality

48. What is the purpose of the simple style of painting D?

(A) To emphasize the contrast between the size of the mother and that of the child
(B) To draw attention to the leaves in the background
(C) To reflect the simplicity and innocence of a mother's love for her child
(D) To indicate the familiarity of a real-life situation

GO ON TO THE NEXT PAGE

"Rather than curse the sea slug, Northern Californians celebrate it with a recipe contest that sends judges gagging, gasping, or on the run home to brush their teeth."

49. The previous sentence should be revised to fix an error in

(A) Subject-verb agreement
(B) Tense
(C) Parallel construction
(D) Comma use

Use the image below of a house designed by architecht Frank Lloyd Wright to answer the question that follows.

50. The architect of the house pictured above most probably designed the layered concrete balconies so that

(A) the sun would enter the house from every window at some time during the day.
(B) the house would look like an impregnable fortress.
(C) their circular form would contrast with the rest of the house.
(D) the house would seem to blend into the site by mimicking the natural outcroppings of rock.

GO ON TO THE NEXT PAGE

Use the excerpts below to answer the three questions that follow.

(A) My name is Otto Dietrich zur Linde. One of my forebears, Christoph zur Linde, died in the cavalry charge that decided the victory of Zorndorf. During the last days of 1870, my maternal great-grandfather, Ulrich Forkel, was killed in the Machenoir forest by French sharpshooters; Captain Dietrich zur Linde, my father, distinguished himself in 1914 at the siege of Namur, and again two years later in the crossing of the Danube. As for myself, I am to be shot as a torturer and a murderer. The court has acted rightly; from the first, I have confessed my guilt. Tomorrow, by the time the prison clock strikes nine, I shall have entered the realms of death; it is natural that I should think of my elders, since I am come so near their shadow—since, somehow, I am they.

(B) At Jan's request, then, I spent almost every Thursday afternoon, from half-past four to shortly before six o'clock, with Sigismund Markus. I was allowed to look through his assortment of drums, and even to use them—where else could Oskar have played several drums at once? Meanwhile, I would contemplate Markus' hangdog features. I didn't know where his thoughts came from, but I had a pretty fair idea where they went; they were in Tischlergasse, scratching on numbered room doors, or huddling like poor Lazarus under the marble-topped table at the Café Weitzke. Waiting for what? For crumbs?

(C) Outside his window he saw the sun dying over the rooftops in the western sky and watched the first shade of dusk fall. Now and then a streetcar ran past. The rusty radiator hissed at the far end of the room. All day long it had been springlike; but now dark clouds were slowly swallowing the sun. All at once street lamps came on and the sky was black and close to the house-tops. Inside his shirt he felt the cold metal of the gun resting against his naked skin; he ought to put it back between the mattresses. No! He would keep it. He would take it with him to the Dalton place. He felt that he would be safer if he took it.

(D) And it was him I'd blame, my dad, my dad Bill. It was him I'd give as my excuse, if I was ever called to account, if I ever found myself slinking back, or being carted in a cop car, to Ollerton Road. I wasn't the first to leave, was I? It was him who set me my example. Maybe he was thinking of me right now, with his floozy in the Isle of Man, if that was where and how it was. Waking up in the small hours, lighting a ciggy. Rain on the window. I wonder what that Mandy's up to, I wonder what that lass is doing right now.

51. Which of these is the best example of an omniscient narrator?

   (A) Paragraph A
   (B) Paragraph B
   (C) Paragraph C
   (D) Paragraph D

52. Which of these excerpts contains a character who refers to himself in both the first and the third person?

   (A) Paragraph A
   (B) Paragraph B
   (C) Paragraph C
   (D) Paragraph D

53. Which of these is the best example of stream-of-consciousness narration?

   (A) Paragraph A
   (B) Paragraph B
   (C) Paragraph C
   (D) Paragraph D

GO ON TO THE NEXT PAGE ➡

Read the excerpt below from Isadora Duncan's *The Philosopher's Stone of Dancing*, written in 1920, and answer the question that follows.

Imagine then a dancer who, after long study, prayer and inspiration, has attained such a degree of understanding that his body is simply the luminous manifestation of his soul; whose body dances in accordance with a music heard inwardly, in an expression of something out of another, profounder world. This is the truly creative dancer; natural but not imitative, speaking in movement out of himself and out of something greater than all selves.

—Isadora Duncan

The Philosopher's Stone of Dancing, 1920

54. Which of the following most closely matches the point of view expressed above?

(A) A thorough education in the foundations of dance is the only way to truly be a successful dancer.
(B) All modern dance has evolved into an art form of feelings, rather than one of movements.
(C) Dance, theater, and poetry are all arts led by the individual rather than societal influences.
(D) Creative dance is done as much by the mind, the soul, and the heart as it is by the body.

55. DORA: For our class project, we are making a model of Monticello, which was built by Thomas Jefferson.

ROBERT: Jefferson is one of the most interesting presidents, because he was an architect, a gardener, and an inventor, as well as a politician.

DORA: We will most likely raise enough money this semester for the whole class to take a field trip to Monticello.

ROBERT: That's a long way to travel, but I guess you will learn a lot.

If neither of the speakers is making false statements, which of the following is an accurate description of the conversation?

(A) Dora states only opinions in both of her statements.
(B) Dora states opinion in her first statement, and fact in her second statement.
(C) Robert and Dora both state opinion and fact.
(D) Robert and Dora state only facts in their first statements.

GO ON TO THE NEXT PAGE

56. Which of the following gives the chateau pictured above the effect of balance and symmetry?

(A) The repetition of rectangular windows on the first and second floors
(B) The central dome
(C) The many chimneys of various heights
(D) The contrast between light and dark

57. Read these sentences:

1. Because of this, the rickshaw is often associated with the Japanese, though it was actually based on an earlier French carriage called the "broutte."

2. The word *rickshaw* is shortened from the Japanese, jin riki sha, which means "manpowered-carriages."

3. The person who created this mix of two cultures was probably an American missionary, Jonathan Goble.

4. From this example, we can see how innovative ideas are born from the merging of three cultures.

5. Goble commissioned a Japanese artisan to use the "broutte" as a model in making a carriage for his wife.

Which of the following is the correct order of the sentences?

(A) 2-3-4-5-1
(B) 1-3-5-2-4
(C) 3-4-5-1-2
(D) 2-1-3-5-4

58. Which of the following is a sentence fragment?

(A) Censorship in the media is an extremely important issue in the twentieth century.
(B) In the 1950s, television programs and movies had to comply with codes that enforced strict standards of propriety.
(C) Couples were shown sleeping in separate beds and the concept of nudity or verbal profanity was unheard of.
(D) In the 1960s and 1970s, the media, in favor of more realistic representations of relationships and everyday life.

GO ON TO THE NEXT PAGE

Read the passage below and answer the five questions that follow.

The writing of the ancient Egyptians, hieroglyphics, had mystified scholars for centuries until a chance discovery by the French army under the command of Napoleon Bonaparte. Owing to his interest in history, Napoleon had brought scientists and historians along with his army as he invaded Egypt. In August 1799, a group of French soldiers in the town of Rosetta discovered a large black stone with writing in three different languages. The stone was inscribed with a message in Egyptian hieroglyphics, another Egyptian form of writing which came to be called *demotic*, and ancient Greek. The scholars knew that this was an important find, because it might allow them to decipher the enigmatic hieroglyphics whose meaning had been lost hundreds of years before. Since they could easily figure out what the Greek writing said, it would simply be a matter of figuring out how the hieroglyphics encoded the same message.

Unfortunately it wasn't an easy matter to unlock the secret of the Rosetta Stone. Most scholars who attempted to solve the puzzle began by working with the demotic script, with varying degrees of success. In 1814, Dr. Thomas Young began studying the Rosetta Stone, and was able to determine that the demotic script was essentially a simpler version of the hieroglyphics, not a completely different form of writing. Young also discovered that certain symbols corresponded to sounds, and not to entire words. His mistake was not in following this idea even further—as it turned out, many more symbols represented sounds than he had suspected. It was up to Jean-François Champollion to make this breakthrough ten years later, which led him ultimately to understand how the system of hieroglyphics worked.

59. The main purpose of this passage is to

(A) explain how people came to understand an ancient language.
(B) describe a military campaign.
(C) praise a remarkable historian.
(D) clarify a common misconception about archaeology.

60. Which of the following can be assumed, based on the information in the passage above?

(A) The Rosetta Stone was intended to help future scholars read ancient languages.
(B) Some scholars in the eighteenth and nineteenth centuries were familiar with ancient Greek.
(C) Understanding the meaning of the hieroglyphics on the Rosetta Stone was an easy task.
(D) The French army remained in Egypt for many years.

61. Which of the following questions is answered by the passage?

(A) Why did Napoleon bring scholars to Egypt?
(B) What was the message written on the Rosetta Stone?
(C) Why was the French army fighting in Egypt?
(D) What is the origin of the word *demotic*?

62. Why was the Rosetta Stone so useful in deciphering the Egyptian hieroglyphics?

(A) The stone's discovery established the French as the leading experts in the study of ancient Egypt.
(B) Scholars knew the meaning of the message on the stone, which helped them figure out hieroglyphic symbols.
(C) The writing on the stone revealed that the ancient name of the town where it was found was "Rosetta."
(D) The stone helped the scholars gain a better understanding of ancient Greek.

63. Which of the following best describes Champollion's intellectual "breakthrough" mentioned in the passage?

(A) He discovered that the texts on the Rosetta Stone each contained the same message.
(B) He realized that most hieroglyphic symbols represented sounds, and only a few represented words.
(C) He pointed out that Dr. Young's work had been completely misguided.
(D) He found the connection between hieroglyphics and demotic script.

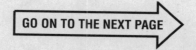
GO ON TO THE NEXT PAGE

Read the excerpts below and answer the five questions that follow.

American schools have come under serious criticism in recent years, due in part to falling test scores and to studies documenting that many students graduate from high school lacking basic knowledge. But what is even more troubling is that many students who perform well in school may not have gained a real understanding of the course material. Further studies have shown that when the format or wording of test questions is altered slightly, these "good" students fail to answer the questions correctly.

Part of the problem, as some have suggested, lies with the emphasis schools place on test performance, and in the very way the tests are constructed. If test questions ask only that students repeat back what has been said in class, they have no chance to demonstrate that they actually understand what they have been taught.

If a history class has been studying revolutions, for example, the usual testing method is to ask specifically about those revolutions covered in class. The test results, therefore, will show how well a student can memorize facts, not how well he can use those facts conceptually. A better testing method might be to ask students to use what they have learned in class to analyze and draw conclusions about a contemporary revolution, which would allow the students to show their mastery (or lack thereof) of the material. It is important to remember that knowing facts is only the first step to understanding; the ultimate goal is to be able to use those facts to solve problems and to reach a full appreciation of the subject.

64. What is the main idea of the passage?

(A) Essay questions are better than multiple-choice questions at measuring a student's proficiency.
(B) The ways in which schools test students do not adequately measure whether the students have a true grasp of the material.
(C) The fact that many students graduate without basic knowledge is a bigger problem than the fact that students who perform well may not thoroughly understand what they have studied.
(D) Factual knowledge is a crucial step in gaining true understanding.

65. The author encloses the word *good* (paragraph one) in quotation marks to

(A) indicate irony.
(B) emphasize approval.
(C) show disinterest.
(D) show that the word was spoken by someone else.

66. Which of the following does the author assert is (are) partly to blame for the failure of students to understand course material?

I. Schools value test scores more than they should.
II. Test questions do not challenge students to recall factual information.
III. Students graduate from high school without fundamental knowledge.

(A) I only
(B) II only
(C) I and II only
(D) II and III only

67. Which of the following testing methods would the author of the passage most likely approve of for a class that has been studying chemistry?

(A) Students are given a list of the elements and a list of abbreviations and asked to match them correctly.
(B) Students are given problems to solve that are very similar to the examples in the textbook.
(C) Students are given an unfamiliar material to experiment with and asked to describe some of its chemical properties.
(D) For a series of chemical terms, students are given five definitions and asked to choose the appropriate one.

68. According to the passage, which of the following will result if a student learns the facts but does not understand the subject?

(A) The student will not be able to take more advanced courses in that subject.
(B) The student will not succeed academically.
(C) The student will develop an acceptable capacity for memorization.
(D) The student will be unable to use those facts to solve problems.

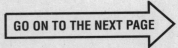

GO ON TO THE NEXT PAGE

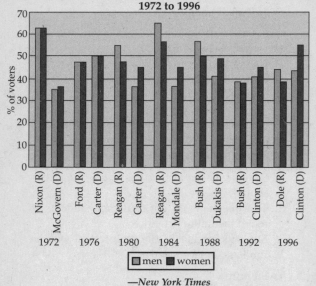

Presidential Vote for Majority Party Candidates, by Gender, 1972 to 1996

—*New York Times*

69. The graph above supports which of the following conclusions about presidential elections?

(A) If only men had voted in the 1980 election, Jimmy Carter would have won.
(B) There is little difference in the level of support that the Republican Party receives from men and women.
(C) The gender gap was more prominent in the 1980s and 1990s than it was in the 1970s.
(D) For a Republican candidate to win, he or she must receive more votes from women than from men.

Read the passage below and answer the question that follows.

The West has been through the trials brought about through excessive nationalism and yet sits idly by while millions of people are ruthlessly oppressed in search of the elusive quality of independence. When will the West learn that it must share its wisdom with these communities that are willing to sacrifice lives for the ability to govern themselves. The West should, and even must, take the lead in enforcing the peace.

70. The passage above is advocating a course of action best described as

(A) isolationist.
(B) interventionist.
(C) colonialist.
(D) nationalistic.

GO ON TO THE NEXT PAGE

Read the passage below to answer the four questions that follow.

Many species of insects have amazingly complex social structures, considering that the individual insects themselves have very simple brains. Army ants, for example, organize themselves for marches in which they devour all plant life in their path. If a stream blocks their path, the ants throw themselves into the water and cling to one another, forming a bridge so that the other ants may cross. Individual ants do not hesitate to give up their lives for the benefit of the colony. It cannot be said, however, that these ants are intelligent. They march by following a chemical trail left by the ants before them. If the ants in the lead can be forced to turn in a circle and march up behind the rear of the group, the ants will continue to march around and around in a circle until they die of exhaustion.

In a certain species of wasp, the mother lays her eggs in a burrow and drags a paralyzed cricket into the burrow for the young wasps to feed upon when they have hatched. When the mother wasp gets the cricket to the entrance of the burrow, she leaves it at the entrance and goes inside to check for intruders. If the cricket is moved away from the entrance while the mother wasp is inside, when she comes out, she drags the cricket back to the entrance, then leaves it and goes inside to check for intruders again. If the cricket is again moved, the mother wasp will again drag it to the entrance and then go inside to check for intruders. She will never notice that she has done the same thing repeatedly. The wasp's brain is not capable of recognizing the pattern of events. It is like a simple computer that can only follow instructions in a set order.

71. What is the main idea of this passage?

(A) Army ants can easily destroy farmlands and forests.
(B) Computers cannot choose to ignore instructions.
(C) Wasps can be tricked into performing repetitive motions.
(D) Insects cannot be considered truly intelligent.

72. According to the passage, army ants communicate through

(A) sound.
(B) marching patterns.
(C) touch.
(D) chemicals.

73. Army ants marching in a circle would do so because the ants that had been marching in the front

(A) did not remember that they were in the front.
(B) had their path blocked by a stream.
(C) had an instinctive understanding of geometry.
(D) wanted to protect the ants in the rear.

74. What is the "pattern of events" mentioned in the second paragraph?

(A) Marching in a circle
(B) Laying eggs many times in a life cycle
(C) Programming a computer to perform calculations
(D) Repeatedly moving the cricket and checking for intruders

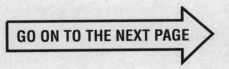
GO ON TO THE NEXT PAGE

Read the passage below to answer the three questions that follow.

Because the Constitution said nothing about education, during the end of the eighteenth century education was left up to the states and towns. The biggest issue at that time was making some minimum amount of education compulsory, although even the states that passed such laws intended them to apply only to whites. Finally, in 1865, a federal bureau began to develop black schools, and land grants were set aside for the formation of black colleges. Since that time, the federal government—including the courts—has become increasingly involved with education, white and black.

In 1896, the Supreme Court ruled in the infamous *Plessy v. Ferguson* that public schools could be "separate but equal," a ruling that severely limited educational opportunities for blacks. Not until 1954, with the Court's *Brown v. Board of Education,* was racial segregation in schools no longer sanctioned.

In later decades, both the states and federal government sponsored programs aimed at providing education to disadvantaged children, and instituted forced busing to try to fix some of the problems caused by years of segregation. Yet the government's success in providing education to all citizens remains mixed, at best; state and federal government, along with teachers, administrators, and parents, continue to battle for control of public schools, often to the detriment of the students themselves.

75. The author's primary purpose is to

(A) criticize the Supreme Court for its rulings on education.
(B) prove that the reason educational opportunities for blacks were limited was that the states did not act responsibly.
(C) argue that education should have been mandatory for all children.
(D) show that government intervention in public education has not been entirely positive.

76. The author implies that the role of the federal government in education has not been clear because

(A) the Supreme Court has historically made conflicting rulings on education.
(B) the states have never willingly ceded control over education to the federal government.
(C) the Constitution failed to include education as one of the government's duties.
(D) the federal government has only been involved in education in the last few decades.

77. The author would most likely agree with which of the following statements about the role of government in education?

(A) Education should be controlled by parents and local governments.
(B) Students should have an active voice in planning their education.
(C) Because the government has made some mistakes in the past, it should not be involved in making education policy today.
(D) The government should be responsible for making sure that all children have access to education.

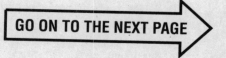
GO ON TO THE NEXT PAGE

Use the passage below to answer the two questions that follow.

My most memorable vacation as a child was a trip I took to the Grand Canyon with my grandfather. I was only eleven at the time; and I'd never been out of the city of Boston.

My grandfather, a true adventurer, decided that it was time for me to discover the great West. My romantic picture of the West, complete with cowboys and Indians, was a little out of date, but the incredible scenery took my breath away.

As I rode along on my mule's back, I noticed that each rock stratum displayed a different hue: gray and violet in some places, dark brown and green in others. The Grand Canyon was truly magnificent.

78. Which sentence, when added to the beginning of the third paragraph, would improve the clarity of the paragraph?

   (A) I had been taking horseback riding lessons since I was a little boy.
   (B) One of the most popular things to do while visiting the canyon is to examine different forms of wildlife in the region.
   (C) On our first day, we decided that the best way to explore the canyon would be to take a mule-packed trip down one of the trails.
   (D) The rock layers of the canyon are mostly limestone, freshwater shale, and sandstone.

79. The second sentence in the first paragraph should be revised to fix an error in

   (A) semicolon usage.
   (B) a misplaced modifier.
   (C) noun-pronoun agreement.
   (D) apostrophe usage.

80. How should the following sentence be revised to fix an error in parallel construction?

Three explanations of Sid's locking himself in his room were a desire to do his homework, a sense that he needed to hone his college essays, and hating his brother Tom, who had been hassling him all evening.

   (A) Sid locked himself in his room because he had a desire to do his homework, a sense that he needed to hone his college essays, and he hated his brother Tom, who had been hassling him all evening.
   (B) Three explanations of Sid's locking himself in his room were desiring to do his homework, sensing that he needed to hone his college essays, and because he hated his brother Tom, who had been hassling him all evening.
   (C) Three explanations of Sid's locking himself in his room were a desire to do his homework, a sense that he needed to hone his college essays, and a hatred of his brother Tom, who had been hassling him all evening.
   (D) Because of Sid's locking himself in his room, he desired to do his homework, sensed that he needed to hone his college essays, and hated his brother Tom, who had been hassling him all evening.

LAST PRACTICE TEST DIRECTIONS FOR THE WRITTEN ASSIGNMENT

DIRECTIONS FOR THE WRITTEN ASSIGNMENT

This section of the test consists of a written assignment. You are to prepare a written response of about 300–600 words on the assigned topic. *The assignment can be found on the next page.* You should use your time to plan, write, review, and edit your response to the assignment.

Read the assignment carefully before you begin to write. Think about how you will organize your response. You may use any blank space provided on the following pages to make notes, write an outline, or otherwise prepare your response. *However, your score will be based solely on the response you write in the following pages.*

Your response to the written assignment will be evaluated on the basis of the following criteria.

- **FOCUS AND UNITY:** Comprehend and focus on a unified, controlling topic.

- **APPROPRIATENESS:** Select and use a strategy of expression that is appropriate for the intended audience and purpose.

- **REASON AND ORGANIZATION:** Present a reasoned, organized argument or exposition.

- **SUPPORT AND DEVELOPMENT:** Use support and evidence to develop and bolster one's own ideas and account for the views of others.

- **STRUCTURE AND CONVENTIONS:** Express oneself clearly and without distractions caused by inattention to sentence and paragraph structure, choice and use of words, and mechanics (i.e., spelling, punctuation, capitalization).

Your response will be evaluated based on your demonstrated ability to express and support opinions, not on the nature or content of the opinions expressed. The final version of your response should conform to the conventions of edited American English. This should be your original work, written in your own words, and not copied or paraphrased from some other work.

Be sure to write about the assigned topic and use multiple paragraphs. Please write legibly. You may not use any reference materials during the test. Remember to review what you have written and make any changes you think will improve your written response.

PART 2: THE WRITTEN ASSIGNMENT

Should the government ration gasoline for both economic and environmental reasons?

In favor of the government rationing gasoline. Think of how many sport utility vehicles there are on the roads today. Each of those trucks consumes an average of twice as much gasoline as one standard car. Fuel efficiency has gone downhill over the past ten years, with people simply taking for granted that they can fill up their gas tanks whenever they want. This excessive use of gas makes our economy dependent on the oil-producing countries. Furthermore, gas is a natural resource, one that can and will be exhausted if we are not more careful with our usage. We need the government to step in and prevent that from happening.

Opposed to the government rationing gasoline. This is a free country in which a person is allowed to purchase a car and purchase the fuel needed to power that car. If the government rations the amount of gasoline a person can use, any industry that relies on transportation will feel the impact. Gas stations will be forced to raise gas prices, and the cost of any product or service that utilizes gasoline will skyrocket. People will have to divert income from other purchases to gas, and the economy as a whole will suffer. Jobs will be lost and the quality of life of millions of people will be negatively affected. Thus, rationing gasoline is not the intelligent means to our end. It would be economically and environmentally smarter for the government to invest in the long-term development of alternate sources of power for automobiles.

Should the government ration gasoline for both economic and environmental reasons?

In an essay written for an audience of educated adults:

- evaluate the arguments related to this question;
- state your position on whether the government should ration gasoline; and
- defend your position with logical arguments and appropriate examples.

13

LAST Practice Test Answers and Explanations

ANSWER KEY

1. B	28. C	55. C
2. D	29. C	56. A
3. C	30. A	57. D
4. A	31. A	58. D
5. D	32. B	59. A
6. D	33. A	60. B
7. C	34. D	61. A
8. A	35. B	62. B
9. D	36. B	63. B
10. B	37. C	64. B
11. A	38. D	65. A
12. B	39. C	66. A
13. B	40. B	67. C
14. C	41. B	68. D
15. B	42. B	69. C
16. B	43. C	70. B
17. D	44. C	71. D
18. D	45. D	72. D
19. B	46. A	73. A
20. C	47. D	74. D
21. B	48. C	75. D
22. D	49. C	76. C
23. C	50. D	77. D
24. C	51. C	78. C
25. C	52. B	79. A
26. A	53. D	80. C
27. D	54. D	

EXPLANATIONS FOR THE LAST PRACTICE TEST

Question 1: If Jack is heavier than Wally, then Jack weighs more than 120 pounds. If Jack is lighter than Theo, then Jack weighs less than 180 pounds. The only answer choice that meets both of these requirements is **answer choice (B).**

Question 2: To figure out the answer to a probability question, you need to set up a fraction. The number on top will be the number of things that satisfy whatever requirement you are given. The number on the bottom will be the total number of things in the group. So in this case, the number on top should be 45 (add the 25 people who have brown eyes to the 20 people who have green eyes). The number on the bottom should be 100 (the total number of people in the group). Therefore, the answer to this question is $\frac{45}{100}$. Expressed as a decimal, this would be .45, **answer choice (D).**

Question 3: The best way to approach this problem is to go directly to the answer choices and use them for the number of runners at the beginning of the race. We know we're going to have to cut one-half of these runners, and then cut one-third of the runners who are left and end up with 24. If you use **answer choice (C)**, 72, and cut that number in half, that means 36 runners drop out and 36 are left. If you take one-third of the remaining 36 runners you find that 12 other runners drop out and you are left with 24 runners.

Question 4: One way to answer this question is to list all the possible ways that Nina can wear the accessories. For example, she can wear the scarf alone, the hat alone, and the belt alone; that's three ways. Since the question says that she can wear more than one accessory at the same time, she can also wear the scarf with the hat, the scarf with the belt, and the hat with the belt; that's three additional ways. (Assigning letters for each accessory makes it easier to list these.) Finally, she can wear all three simultaneously. Therefore, **answer choice (A)** is correct because Nina can wear her accessories seven different ways.

Question 5: The passage discusses how Pythagoras applied mathematical proportions to a broad variety of things and ideas, such as music, astronomy, and philosophy. Therefore, **answer choice (D)** is the best from those provided.

Question 6: This one is a little tricky because it is a Roman numeral question and because it is asking you about what is NOT mentioned in the passage. Since the experiments were conducted on calm days, the effects of wind on the termites' reactions were not measured. You can therefore eliminate answer choice (B) because it is missing statement I. Statement II is something that is measured in the experiment (soldiers exhibited "a uniform number of convulsions, regardless of the distance" from the danger source), so it is NOT a part of the answer. You can now eliminate answer choice (C) because it contains a statement that the credited response will not contain. Since the "experience" of a soldier is never discussed, you can safely assume that this phenomenon wasn't measured. So, since what you are looking for is what the scientists *did not* do, the credited response is **answer choice (D)**.

Question 7: What you know is that two items of different weights fell at the same speed. That's all you're told, so you should focus on finding an answer that most closely matches that information. Since there's nothing about air resistance discussed in the experiment, you can eliminate answer choice (A). Answer choice (B) can be eliminated because it contradicts the information you were given in the question. Answer choice (C) looks very good since it matches up well with the information provided in the question. Answer choice (D) looks good if you don't read it carefully. Although we know that the two items dropped at the *same* speed, we don't know if that speed was *limited*. The answer is **(C)**.

Question 8: Of the four answer choices, the only one in which one variable increases while the other decreases is **answer choice (A)**. Notice that as the volume of soda increases, the cost of soda decreases. This is an example of an inverse relationship.

Question 9: Answer choice (A) can be eliminated because the use of the word *best* isn't justified by the data you have in front of you. Since the issue of soil depletion is never mentioned, you don't have sufficient information to justify answer choice (B). Answer choice (C) can be eliminated for pretty much the same reason that you can get rid of (A): The word *all* in this answer choice isn't justified by the information provided in the table. **Answer choice (D)** is the credited response. For all plants except for eggplants, the presence of compost noticeably increased yields.

Question 10: This question is asking you to find something that would cause you to question the experimental results. Remember, a good experiment only introduces one variable at a time so observed results can be properly attributed to that variable. The credited response to this question is **answer choice (B)** because it would cause one to question whether the difference in yield for the two sets of tomato plants was due to the presence of compost or the difference in the amount of rain the two plants received. Remember, to weaken a proposed cause-effect relationship (in this case, the claim that compost is what caused higher tomato yields), demonstrate that other possible causes are present.

Question 11:   In this question, you are asked to weaken the claim that one needs to cut back on the consumption of complex carbohydrates to lose weight. The argument assumes that weight loss cannot be accomplished in any other way. In this case, **answer choice (A)** weakens the argument by pointing out that there is an ameliorative effect against the impact of complex carbohydrates if one consumes certain other foods. If answer choice (A) were true, then it wouldn't necessarily be true that a person would have to cut back on complex carbohydrates to lose weight. Instead, an individual could simply add other types of food to the diet to counter those negative effects.

Question 12:   By applying the conditions to the answer choices one at a time, you can eliminate answer choices as you go. Since you know that Buddy and Frank cannot sit next to each other, you can eliminate answer choices (A) and (D). Next, since you are told that Frank and Martha must sit next to each other, you can eliminate answer choice (C). The only choice left is **answer choice (B).**

Question 13:   In this experiment, the wooden block and the length of the ramps do not change, thus eliminating answer choices (A) and (C). The material of the ramps changes, but since it does not depend on anything else to change, it is the independent variable. **Answer choice (B)** is the credited response because the speed of the wooden block depends on the material of the ramp.

Question 14:   If you need 3 cups of lemon juice to make 4 quarts of lemonade, you will need more than twice as much to make 10 quarts of lemonade (since 10 is more than twice as big as 4). So, the answer you pick needs to be bigger than 6. You can therefore eliminate answer choices (A) and (B). So even without doing much heavy lifting mathwise, you can get this down to two choices. To solve the problem mathematically, you need to set up an equation where $3/x = 4/10$. After doing the arithmetic, you should find that $x = 7\frac{1}{2}$ and you should therefore pick **answer choice (C)** as your response.

Question 15:   In a right triangle, the hypotenuse is always the largest side. (In any triangle, the largest side is opposite the largest angle.) There is no information given about the lengths of the two legs of the right triangle, so the only answer that MUST be true is **answer choice (B).**

Question 16: The trick here is to sketch a quick diagram that relates everything. You should get something that looks like this:

TEAL————RED————PURPLE

ORANGE————BLUE

So teal and orange are both greater than red and purple. While you do know that teal and orange are both greater than blue, you don't have enough information to know how blue relates to red and purple. Answer choice (A) might be true, but you don't have enough information to establish that it is definitely true. **Answer choice (B)** must be true. If orange and teal are the same, and if teal is greater than red, which is greater than purple, then orange must be greater than purple. Answer choice (C) cannot be true, and answer choice (D) might be true but also might be false.

Question 17: Why do health care professionals think that the current standards are not adequate to protect the public? Look for an additional consideration that would explain why they might still be concerned. Answer choices (A) and (B) don't really look like they are related to concerns about health effects of loud noises, so you should look to the other answer choices to see if there's a better choice. Answer choice (C) looks better than the first two, but it's not entirely clear that a lack of government effort to regulate noise necessarily means that noise poses some kind of physical hazard beyond what's already been described. **Answer choice (D)** is the credited response. It describes physical hazards from loud noises that are not currently regulated by the government recommendations.

Question 18: Why does the kid think the pool is warm when the parents think the pool is cold? What else do you notice that is different about them? Well, the kid was in an air-conditioned environment and the parents have been sitting in the hot sun. Does one of the answer choices touch on these issues? Yes, **answer choice (D)** explains that the difference in perception of the temperature of the pool is related to the difference between being in an air-conditioned room and being out in the hot sun. Notice how answer choices (A) and (B) can be eliminated from a very careful reading of the material. All three of them agree that the temperature of the pool is 80 degrees. It's just that the parents think that it feels cold and the son thinks it feels warm. They do not, however, sense an actual difference in the temperature of the water (which is something that (A) and (B) both claim is going on).

Question 19: What does the author mean by *treatment*? While *strategy* is close, it would be more appropriate to say that a strategy is something that you would implement for the *prevention* of Lyme disease rather than for Lyme disease itself. The best answer in this case is actually **answer choice (B).** Antibiotics are being used as a remedy for the disease.

Question 20: Notice from the passage that the author indicates that casual outdoor-bound individuals are probably better off using tick repellant. So, the kind of person who should be getting a vaccine would be someone who doesn't fit this description. In this case, the best answer choice would be **answer choice (C)** because it parallels the contrast that the author is making in the passage.

Question 21: A secondary source is something that was written after an event occurred. Therefore, **answer choice (B)** is the only source that can be considered as a secondary source, since the article was written seventy-five years after the strike.

Question 22: What statement about the abolition of the poll tax can be most appropriately applied to the amendment itself? Since the amendment is more about voting than about taxes, you can eliminate answer choice (A). Next, since northern or southern states are not mentioned, you can safely eliminate answer choice (C), if you hadn't already eliminated it because you knew it was historically incorrect. So now you're down to two. The trick is to focus on what the question is asking you. While answer choice (B) accurately describes the *conditions* under which the amendment was passed, it doesn't describe the reasoning behind the amendment. **Answer choice (D)** provides the legal justification behind the passage of the amendment.

Question 23: You may have heard of the Irish potato famine. If you haven't, this is a great example of a question where you pretty much have to guess and keep moving. If you have heard of the Irish potato famine, then the next trick is to figure out which one of these places on the map is Ireland. I is Turkey, II is the border area between Germany and Poland, III is Ireland— **answer choice (C)**—and IV is Italy.

Questions 24–26: As with many poems, the poem is not about what it seems to be literally about. This poem is not about a falcon; it is about society falling apart.

Question 24: What's the poem's mood? It's sure not excited and happy. The poem is gloomy and pessimistic in its view of the world. The presence of the word *lethargic* is enough to allow you to eliminate answer choice (B) and the presence of the word *unfeeling* is enough to allow you to eliminate answer choice (D). *Apprehensive and pessimistic* is an excellent summary of the foreboding tone of this particular poem, so the best choice is going to be **answer choice (C).**

Question 25: The words *intentional overstatement* can't be justifiably defended from the information you have been given, so you can go ahead and eliminate answer choice (A). No words seem to be capturing sound or motion, so answer choice (B) doesn't look particularly compelling. **Answer choice (C)** isn't a very ambitious answer choice and is therefore pretty easy to defend. It's not much of a stretch to say that certain vowel sounds are repeated (*turning and turning*; *falcon* and *falconer*). Answer choice (D) would require far more knowledge of poetry than you would ever be expected to have for this answer choice to be correct. Rest assured that you are not expected to know the poetry styles of different poets to the degree that you would be expected to recognize a satire of any particular style.

Question 26: Answer choices (B) and (C) should be pretty easy to eliminate. The poem is pretty clearly a figurative expression rather than a reference to any specific event or to the poet. To say that the theme of a poem is less important than a poem's imagery is to miss the point of why poems have imagery. Poems generally engage in imagery in support of the poem's theme. Therefore, the most appropriate answer choice is **answer choice (A)**.

Question 27: Paragraph E is the one that uses vivid examples to describe a character trait. The brother's aversion to overripe papayas, revulsion of men in short-sleeved shirts, and horror of clip-on ties reveals a certain squeamishness that stands in stark contrast to his behavior of kneeling down next to the dog, which might be expected to evoke these feelings. The credited response is therefore **answer choice (D)**.

Question 28: Paragraph D is the most appropriate answer. "Such were the extremes of emotion that Mr. Ramsay excited in his children's breasts by his mere presence" is a quote from that paragraph that absolutely justifies the selection of **answer choice (C)**.

Question 29: From question 27, you should remember that the narrator was surprised by his or her brother's behavior in paragraph E, so you should select the only answer choice containing that paragraph as part of the answer. This would of course be **answer choice (C)**.

Question 30: From stanza A comes the line, "In which I have lived like a foot." This compares the writer to a part of the body, and so the best answer is **answer choice (A)**.

Question 31: Also from stanza A comes the line, "You do not do, you do not do." That repetition does indeed create a rhythmic effect and is your justification for selecting **answer choice (A)**.

Question 32: You must carefully read the passage in order to understand how it is structured. As you read the passage, you should sketch an outline showing what each paragraph says and does. The first paragraph describes what was happening in Europe in the mid-fourteenth century. The second paragraph briefly discusses the changes that occurred in Europe because of the Bubonic Plague, and the third paragraph describes the conditions in Europe that allowed the Plague to hit so virulently. Therefore, **answer choice (B)** is the best answer. Don't let the fancy terminology in the answer choices intimidate you; use POE if you're unsure of the words. None of the other answer choices follow the outline we made, so (B) has to be the correct answer.

Questions 33–34: If you've never heard of apartheid, then question 33 is not going to be something you can do more than guess at. Don't be discouraged into thinking that you couldn't do question 34 anyway.

Question 33: Apartheid is of course something that was a feature of South Africa. Even if you're not an ace at African geography, a good guess as to the location of South Africa would be Roman numeral I (since it's the southernmost tip of the continent). The best answer choice to this question is therefore **answer choice (A).**

Question 34: This question is asking you to parallel the theme of the original quote to a theme in one of the answer choices. Since the original quote is about keeping the races separate but equal, you should find a quote that touches on that same idea. The most appropriate parallel can of course be found in **answer choice (D).**

Question 35: This is a supply and demand question. Prices tend to be highest when supply is lowest. Therefore, the best answer to this question would be **answer choice (B)** because it reflects the time period when the oil supply was at its lowest.

Question 36: Which building *looks* the oldest? **Answer choice (B)** would be an excellent choice.

Question 37: Which building looks most like its usefulness was the most important feature? That would be **answer choice (C).** Notice how the building is not at all ornamental but instead is built purely for function.

Question 38: This is an excellent reminder of basic test-taking strategy. Notice how in answer choices (A) through (C), the word *all* is prominently featured. In answer choice (D), the words *at least one* replace the word *all*. Is it fair to say that at least one of the buildings was intended to be a place of worship? Building B looks enough like a church or cathedral to make **answer choice (D)** a good choice.

Question 39:   Answer choice (C) is correct since the passage deals with two aspects of the ancient site: health and wealth. The phrase, "revealed a greater prevalence of cavities and other dental pathologies among those in the decorous burial," is a clue that there is a relationship between health and wealth. Choice (A) is an incorrect reading of the passage since the number of grave goods doesn't lead to dental pathologies. The word *best* in choice (B) is too extreme, and choice (D) contradicts the passage.

Question 40:   Since mosquitoes are both ecologically beneficial and bothersome to humans, the best response is **answer choice (B)**.

Question 41:   Another supply and demand question. Increases in demand will, in the short term, lead to increases in price. The credited response is therefore **answer choice (B).**

Question 42:   There's nothing in the graphs that would enable you to predict the future development of the railroads, so you can't support answer choice (A). **Answer choice (B)** looks very good. The north had many more miles of railroads, and notice that the time period shown on the chart is the time leading up to the Civil War. Furthermore, the ability to move troops and equipment would seem to have some bearing on each side's ability to fight the war. As far as answer choice (C) goes, without knowing how much cargo was being shipped or how many trains were traveling on the existing rails, there is no way for you to be able to determine if the amount of development was *adequate* for the south's needs. Finally, answer choice (D) is contradicted by the information in the chart.

Question 43:   It's impossible to say if answer choice (A) is true or not. While it appears that Republicans will eventually hold more seats *total* when all states are considered together, the graph doesn't provide enough information for you to be able to tell what might be happening on a *state-by-state* basis. As for answer choice (B), since the graph indicates relative numbers of elected officials, you cannot use it to determine anything about numbers of registered voters. Registered Republicans can theoretically vote for a Democrat and vice-versa. **Answer choice (C)** is the credited response. The chart indicates that, at least in the early 1990s (you should be looking at only the top two in each set of four bars), Democrats outnumbered Republicans in state legislatures. Notice how this statement is plainly true and requires no additional assumptions. (A) and (B) *might* be true depending on other circumstances, but (C) *has* to be true no matter what. Answer choice (D) is not going to be credited because this answer choice is talking about governors and the graph is talking about the composition of state legislatures. The two ideas are not necessarily related to each other, and of course neither is necessarily related to proportions of registered voters. While experience might lead one to believe that they are related, they are not objectively true in the way that answer choice (C) is. Understanding this difference will definitely increase your chances of passing this test.

Question 44: What's wrong with this plan? Unlike the situation that was taking place during the War of 1812, the cargo the smugglers are carrying is illegal drugs. So, if the modern-day privateers were to sell the cargo they had seized, then the modern-day privateers would be selling the illegal drugs that the government is trying to keep off the streets. The credited response to this question is therefore **answer choice (C).**

Question 45: What David Hume is saying is that if an idea is not supported by abstract or experimental reasoning, then the idea should be discarded. You should be looking for an answer choice that most closely parallels that idea. Answer choices (B) and (C) can be discarded because the quote makes no reference to either the church or the monarchy. Answer choice (A) doesn't seem to match the theme of the quote presented with the question. Hume isn't saying that everything knowable had been discovered. Instead, Hume is making a statement that reason is the means by which real knowledge is gained. This is best paraphrased in **answer choice (D).**

Question 46: Paintings B and C both utilize foreshortening to create the illusion of space. The painting that creates space by utilizing overlapping layers is painting A, which is **answer choice (A).**

Question 47: The best way to arrive at the answer to a question like this, in which you are being asked to compare or contrast pieces of artwork, is to utilize POE. For each answer choice, can you find a painting that *doesn't* do what the answer choice says it does? If so, you can eliminate that choice. Painting A doesn't seem to reflect an obsessive attention to small details, painting D doesn't appear to elevate linear over curved forms, nor does painting D seem to reflect a pessimistic attitude toward society. However, it would not be much of a stretch to say that each painting presents a highly subjective rendering of reality. For that reason, you are best served by selecting **answer choice (D).**

Question 48: Why does the author use a simple style in painting D? You should be looking for an answer choice that ties the simplicity of the painting to what is likely to be the author's theme for the painting. In this case, the best choice of the group can be found in **answer choice (C).** Even if you felt totally lost on this question, you should at least be able to eliminate answer choice (B), because it doesn't seem from looking at this particular painting that your attention is being drawn to the leaves in the background. Remember, no matter how lost you feel on any question, you should always eliminate what you can and pick something from the remaining choices before moving on.

Question 49: This sentence contains a parallel construction error. The part of the sentence that needs correction should say "gagging, gasping, or *running* home to brush their teeth." The credited response to this question is therefore **answer choice (C).**

Question 50: Answer choice (A) seems like a pretty fair candidate for elimination since you can't really see all the windows and have no idea which direction the house is facing. How would you be expected to know if the sun is going to shine into *every* window of the house without knowing this stuff? Answer choice (C) is also pretty easy to eliminate because the picture doesn't seem to match up with the description of a *circular form*. The balconies look pretty rectangular to us. Of the remaining two choices, **answer choice (D)** seems a better choice because the house seems to be designed to look as if it fits right into the rocks. The waterfall emerging from under the balconies would be another reason you would want to steer toward the answer choice that talks about nature rather than the answer choice that talks about a fortress.

Question 51: An omniscient narrator is different from a first-person narrator. Notice how three of the paragraphs are being told from the point of view of a character in the story, while the fourth (paragraph C) is being told from the point of view of a narrator. Since the narrator can see and know everything that is happening in the story, then it would be correct to describe the narrator as omniscient. **Answer choice (C)** is therefore the answer.

Question 52: This one takes a bit more reading, but what you are looking for is a paragraph in which the first-person narrator refers to himself as both "I" and by a name. Paragraph A is close because the narrator introduces himself by name ("My name is Otto Dietrich zur Linde"). However, this is not an example of the narrator referring to himself in the third person. In paragraph B, however, there is an example of a first-person narrator referring to himself in the third person ("where else could Oskar have played several drums at once?"), so **answer choice (B)** is correct.

Question 53: Stream-of-consciousness narration is a writing style that tries to mimic the various thoughts running through the narrator's mind. This effect is most clearly present in paragraph D, **answer choice (D)**.

Question 54: Isadora Duncan is saying that a truly creative dancer engages in movements that are a manifestation of the dancer's soul. The "body dances in accordance with a music heard inwardly." Answer choice (A) doesn't look so great because of the presence of the word *only*. Be careful that you don't confuse statements that talk about *one* way of doing something with answer choices that claim the author says it's the *only* way of doing something. In answer choice (B), the presence of the word *all* is suspicious, and you should be eliminating this answer choice because it presumes that the quote from Isadora Duncan is saying more than it actually does. Answer choice (C) can be eliminated because the quote makes no mention of theater or poetry. Finally, **answer choice (D)** looks very strong because it touches on the same themes as are present in the quote.

Question 55: This is another one of those questions that requires you to work carefully through the choices and compare what they are saying with what is going on in the source material. Since Dora's first statement is a fact rather than an opinion, you can go ahead and eliminate answer choices (A) and (B). **Answer choice (C)** looks very good, since both Dora and Robert state opinions (Dora—"we will most likely raise enough money" to go to Monticello; Robert—"I guess you will learn a lot") and facts (Dora—"we are making a model of Monticello"; Robert—Jefferson "was an architect, a gardener, and an inventor, as well as a politician"). Since both Dora and Robert state opinions in addition to facts, you can also eliminate answer choice (D).

Question 56: Symmetry and balance are achieved by having equal things on all sides. In this case, there is an equal number and equal type of windows on both rows of the chateau, so **answer choice (A)** is the credited response.

Question 57: From surveying the answer choices, you know that the first sentence has to be either 1, 2, or 3. Since sentences 1 and 3 both have a "this" that they refer to, neither of them is going to be a strong candidate for the first sentence. So, you can safely eliminate answer choices (B) and (C). From the remaining two choices, you now know that the sentence following sentence 2 will be either sentence 1 or 3. In this case, it makes more sense for sentence 1 to be second. Why? Because the "this" in sentence 1 would now refer to the idea that the rickshaw got its name from the Japanese language. Consequently, **answer choice (D)** is the most appropriate answer choice.

Question 58: A complete sentence is going to need a subject and a verb. **Answer choice (D)** is a sentence fragment because the subject (the media) is described but there is no action in the sentence. The rest of the sentences all have subjects taking some form of action.

Questions 59–63: The passage discusses the discovery of the Rosetta Stone and how we came to understand hieroglyphics through the work of scientists in deciphering the writing found on the stone.

Question 59: **Answer choice (A)** pretty much captures the idea of the passage as summarized above.

Question 60: Answer choice (A) can be eliminated because although we know that the Rosetta Stone enabled scholars to decipher ancient languages, we cannot say with certainty that that was the intended purpose of the people who made the Rosetta Stone. **Answer choice (B)** looks very strong. Notice how in the first paragraph it mentions that the Rosetta Stone contained ancient Greek writing and that scholars "could easily figure out what the Greek writing said." This must mean that some scholars could read ancient Greek. Answer choice (C) is contradicted by the passage, which claims that translating the hieroglyphics was *not* an easy task. Not enough is said about the French army to know whether answer choice (D) is true.

Question 61:   **Answer choice (A)** is answered in the passage. Napoleon brought scholars to Egypt because of his interest in history. None of the other answer choices are explicitly addressed in the body of the passage.

Question 62:   From the very end of the first paragraph, you are told that since the scholars could read the ancient Greek, they would be able to use their understanding of what the message on the stone said to enable them to figure out how hieroglyphics were used to represent language. This idea is best captured in **answer choice (B)**.

Question 63:   In the latter part of the second paragraph, it is revealed that Jean-Francois Champollion's main contribution was to realize that many more hieroglyphics represented sounds than had been previously thought. This idea is best summarized in **answer choice (B)**.

Questions 64–68:   This passage examines a problem in education. Students are taught a series of facts that are generally tested in terms of what they have memorized. The author points out that these students haven't really engaged in "real" learning because they lack the skill to utilize the information in any way beyond simply parroting back what they have been taught.

Question 64:   Since essay questions are never mentioned in the passage, answer choice (A) is not the one you want to pick. **Answer choice (B)** looks very solid because it focuses on the issue of testing and how the kinds of testing that are commonly used do not test student understanding of the material. While the two problems mentioned in answer choice (C) are discussed in the passage, there is no clear indication in the passage that the author sees one problem as more or less serious than the other. It's unclear whether the author would even agree that answer choice (D) is true. The only comment that the author makes regarding factual knowledge and true understanding is that factual knowledge by itself doesn't guarantee true understanding.

Question 65:   The author is discussing the fact that students who have passed a test will fail a test on the same material if the test is changed slightly. So, the author is using the word "good" ironically because what the author really means is that these students haven't really learned. Therefore, the most appropriate answer to this question is **answer choice (A)**.

Question 66:   The beginning of the second paragraph is sufficient to support your including statement I in your answer. At this point you can eliminate answer choices (B) and (D). You should see that you don't have to check statement III because it isn't in any of the remaining answer choices. You do have to check statement II, and you should notice that this statement is directly contradicted by information in the passage. Therefore, the most appropriate response to this question is **answer choice (A)**.

Question 67: Remember, the author's idea of what makes a good test is that the test will challenge students' ability to apply what they have learned to seemingly new situations. The author would resist using a test that is simply a review of factual information that could be retrieved from memory. The answer choice that most closely meets the author's criteria for a good test question can be found in **answer choice (C).**

Question 68: If the student learns the facts but does not understand the subject, that student will not be able to apply the facts in any kind of meaningful way. This idea is best captured in **answer choice (D).**

Question 69: Answer choice (A) is directly contradicted by the information in the graph. The voting behavior through the 1980s seems to be reason enough to steer clear of answer choice (B). **Answer choice (C)** looks very strong. Notice how there is almost zero gender difference in voting behavior in the 1970s, but differences start to become apparent in the 1980s and 1990s. Answer choice (D) is also contradicted by information in the graph (see the election data from 1980 and 1984, for example).

Question 70: This quote states that the West should "share its wisdom" and "take the lead." The author is a believer in the idea that the West should get involved in helping other nations. The answer choice that best captures this is **answer choice (B).**

Question 71: Since one paragraph is about army ants and the other paragraph is about wasps, it would be incorrect to say that the main idea is strictly about one or the other. For this reason, you can eliminate answer choices (A) and (C). Answer choice (B) would seem to be a strange answer to pick since the passage barely mentions computers. The best answer—the one that best captures the theme of the passage as a whole—is **answer choice (D).**

Question 72: In the first paragraph, the author says that army ants follow a *chemical* trail left by the ants at the head of the column. That's ample reason to select **answer choice (D)** as your response.

Question 73: Why do the ants keep marching in a circle? Because the ants are basically stupid and they are following the chemical trail laid down in front of them. So, when the chemical trail forms a circle, the ants will simply keep marching around. The best answer choice to select here is **answer choice (A).**

Question 74: The "pattern of events" that the author is mentioning is the wasp dragging the cricket to the burrow's entrance and then going inside to check for intruders. This of course is perfectly paraphrased in **answer choice (D).**

Question 75: The author mentions the Supreme Court in the second paragraph, but that mention is not wholly critical. Therefore, answer choice (A) can be eliminated. The presence of the word *prove* in answer choice (B) is sufficient to eliminate that answer choice. Answer choice (C) isn't entirely appropriate either, since the theme of the passage as a whole is government involvement in education. **Answer choice (D)** is the closest parallel to the author's point of view, as revealed in the last few lines of the passage.

Question 76: The first couple of lines of the first paragraph are sufficient to support **answer choice (C).**

Question 77: The author examines the role that the federal government has played through history in making education accessible to a wider group of people. Answer choices (A) and (B) don't seem to match up with the author's thesis regarding the need for government to be involved in the education process. A close reading of answer choice (C) will reveal that it says the opposite of what the author thinks. Therefore, the most appropriate answer choice of the group is **answer choice (D).**

Question 78: The third paragraph is missing a sentence that establishes the scene. **Answer choice (C)** would establish that the narrator and his grandfather are riding mules down into the canyon.

Question 79: The second sentence in the first paragraph has a semicolon where a comma should be. Therefore, the most appropriate response to this question is **answer choice (A).**

Question 80: The verb *hating* breaks the parallelism in the sentence. The parallelism should read "a desire," "a sense," and "a hatred." This structure can be found in **answer choice (C).**

14

ATS-W Practice Test

ATS-W PRACTICE TEST DIRECTIONS FOR MULTIPLE-CHOICE QUESTIONS

DIRECTIONS

This test contains a multiple-choice section and a section with a single written assignment. You may complete the sections of the test in the order you choose.

Each question in the first section of this test is a multiple-choice question with four answer choices. Read each question CAREFULLY and choose the ONE best answer. Record your answer on the answer sheet in the space that corresponds to the question number. Completely fill in the space that has the same letter as the answer you have chosen. *Use only a No. 2 lead pencil.*

Sample Question: 1.   What is the capital of New York?

          A.   Buffalo
          B.   New York City
          C.   Albany
          D.   Rochester

The correct answer to this question is C. You would indicate that on the answer sheet as follows:

1.

You should answer all questions. Even if you are unsure of an answer, it is better to guess than not to answer a question at all. You may use the margins of the test for scratch paper, but you will be scored only on the responses on your answer sheet.

The directions for the written assignment appear later in this test.

The words "End of Test" indicate that you have completed the test. You may go back and review your answers.

PART 1: MULTIPLE CHOICE QUESTIONS

Use the information below to answer the four questions that follow.

Ben Jones teaches Algebra I to ninth-grade students. When introducing new mathematical concepts, he uses an assortment of presentation methods, including demonstrations on the chalkboard or overhead projector, computer software, and group activities.

1. Kara Jackson is a student in Ben's class. She does not participate much in class, and has little success in algebra. Ben would like to improve her confidence level in algebra, in the hopes that more confidence in math will result in more successful algebra problem solving. When doing exercises that involve students' coming up to the board, he should

   (A) not call on Kara to come up to the board, so that she does not become embarrassed if she solves the problem incorrectly in front of her classmates.
   (B) have another student come up to the board with her to guide her through successful problem-solving.
   (C) have the students complete problems at their seats first, while Ben circulates among them to offer individual help, then call on Kara to do a problem on the board that he already knows she can do correctly.
   (D) ask Kara and several other students to each present a different problem on the board as best they can, and then ask the rest of the class for corrections to work on the board.

2. Ben has shown students how to multiply binomials and is doing a drill on the overhead projector when Nicola White raises her hand and says, "Mr. Jones, we had all of this last year in eighth-grade math. We know how to do it. Don't waste our time."

   Mr. Jones says to the entire class, "Is that true, folks?"

   He hears a loud chorus of "yes" in response. What should he do next?

   (A) Rush through the rest of the drill to get it over with quickly.
   (B) Skip the rest of the practice problems and go on to the next lesson.
   (C) Assign the rest of the drill to do in class with partners.
   (D) Give a pop quiz.

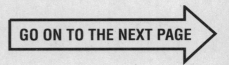
GO ON TO THE NEXT PAGE

3. All of the following would be appropriate audiovisuals in Ben's class EXCEPT

(A) a video that glamorizes how a bookmaker uses his knowledge of mathematics to amass great wealth.
(B) posters portraying mathematicians at work.
(C) an interactive CD-ROM that allows students to question people who are not mathematicians but who use math in their work.
(D) a film about a mathematician and her mathematical discoveries.

4. Ben uses a final examination that will represent a significant portion of each student's final grade. Which of the following is true of exams in general?

I. Norm-referenced tests are competitive and therefore more accurately determine what students have learned, since high school students work well under pressure.
II. Criterion-referenced tests can allow all students in a class to earn high scores.
III. The final exam should represent nearly 100 percent of each student's grade since the material will be cumulative and all-encompassing.
IV. A performance-based test can allow students to demonstrate higher-level thinking skills.

(A) I and III only
(B) II and IV only
(C) II, III, and IV
(D) I, II, III, and IV

GO ON TO THE NEXT PAGE ⟩

Use the information below to answer the seven questions that follow.

Dave Maloumian teaches kindergarten in an urban residential neighborhood. His large classroom includes several areas for dramatic play: play house, play kitchen, and an unused walk-in closet. In January, he notices that many of the children have been pretending that the closet is a "workshop" for fixing things. Dave uses an emergent curriculum and decides to implement a unit on tools into the curriculum. One activity that he would like to do is a field trip to the neighborhood hardware store.

5. The students' current dramatic play indicates that

(A) Dave needs to create a highly motivating initial activity for this unit to motivate his students.
(B) Dave's students are already motivated to learn about tools.
(C) Dave should wait until later in the school year to take the students on a field trip since the weather will probably be more agreeable in the spring.
(D) the students already know a great deal about tools and therefore a unit on them would not be teaching them anything new.

6. Dave knows that one way children learn is by imitating what they see adults doing. He also knows that kindergartners learn through their own actions. He would like to teach the children to use real, child-sized tools in a woodworking area, as he saw a colleague in a neighboring school teach children to do. The most important consideration in determining whether to undertake this activity with the children is

(A) whether the school is willing to pay for the tools.
(B) if Dave has enough room in his classroom to set up a woodworking area.
(C) whether he can provide enough close adult supervision so that the children can use the tools safely.
(D) if the students will be able to create something useful with the wood and the tools.

7. Dave plans for the students to take a five-minute train ride to the hardware store. He secures enough parent chaperones to guarantee a 4:1 ratio of students to adults. Before the date of the trip, Dave needs the explicit permission of

I. the principal.
II. the chaperones.
III. the students.
IV. each student's parent or guardian.

(A) I only
(B) I and IV only
(C) II, III, and IV only
(D) I, II, III, and IV

8. Dave does not tell his students that he is planning a trip to the hardware store. Instead, he holds a brainstorming session with them to come up with a list of everything they know about hardware stores. He asks the class, "How do you think we could determine whether this is an accurate list?"

Several students raise their hands and offer suggestions.

"We could call the store and ask," says William Payne.

"We could ask my dad, because he goes there all the time," says Graham LaRue.

"We could go to the store and see for ourselves," says Georgia O'Lynn.

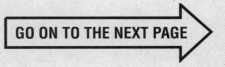

GO ON TO THE NEXT PAGE

Dave repeats each option to the class, asking for a show of hands for which one the students think is the best option. When the students see that most children agree that going to the store is the best way, several call out, "Can we go?"

Which of the following statements is most likely the main reason that Dave led this discussion?

(A) Students feel a sense of ownership in activities that they develop themselves.
(B) He wanted to see how much they already know about hardware stores.
(C) He wanted to teach students the critical thinking skill of how to brainstorm ideas.
(D) Kindergarten students need practice in discussion skills such as raising hands and taking turns talking to prepare them for first grade.

9. Dave wants this trip to make a lasting impression on the students and to relate to other curriculum areas. To best ensure achieving this goal, during the trip he could

(A) take photos for the class photo album.
(B) make an audiotape record of the students' comments at the hardware store.
(C) have the students raise money and use it to purchase items that the class will use throughout the year, such as seeds for the garden and bookbinding supplies.
(D) ask each student to remember three things about the trip to tell his or her parents at the end of the day.

10. Dave would like to make an assessment of how much the students learned from their trip to the hardware store and from the unit on tools. Which of the following would be the best method for Dave to accurately assess what the students have learned?

(A) Observation of the children's dramatic and independent play after the trip
(B) Portfolios that include students' drawings of the hardware store
(C) Student-written reports on what they learned on the trip
(D) Oral testing in which each child tells which tools should be used for which projects

11. Earlier in the school year, Dave took his students to the local library and the animal shelter. Later in the school year he plans to take them to the local pizza parlor for a lesson in dough-making. The main reason that Dave believes trips to be an important part of the curriculum is that

(A) trips are fun for the children, teacher, and chaperones.
(B) trips are a good way for children to learn a lot without too much work on the teacher's part.
(C) the students need to decide what they will do with their futures.
(D) Dave wants to build stronger ties to the community, and to make his curricular content personally meaningful for his students.

GO ON TO THE NEXT PAGE

Use the information below to answer the five questions that follow.

Joanne Sparks utilizes theme-based learning in her sixth-grade classroom. She would like for her final theme of the academic year to be bicycles. With this theme, she hopes that her student teacher, Jerry Grant, will demonstrate clear mastery of theme-based curriculum planning.

12. Jerry begins the unit planning by writing the word "bicycle" in the middle of a posterboard. He then circles the word. Near this word, he writes "how gears work (science)" in a smaller circle, and draws a line to connect it to "bicycle." He also writes and connects to "bicycle" the following: "its invention (history)," "Tour de France (geography)," and "fitness (health)." Jerry's students help him add items related to literature, art, and math. They also start to draw lines and circles connecting more ideas to the ideas already listed. This is an example of

   (A) facilitation.
   (B) webbing.
   (C) synthesis.
   (D) district-wide curriculum guidelines.

13. Jerry proposes to Joanne that students bring their bicycles to school for one day. Joanne advises him to most importantly consider

   (A) whether all of the students have bicycles.
   (B) if the physical education teacher will collaborate in a bicycle-related activity.
   (C) how much the students would enjoy this activity.
   (D) how this activity will affect the final student-teaching evaluation that Joanne will give Jerry.

14. On the day that the class is to begin the unit on bicycles, Joanne gets the children seated and then Jerry rides into the classroom on his bicycle, attired in bike-racing clothing and safety equipment. He does this to

   (A) get the children to laugh.
   (B) get the students' interest and attention.
   (C) demonstrate his bicycling skill.
   (D) impress Joanne with his creativity.

15. Jerry shows the students a biographical film on the life of competitive bicyclist Lance Armstrong. At several points during the presentation, he stops the film and discusses what has just appeared. Which of the following is a likely and significant effect on the students?

   (A) The students become annoyed and distracted.
   (B) The breaks are helpful to students' focus and comprehension.
   (C) The students remember and comprehend less than they would if Jerry were to show the film uninterrupted.
   (D) The breaks add time to the presentation, so that the class may end before Jerry gets to the end of the film.

16. When Jerry first came to Joanne's class earlier in the year, he asked her to tell him who were the brightest students in the class, who were average, and who were below average. Joanne was reluctant to tell him because

   (A) student teachers should learn everything about teaching by themselves to maximize their long-term learning.
   (B) Joanne was uncooperative.
   (C) the students were all of the exact same level of academic ability.
   (D) teachers' expectations of student performance can have negative consequences.

GO ON TO THE NEXT PAGE

Use the information below to answer the five questions that follow.

Ruth Augusto-Correia and Marcelo Augusto-Correia are both high school teachers in the same school. They are also married to each other.

17. The Augusto-Correias often discuss instructional matters with each other at home, but they are unsure whether they should discuss the performance of specific students, since they have no students in common. Mr. and Mrs. Augusto-Correia ask their principal for advice, and she tells them that

   (A) it is illegal for teachers to discuss specific students with anyone other than the student's parents or guardians.
   (B) it is fine for them to discuss students together only because Ruth and Marcelo are a married couple.
   (C) it is fine for them to discuss any students in the school since both teachers are employed by the same school.
   (D) it is legal for them to discuss any of the school students, provided that the discussions take place on school property, and not in the home.

18. The Augusto-Correias and 40 percent of the students in their school are of Brazilian descent and are fluent in Portuguese. Both Augusto-Correias speak only English in their classrooms; they respond in English when students address their teachers in Portuguese. This is mainly because

   (A) children in the United States should speak only English.
   (B) responses in Portuguese would alienate the non–Portuguese speaking students in their classrooms.
   (C) speaking only English in school is a legitimate ESL instructional technique.
   (D) it is disrespectful for students to address their teachers in a different language, and the teachers are trying to teach respect.

19. Mr. Augusto-Correia teaches high school civics, for which there are daily class discussions. Frequently during the discussions, he asks a student to paraphrase what the previous speaker said. He does this because

   (A) it helps students to enunciate clearly.
   (B) he wants to make sure no one is dozing.
   (C) he wants to further develop students' listening skills.
   (D) it helps Mr. Augusto-Correia to remember and keep track of what everyone says.

20. Mrs. Augusto-Correia teaches ninth-grade English. She is planning a research project to enable her students to develop lifelong research skills. The project will take three months to complete. Most of her students have never done such a project. Which of the following would be the best way to assign research topics?

   (A) She should assign a topic or topics unrelated to the current theme in the classroom.
   (B) She should assign a topic or topics related to the current theme in the classroom.
   (C) The students should choose their own topics, as long as the topics are related to the current theme in the classroom.
   (D) The students should choose their own topics, regardless of whether the topics are related to the current theme in the classroom, as long as the topics meet the teacher's expressed guidelines.

21. Which of the following types of assessment would be best for Mrs. Augusto-Correia to use during the research process?

   (A) Biweekly conferences with each student
   (B) A requirement that each student turn in one rough draft per month
   (C) A scheduled time each week for students who have questions to ask
   (D) A checklist at the beginning and the end of the project for students to submit to Mrs. Augusto-Correia

GO ON TO THE NEXT PAGE

Use the information below to answer the five questions that follow.

Ms. Singh's high school history class is studying the Great Depression. She uses learning centers to complement more traditional secondary school teaching methods.

22. While students in her class are not required to read Steinbeck's book *The Grapes of Wrath*, Ms. Singh allows students to spend time reading this novel when they have finished all of their other class work. This is an example of

(A) an extra credit assignment.
(B) collaboration between the English and history departments.
(C) enrichment.
(D) a classroom management technique to keep students busy.

23. Since some students never finish assignments early, those students might never get a chance to read *The Grapes of Wrath* in class. To give everyone a chance to read it, Ms. Singh should

(A) include reading as an acceptable activity during learning center time.
(B) assign it for homework.
(C) devise a separate activity for the faster-paced students to do with Ms. Singh while the slower-paced students read the novel.
(D) tell the students who have not read it yet that they shouldn't worry about it.

24. Ms. Singh discusses all of the following questions during her unit on the Great Depression:

I. "Which New Deal programs would work today if there were a depression in the twenty-first century United States?"
II. "When did the Great Depression occur?"
III. "What type of programs helped the country to get out of the Great Depression?"

She wants to build up to the evaluation level of educational objectives. In which order should she ask these questions to enable the students to experience success?

(A) I, then II, then III
(B) II, then I, then III
(C) III, then II, then I
(D) II, then III, then I

25. Ms. Singh uses one handout per day during this unit. On each handout, she includes a political cartoon that was first published during the Great Depression. The main reason she does this is to

(A) demonstrate her skill at desktop publishing.
(B) use humor to entertain her students.
(C) appeal to visual learners.
(D) give the students another content-related topic of conversation.

26. Ms. Singh wants to assess how well her students understand the causes and effects of the Great Depression in terms of society, the economy, and foreign affairs. Which of the following forms of assessment would be the most appropriate for her to use?

(A) A fill-in-the-blank test
(B) An essay test
(C) A true-false test
(D) A multiple-choice test

GO ON TO THE NEXT PAGE

Use the information below to answer the five questions that follow.

Through his professional organization, Gary Patten recently attended a seminar on writing across the curriculum. He is excited to implement this concept at Blackwood High School, where he teaches English. He feels inspired by a book he's read recently—*The Riddle of the Compass: The Invention That Changed the World*, by Amir. D. Aczel. Mr. Patten thinks that the history, science, and English departments could work together to study the invention of the compass. After the seminar, he ran into his department chairperson, Michael St. George, in the school parking lot and had the following conversation:

"Mr. St. George, I just attended this great seminar on writing across the curriculum, and I think we should try it here. Studies have shown that in such a program, students' academic performance not only improves in their English classes, but also in the content areas."

"We've never done anything like that here, Mr. Patten, and our students are already scoring above statewide averages on standardized tests."

"That's to our credit, Mr. St. George. I think that with this program, however, we could meet our educational objectives and possibly even exceed them, based on what I've heard from other teachers. I even have a specific project in mind."

"Well, that might be something worth pursuing. Even if the English department does stand behind this program, however, I doubt whether the other departments would be as enthusiastic. I should give you some tips on dealing with other departments before you approach them."

"Thanks for your input, Mr. St. George. I'll talk to you more about it at another time."

27. Mr. Patten's exchange with Mr. St. George was professional because

I. he acknowledged Mr. St. George's viewpoint.
II. Mr. Patten initiated the discussion in the school parking lot.
III. Mr. Patten exhibited confidence, enthusiasm, and competence.
IV. Mr. Patten kept the unscheduled conversation brief.

(A) III only
(B) I and III only
(C) I, II, and IV only
(D) I, III, and IV only

28. What should Mr. Patten's next step be in pursuing this project?

(A) Send Mr. St. George a note requesting a scheduled meeting so that the two of them can discuss the project.
(B) Write up a detailed proposal and send it directly to the heads of the history and science departments.
(C) Go to the principal and ask that she require all three departments to participate in this project.
(D) Tell the other teachers in the English department that Mr. St. George did not wholeheartedly endorse the project, and get their advice on how to deal with him.

GO ON TO THE NEXT PAGE >

29. Mr. Patten would like for his students to write a research paper on any aspect of the compass. He wants to conference with them weekly. After each conference, he plans to give each student an index card with his observations on his or her progress. These index cards are an example of

(A) journal entries.
(B) formative evaluation.
(C) portfolio assessment.
(D) summative evaluation.

30. Mr. Patten would like to suggest to the science department that students experiment with magnets to derive the principles of magnetism. Students could then couple this with their knowledge of geography to design their own compasses. The experimentation with magnets is an example of

(A) a deductive method.
(B) an inductive method.
(C) the scientific method.
(D) Pavlov's method.

31. The school did use Mr. Patten's proposal for a multi-subject unit on the compass. Later in the year, a science student was having trouble understanding how a weathervane works. Her teacher, Ms. Burke, told her, "Think of how a compass works. Do you remember and understand that?" Why did Ms. Burke make this comparison?

(A) A comparison between something unfamiliar and something known is a cognitive tool that aids in memory and comprehension.
(B) The science class material was cumulative, so each topic was a prerequisite for the next.
(C) Ms. Burke could not think of a better way to explain the weathervane.
(D) Ms. Burke wanted to make sure the student understood how a compass works.

GO ON TO THE NEXT PAGE

Use the information below to answer the three questions that follow.

Martha Hould has begun her teaching career in a first-grade classroom at Bluebell Elementary School. She would like to continue an annual visitation program instituted by her predecessor. In this program, the first graders of Bluebell Elementary visit a first-grade class at Greentree School for the Deaf on the first and third Fridays of each month. On the second and fourth Fridays, the Greentree students visit Bluebell. When together, the students play in the playground, have a snack, and participate in an activity or story time.

32. Martha's first step is to write a note to Joe McBaron, Greentree's long-time first-grade teacher. In the note, Martha

 (A) creates a detailed schedule with all activities planned for the first month of the program.
 (B) introduces herself, expresses her enthusiasm about the program, and proposes a planning meeting.
 (C) tells Joe that whatever was done last year is fine with her, and asks him to contact her with the plan.
 (D) expresses her concern that she wants to participate in the program, but does not know sign language.

33. As Martha and her students study American Sign Language, she notices that student Jenny Singer is not positioning her hands correctly for many of the words. Martha knows that Jenny is an auditory learner. Which of the following strategies should Martha use to most help Jenny learn the hand signs?

 (A) Martha should give Jenny spoken descriptions of how to make the signs while they make the signs together.
 (B) Martha should show Jenny a book that depicts people signing the words that the class is learning.
 (C) Martha should use her own hands to put Jenny's hands in the proper positions.
 (D) Martha should give Jenny an audiotape about Helen Keller.

34. When the students from both schools are together, all adult communications are conducted in both spoken English and ASL. Martha and her assistant speak out loud, Joe signs, and Joe's assistant speaks and signs simultaneously. The main reason that the teachers communicate with one another and the children in this manner is that

 (A) this is the best way for each group of students to learn one another's languages.
 (B) it is required by law.
 (C) it is important for the teachers to comprehend everything that is communicated in the classroom.
 (D) the teachers want to impress one another with their communication skills.

35. Ms. Slovava has recently moved from an affluent Pennsylvania suburb to a small city in New York State. Her school, Carver Elementary, is in the same neighborhood as a soup cannery, and many of her students' parents work in the cannery. Many different racial groups are represented in the community and, therefore, are represented in the classroom. In her first year at Carver, Ms. Slovava notices that most of the books and posters in the school portray only people of European descent. She would like for her classroom and curriculum to reflect the rich diversity found in the community. Given that Ms. Slovava has a chance to attend one of the following four in-service trainings, which one would best suit her needs?

 (A) "Language Skills with ESL Students: Teachers will learn recent recommendations about working with students who do not speak English."
 (B) "A City Snapshot: Teachers will discuss the demographic traits and cultural practices of the many different types of people in our district."
 (C) "The Three Winter Holidays: Teachers will brainstorm ideas for curriculum-enhancing projects involving Christmas, Kwanzaa, and Hanukkah."
 (D) "Literature from Central America: An experienced teacher who has used the novels of Julia Louise Alvarez in her classroom will share her curriculum."

GO ON TO THE NEXT PAGE

Use the information below to answer the two questions that follow.

Toi Ford is a fifth-grade teacher. She is using learning centers and cooperative learning to teach her students geography. Most of the children have rarely worked in groups before, so Toi is teaching them how to work together. They are a very competitive group of high-achieving children, and have been working in their groups for one month.

36. During the past two weeks, four of the five members of one class cooperative group have come to Toi individually to complain about Zachary Kelly, the fifth member of the group. All four complaining students say that they want Zachary out of the group. Which of the following courses of action should Toi take first?

(A) She should meet with the entire group to find out what the specific grievances are, and also elicit feedback on the group's functioning from Zachary—then give the children suggestions on how to resolve the problems.

(B) She should tell the students that the assigned groups are final and they have to work out problems themselves as they would in the real world.

(C) She should assign Zachary to a different group in hopes that he will get along better with other children who might be more accepting of him.

(D) She should offer all group members extra credit if they can work out the problems themselves, or if they attempt it themselves for three days and then schedule a conference with the teacher to evaluate their attempts and get feedback.

37. Toi wants to effectively manage the collaborative learning process as she teaches students cooperative skills. All of the following would be effective management techniques for Toi EXCEPT to

(A) require the group to submit one completed assignment for the entire group instead of one per student.

(B) require a specific group spokesperson to bring all group questions to the teacher's attention.

(C) use predetermined and explicit time limits for assignments.

(D) make group participation optional, since some students prefer to work alone.

Ms. Frederick is a fourth-grade teacher. In social studies, she and her students have been learning about the geographic and demographic characteristics of the different states in the United States.

38. She assigns her students to choose five states, write a paragraph about each one, and draw a bar graph comparing the populations of each state. In this activity, students could utilize skills in which of the following areas?

I. Research
II. Mathematics
III. Reading
IV. Computers

(A) I only
(B) I and II only
(C) II and III only
(D) I, II, III, and IV

GO ON TO THE NEXT PAGE

Use the information below to answer the five questions that follow.

Ms. Hernandez teaches at a rural elementary school in Finleyville. She has been teaching her sixth-grade class about how some people gain political influence or power through community involvement. She mentioned that in England, when a person involved in fox hunting became the Master of the Fox Hunt, that person, if clever enough, might be on his way to the House of Commons. The students began asking Ms. Hernandez questions about fox hunting.

39. The children have asked Ms. Hernandez so many questions about fox hunting that she is considering a class study of the sport. The first thing she should consider in her decision is

(A) whether she could meet her educational objectives while pursuing this topic.
(B) whether fox hunting is something in which sixth graders would be interested.
(C) whether the school library has significant resources to enable a study.
(D) whether people in the community engage in fox hunting.

40. After considering the idea and consulting with her principal and department, Ms. Hernandez decides that she will teach a unit on fox hunting. Her first unit activity involves a flip chart at the front of the classroom. She asks each student to come up to the flip chart and write down one thing that he or she would like to learn about fox hunting. Students who do not have questions are asked to find a question already posted that they are curious about and put their initials next to it. She mainly does this because

(A) she wants her students to participate in class more.
(B) she wants her students to learn how to set and achieve their own educational objectives.
(C) she can save preparation time if the students get more involved in the planning of the unit.
(D) a flip chart is a nice alternative to using the chalkboard all the time, and she can easily save and post the result.

41. Ms. Hernandez always writes formal lesson plans. All of the following are components of a formal lesson plan EXCEPT

(A) an objective.
(B) a list of materials and preparation required.
(C) a seating assignment.
(D) a motivation.

42. Fox hunting is not actively pursued in Finleyville, although it is done in a nearby county. Ms. Hernandez asks her students to work in groups to create a map of a hunt field that could theoretically be used in Finleyville. She would like each group to submit a computer-generated color map. What computer software should students use to create their maps?

(A) A database
(B) A spreadsheet
(C) A word processing program
(D) A graphics program

43. Because Ms. Hernandez knows that children are motivated by games, she designs a game in which the students simulate a fox hunt on the school playground. She tells them that they can each take a role: first whipper-in, huntsman, fox, hound, master, an so on. She asks for a volunteer to be the first whipper-in, and nobody volunteers. This is most likely because

(A) the students don't want to play a game.
(B) none of the students wants to be the first to volunteer.
(C) Ms. Hernandez needs to further explain the unfamiliar vocabulary.
(D) the students first want to know what the prizes for winning will be before choosing parts.

GO ON TO THE NEXT PAGE

Use the information below to answer the three questions that follow.

Diane Scutti is a middle school science teacher. She graduated from college three months ago, and this is her first teaching job. Her principal has asked master teacher Elaine Teitelbaum to engage in a mentoring relationship with Diane before school begins and throughout the school year.

44. Diane tells Elaine how she remembers getting a certain look from teachers—a look that makes students instantly behave appropriately. She is wondering if she should use that look herself in dealing with students. Elaine tells her

   (A) using such a look will make students think she is mean.
   (B) it is important for teachers to utilize nonverbal cues such as this in the classroom.
   (C) it is very difficult for a new teacher to use this look successfully since students do not respect young teachers.
   (D) she should only use it as a last resort.

45. Diane wants to be in control of the class and also to make the students feel comfortable on the first day of school. The students in her class were together for the previous year and are accustomed to sitting in rows in alphabetical order. Which of the following suggestions would Elaine most likely recommend to Diane?

   (A) Require students to choose their own seats.
   (B) Stand at the door and warmly introduce yourself as each student enters.
   (C) Use name tags to be sure to remember each child's name.
   (D) Dress in a casual style of attire that is similar to that of the students.

46. During the first week of school, Elaine observes Diane's class. During a class discussion, a student talks out of turn to insult another student's point of view. Diane makes a rule on the spot that there is to be no speaking out of turn, and that students must be respectful of one another's opinions and feelings. When they discuss the incident after class, Elaine would most likely tell Diane that

   (A) Diane should have required the offending student to apologize in class in front of his peers.
   (B) while Diane's new rule is an appropriate rule, it is important to have rules in place beforehand so that students are less likely to engage in undesirable behavior.
   (C) Diane should have explicitly explained to the class the reasons for the rule and the reason why the student's remark was offensive.
   (D) Diane should have waited until a later time to correct the offending student.

GO ON TO THE NEXT PAGE

Use the information below to answer the five questions that follow.

Kyung Kim is a second-grade teacher who is using fairy tales in his reading instruction. Kyung's lessons include asking the students to build models of *The Three Little Pigs'* houses, and to rewrite the ending of *The Three Billy Goats Gruff.*

47. Kyung plans to formally assess how well students are reading at the end of the unit. Which of the following types of assessment would be the most valid?

    (A) Performance-based testing
    (B) A standardized test
    (C) Student portfolios
    (D) Student self-assessment

48. Kyung asks the school's art teacher to collaborate with him on the model-building project. The most important reason for this collaboration is that

    (A) it satisfies the educational goals of both teachers.
    (B) it is an efficient use of time, which gives the teachers more time to plan future lessons.
    (C) the teachers' principal requires collaboration at all grade levels.
    (D) collaboration is motivating for the students.

49. Kyung would like to use technology to aid his reading instruction. All of the following are important considerations in choosing computer resources EXCEPT

    (A) how well the program meets educational objectives.
    (B) whether the teacher already knows how to use the program.
    (C) whether students would be motivated to use it.
    (D) whether it runs smoothly enough so that students do not become easily frustrated.

50. Vaughn Brown is a student in Kyung's class. Vaughn does not have any friends in the class, and when the students work together on projects, they do not ask Vaughn to join them. Kyung usually assigns groups or partners for such activities so that Vaughn does not feel more isolated. Kyung models and explicitly teaches good social skills, and strives to treat all of his students warmly. Kyung mainly engages in such behavior because he knows, according to Erikson's theory of psychosocial development, that

    (A) children tend to avoid those whom they pity.
    (B) children who are not accepted by their peer groups do not do as well in school as those who are accepted.
    (C) Vaughn has just moved to the area and doesn't know anyone yet.
    (D) Vaughn is likely to have better social skills by the time he enters junior high school.

51. Kyung has invited Vaughn's father, Mr. Brown, in for a conference. Which of the following opening statements would be the best one for Kyung to use?

    (A) "No one likes your son, Mr. Brown, and I'd like to find out why."
    (B) "Your son shows great potential, Mr. Brown. I was hoping that together we could come up with some ideas to help him socially."
    (C) "Mr. Brown, I have absolutely no concerns whatsoever about Vaughn's performance in class."
    (D) "I suspect that family problems might be making it hard for Vaughn to make friends, and I'd like more information so that I can help him."

GO ON TO THE NEXT PAGE

Use the information below to answer the two questions that follow.

Dina Monticelli teaches kindergarten.

52. Every day, Dina and the students sing the same clean-up song as they straighten up the room at the end of playtime. She wants the room to be clean and organized before the next activity, snack time. Dina sings the song mainly to

    (A) integrate music into the curriculum.
    (B) facilitate a transition.
    (C) teach responsibility.
    (D) make students think that cleaning up is fun.

53. Dina often begins to clean up the room herself a few minutes before singing the song. She notices that some students who see her do this begin to hum while they play. The humming is most clearly an example of which theory of development?

    (A) Reinforcement
    (B) Stage theory
    (C) Conditioning
    (D) Pre-conventional morality

GO ON TO THE NEXT PAGE

Use the information below to answer the four questions that follow.

Tom Connors teaches high school music. His classes include Music Theory, Introduction to Music, and Instrumental Music. His Music Theory class has 32 students in it. Tom finds this class to be a challenge to manage because of its large size.

54. Tom finds that when he assigns written class work, each student finishes at a different time. Which of the following is the LEAST appropriate way for Tom to deal with a student who completes in-class written assignments early?

(A) A student who finishes early can help a partner complete the assignment if the partner desires help.
(B) A student who finishes early can work on an independent teacher-assigned supplemental activity.
(C) A student who finishes early can talk quietly with other students who have finished early.
(D) A student who finishes early can read quietly.

55. Which of the following would be the most effective way for Tom to make sure that students obey classroom rules?

(A) Involve students in the process of developing rules.
(B) Have many very specific rules.
(C) Hand out a printed copy of the rules to each student early in the school year.
(D) Promise severe consequences for infractions.

56. Which of the following instructional techniques would help Tom to manage the large group in his Music Theory class?

I. Learning centers
II. Cooperative learning
III. Peer tutoring
IV. Worksheets to keep students busy

(A) I and II only
(B) I, II, and III
(C) II, III, and IV
(D) I, II, III, and IV

57. One basic skill Tom teaches in his Introduction to Music class is how to read and write sheet music. He teaches students mnemonic devices such as, "Every good boy does fine." This is an example of

(A) a memory aid.
(B) comprehension.
(C) a metaphor.
(D) cramming.

GO ON TO THE NEXT PAGE

Use the information below to answer the three questions that follow.

Christine Bush teaches Advanced Placement European History. She shows her students respect and strives to create a safe and unbiased atmosphere so that students feel secure about class participation.

58. Her students are engaged in a lively class discussion on the Reformation, and one student asks what Christine's personal religious views are. Christine most likely

   (A) tells the class, "I participate in community service projects with my congregation. I believe that it is important to be kind, and to help those less fortunate than ourselves."
   (B) says, "What I believe is unimportant, so let's get back to the lesson."
   (C) decides not to acknowledge the question, in hopes that the students will forget about it.
   (D) explains in detail the tenets of her religious beliefs and the specific reasons that she feels strongly about them.

59. Tom Sears is a student in Christine's class. Tom has recently taken on a before-school shift at the local supermarket. His shift ends 15 minutes before school starts, and he is late for homeroom if his bus encounters traffic. However, he always makes it to Christine's first period class in time. Christine has observed that since Tom started working, he is participating less in class and the quality of his work has declined. This is most likely because

   (A) students who work are more motivated to do their jobs than to do schoolwork.
   (B) Tom is going out in the evening now that he has money to spend; as a result, the quality and quantity of his homework has declined.
   (C) Tom's physiological needs for enough sleep and breakfast are no longer being met.
   (D) Tom is not a morning person, and would do better if Christine's class met later in the day.

60. Tom has taken on this job because his family needs the money. Tom's father left the family, and his mother suddenly became the sole supporter of five children. Tom has kept his family situation a secret from everyone at school. He told his friends that he got the job so that he could save up for the prom. Tom thinks that no one at school would understand his situation. He also thinks that his peers do not believe that he is really saving for the prom; he thinks that they are talking amongst themselves about the real reasons that Tom needs the money. Which of the following statements are likely to be true about Tom's behavior?

   I. Tom is in danger of becoming a habitual liar, if he is not one already.
   II. It is normal for adolescents to think that others are scrutinizing them.
   III. Tom needs professional help to deal with his paranoia.
   IV. Tom is exhibiting the typical adolescent view that he is the only one who has ever been in his situation.

   (A) III only
   (B) I and III only
   (C) II and IV only
   (D) I and II only

GO ON TO THE NEXT PAGE

Lillian Edelstein is a new teacher in a large suburban school. She plans on spending her free time getting to know the community, planning her curriculum, evaluating student submissions, and attending professional development seminars.

61. Because of Lillian's excellent recommendations from her university and previous employer, the principal asks Lillian to be grade-level chairperson for the year. Lillian is worried that this position might compromise her quality of instruction by cutting into the time she has allocated for the above-mentioned activities. However, she is anxious to find ways to develop professional relationships with her colleagues and principal. Lillian should tell her principal that

   (A) she cannot take on the position in her first year of teaching, but would be glad to reconsider it next year.
   (B) she wholeheartedly accepts the position.
   (C) she would like to find out exactly what responsibilities and time commitment the position entails.
   (D) she is flattered by the offer, and accepts with the condition that she can promise to put in only one hour per week.

62. Jeremy Walsh is a student in Lillian's homeroom. His parents sent Lillian a note informing her that Jeremy's religion forbids him from pledging allegiance to the flag. When it comes time to recite the Pledge of Allegiance, Lillian

   (A) tells Jeremy to sit quietly during the Pledge, and sits it out with him to be supportive.
   (B) asks Jeremy to explain to the rest of the class why he is not reciting the Pledge.
   (C) tells Jeremy to stand up with the other students but not to recite the Pledge, so that he does not feel alienated from the group.
   (D) tells Jeremy that all students are required to recite the Pledge of Allegiance no matter what.

Gregory Sinclair is certified to teach elementary school. He has been teaching sixth grade in New York City for five years. This year, he has returned to graduate school to obtain an additional certification as a reading specialist.

63. Throughout the semester, Mr. Sinclair tells his sixth-graders about his own coursework. Specifically, he shares with them the strategies he uses for studying, taking notes, and writing papers. He does this because

   (A) he wants to model effective study skills.
   (B) students will respect him more when they see how smart he is.
   (C) he wants students to understand why he is so tired on some days.
   (D) he wants advice from them on how to study effectively.

64. Which of the following institutions is directly responsible for Mr. Sinclair's pending certification as a reading specialist?

   (A) The New York State Education Department
   (B) The Board of Cooperative Educational Services
   (C) The New York City Board of Education
   (D) The principal of Mr. Sinclair's school

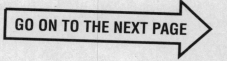

GO ON TO THE NEXT PAGE

Use the information below to answer the two questions that follow.

Rasheed Jones teaches at Johnstown Regional High School. This winter, the weather in the Johnstown area has been unseasonably warm. Rasheed has been holding class outside on any day that the temperature exceeds 60 degrees. On January 18, the townspeople wake up to a blustery wind and forecast of snow. By 10:00 A.M., snow is falling heavily.

65. From 10:30 until 11:20 A.M. each day, Rasheed teaches a group of students who learn well through class discussions. On January 18, however, the students only want to discuss the weather. An announcement comes over the public address system informing the students that they will be dismissed two hours early because of a blizzard. Some students jump out of their seats and cheer. Rasheed knows that a discussion of the weather will not meet his students' educational needs. However, they do not seem able to concentrate on the academic topic under discussion, or even to sit still in their seats. Rasheed

(A) tells the students to stop talking about the weather and to start discussing the planned topic, or else they will each lose 10 points.

(B) allows them to work quietly on their homework.

(C) plays a participatory, fast-paced game with them that requires rehearsal of content-area material.

(D) shows a video of the high school championship football game that Johnstown Regional won last fall.

66. Janelle McPherson is a student in Rasheed's class. She has physical limitations that require her to spend part of her school day in a resource room instead of a mainstream classroom. If Janelle had been a student before Public Law (PL) 94-142 was enacted, she would have spent all of her instructional time in the school's resource room. Janelle only spends part of her time in the resource room because

(A) Rasheed is a special education teacher.

(B) a resource room is the most appropriate place for handicapped students.

(C) PL 94-142 requires that all students be educated in the least restrictive environment.

(D) her full-time presence in the mainstream classroom would have diminished the educational experiences of the non-handicapped students.

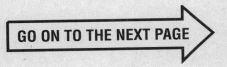

GO ON TO THE NEXT PAGE

Use the information below to answer the five questions that follow.

The Colonial School District is undertaking a district-wide anti-bullying initiative. The administration has asked every teacher at every grade level to participate. The teachers are on alert to identify bullying situations, intervene when appropriate, and notify the guidance department of all incidents. Also, the teachers are instructed to use class time to initiate dialogue on bullying. Karen McGuire teaches English at Colonial Senior High School. She wants to make discussions on bullying part of her regular English lessons, so that a single unit can meet the objectives of both the anti-bullying initiative and her English curriculum. She decides to use Orson Scott Card's novel *Ender's Game* for these purposes. In this novel, Ender, a child who is bullied by his brother Peter, is required by his government to leave his family at age six to attend military training.

67. Before asking the class to begin reading the book, Karen assigns the following pre-reading written assignment: "Write a one-page description of a time when you were either (1) separated from your family for a significant period of time, or (2) asked to do something important that you didn't want to do. Describe how you felt during the situation, and compare that with how you feel about it now." The primary purpose of this prereading assignment is to

(A) develop reflective writing skills.
(B) focus students' attention on themes they will encounter in the book, therefore improving comprehension.
(C) convince students to read the book.
(D) train students to be more sensitive so that bullying is less likely to occur in the school.

68. Karen tells the students to read the first 50 pages of the book. Her plan is then to discuss the characters Peter (the bully) and Ender (the victim). She will ask students two questions: (1) "What should Ender do about the bullying?" and (2) "What factors could be responsible for Peter's behavior?" Karen plans to lead the class discussion from bullying in the book to bullying at Colonial Senior High School. She knows that if students do not feel safe in her classroom, they will not feel safe discussing bullying. Karen has worked hard all year to make her classroom a safe environment for her students. The characteristics that most likely make students feel safe in Karen's classroom are

I. Karen's rule that all student opinions are to be respected.
II. the metal detector in the doorway leading into the building.
III. students' knowledge that Karen keeps her promises about confidentiality.
IV. Karen's willingness to involve the principal in conflict resolution.

(A) I only
(B) I, II, and IV only
(C) II, III, and IV only
(D) I and III only

GO ON TO THE NEXT PAGE

69. Jamie Watterson and Joe Hillanbrand are students in Karen's English class. On two occasions, Karen notices that Jamie has bruises on his face and arms. She suspects that abuse or bullying may be involved; Karen has seen Jamie's father yell at him in public, and she has also seen Joe, who is on the wrestling team, tease Jamie. However, she has not witnessed any violent incidents, nor has Jamie ever mentioned the bruises. In a supportive and private way, she asks Jamie how he got the bruises, and he tells her that he fell several times. At this point Karen should

(A) accept Jamie's explanation and watch to see if he gets any more bruises.
(B) accuse Joe of hurting Jamie and ask Joe for his side of the story.
(C) report her observations to the principal.
(D) ask the other students in the class if they know what happened to Jamie.

70. When the students are nearly done reading the book, Karen gives the following assignment: "Write a position paper on the methods that Colonel Graf used to get Ender back into Battle School. Discuss whether you think it was okay for him to use Ender's sister Val to achieve this objective. Defend your position with three specific reasons." A class debate is to follow this written assignment. The main purpose of this assignment is to

(A) give students a chance to develop skills required for a certain type of writing and speaking.
(B) assess student comprehension.
(C) determine which students have the right opinion.
(D) make sure that students have been reading the book.

71. When the students have finished the book, Karen calls on students in class to answer questions. She wants to make sure they all comprehend the book's conclusion—not only what happened but also the characters' intentions. When she calls on Jill Greer to answer a question, Jill does not say anything immediately. After five seconds, she still has not answered; Karen thinks that Jill is still thinking about the answer. At this point, Karen should

(A) repeat the question because Jill probably didn't understand it.
(B) call on another student to answer it.
(C) tell Jill the answer to the question.
(D) give Jill a little bit more time to formulate her response.

GO ON TO THE NEXT PAGE

Use the information below to answer the three questions that follow.

Jean Jackson's students in tenth-grade English at Seaside High School tutor students at Seaside Elementary School twice per month. After a recent visit to the elementary school, Ms. Jackson's students have the following discussion in class:

"Those kids were so antsy today," said John.

"As usual," replied Sam.

"I know, they couldn't sit still for five minutes!" said Priya. "It's a shame they don't have a playground to run around on. They need a way to release all that energy. Ms. Jackson, why doesn't that school have a playground?"

"The district doesn't have the money for it. People have been complaining about this for years," said Ms. Jackson.

"I wish there was something we could do about it," said Sam. "My brother goes to that school."

"There's nothing we can do," said John. "Playgrounds are very expensive."

"Maybe if we make people in the town aware of the problem, we could get people to contribute money for a playground," suggested Priya.

The class decides to write a letter to the editor of the local newspaper about the problem. In the letter, they ask people in the community to send donations to a special fund for a Seaside Elementary playground. They also plan a student-run car wash to raise money for the cause.

72. Which of the following statements would Piaget most likely use to explain the situation above?

I. The high school students are learning because they are actively involved in their environment.
II. A playground is beneficial to young children because they learn through using concrete materials and images.
III. It is more appropriate for the high school students to seek funding and action on a new playground than it is for the elementary students to do so because complex reasoning skills will be involved.
IV. The older elementary students are at a level of thinking at which they could be involved in the design of the playground.

(A) II only
(B) II and III only
(C) I, II, and III only
(D) I, II, III, and IV

73. When Ms. Jackson's students continue to seek money for a new playground, Priya Allen investigates the reasons that Seaside Elementary has never had a playground. She discovers that the principal of the school is paid a salary that is nearly double that of any other principal in the area. Priya is outraged. On her own time after school, Priya writes a letter to the town newspaper expressing her outrage. She also enlists other students, parents, and community members to carry peaceful protest signs at the next school board meeting, which is open to the public. Which of the following disciplinary measures can the school district take because of Priya's actions?

(A) Priya can be suspended from school.
(B) Priya can be barred from attending the school board meeting.
(C) Priya's actions are within her legal rights so she cannot be punished or prevented from engaging in this behavior.
(D) Priya can receive a lower grade in English because the protest was a direct result of her English class activities.

GO ON TO THE NEXT PAGE

74. Ms. Jackson is proud of Priya and the other high school students for standing up for their beliefs. Ms. Jackson also thinks that the elementary principal should be paid less money so that the school can afford a playground, although she is not aware of the details of that principal's contract. However, she is aware that Seaside Elementary is not her school, and she does not want to alienate people in the administration by complaining. What should Ms. Jackson do at this point?

(A) She should be supportive of Priya and praise her strong research skills.
(B) She should go along with whatever her own principal does in this controversy, if anything.
(C) She should encourage the teachers who work at the elementary school to protest.
(D) She should earn the respect of her colleagues by organizing her own protest.

75. The halls of Overbrook High School are filled with posters that warn students about the dangers of drugs, alcohol, and cigarettes and at the same time portray students who don't indulge as popular. The main reason that the school administration hung up these posters is that

(A) drugs, alcohol, and cigarettes are illegal.
(B) drugs, alcohol, and cigarettes negatively affect students' health and learning.
(C) school officials want to show students how to become popular.
(D) the school has a significant problem with drugs, alcohol, and cigarettes on campus.

76. Allison McFall is a physical education teacher. Her first period class consists of 12 girls and 12 boys. Allison asks the boys to stand in one line and the girls in another for a game. The two rows of students face each other. She asks the boys to stand with their arms outstretched to their sides, touching each others' fingertips. She asks the girls to stand with their arms outstretched to their sides, touching each others' shoulders. When the students are lined up correctly, several comment that they didn't realize their class had so many more boys than girls. This remark indicates that, according to Piaget's work, the students are

(A) primary-school age.
(B) older elementary-school age.
(C) middle-school age.
(D) high school age.

GO ON TO THE NEXT PAGE

Use the information below to answer the two questions that follow.

Linda Quiring teaches the same curriculum in both regular and honors biology. At the beginning of the year, the principal's secretary, Mrs. Bloggs, made a mistake with Linda's schedule. Mrs. Bloggs gave Linda a printed schedule that said Period 1 was regular biology and that Period 2 was honors biology. Honors students showed up for Period 1 and average students showed up for Period 2. No one noticed the mistake, so Linda thought that she was teaching honors students in Period 2, as apparently scheduled.

77. The Hawthorne effect would predict which of the following outcomes in Linda's students?

   I. The average students' performance was above average.
   II. The honors students' performance was average.
   III. The average students' performance was average.
   IV. The honors students' performance was above average.

   (A) I only
   (B) I and II only
   (C) IV only
   (D) III and IV only

78. Linda always begins each new topic of study with a motivational activity. She mainly does this to

   I. get students' attention.
   II. arouse students' interest.
   III. give students an outlet for their mental and physical energy.
   IV. make it easier for her to manage the class.

   (A) II only
   (B) II and IV only
   (C) I and III only
   (D) I, II, and III

Use the information below to answer the two questions that follow.

Nancy Silpa teaches high school art.

79. Nancy wants to use modeling to teach her students how to use the potter's wheel. Which of the following instructional methods would correctly teach this through modeling?

   (A) Ms. Silpa uses the potter's wheel herself.
   (B) Ms. Silpa lets the children learn through doing.
   (C) Ms. Silpa gives students a handout with instructions on proper use of the potter's wheel.
   (D) Ms. Silpa shows students a video on proper use of the potter's wheel.

80. Ms. Silpa and several other teachers are collaborating on a unit about whether art imitates life or life imitates art. The objective is for students to be able to answer this question and explain their answers. Ms. Silpa shows her students examples of pottery from different cultures. One student, Andre, says, "We have a lot of pottery at home. My mother made it before we moved here from South America." His statement causes Ms. Silpa to wonder whether Andre and his mother could be involved in the curriculum. Which of the following is the most appropriate way to get Andre and his mother involved in the class?

   (A) Andre should not be singled out in any special way because students from other cultural backgrounds need help assimilating into the dominant American culture.
   (B) Ms. Silpa should tell Andre to ask his mother to teach the class how to make pottery like hers.
   (C) Ms. Silpa should ask Andre's mother whether she would like to show the class her pottery and talk with the students about how it relates to the family's culture.
   (D) Ms. Silpa should first ask Andre whether his mother speaks English, and only if the answer is yes should Ms. Silpa consider involving her in the class.

DIRECTIONS FOR THE WRITTEN ASSIGNMENT

This section of the test consists of a written assignment. You are to prepare a written response of about 300–600 words on the assigned topic. *The assignment can be found on the next page.* You should use your time to plan, write, review, and edit your response to the assignment.

Read the assignment carefully before you begin to write. Think about how you will organize your response. You may use any blank space provided on the following pages to make notes, write an outline, or otherwise prepare your response. *However, your score will be based solely on the response you write in the following pages.*

Your response will be evaluated on the basis of the following criteria.

- **PURPOSE:** Fulfill the charge of the assignment.

- **APPLICATION OF CONTENT:** Accurately and effectively apply the relevant knowledge and skills.

- **SUPPORT:** Support the response with appropriate examples and/or sound reasoning reflecting an understanding of the relevant knowledge and skills.

Your response will be evaluated on the criteria above, not writing ability. However, your response must be communicated clearly enough to permit valid judgment of your knowledge and skills. The final version of your response should conform to the conventions of edited American English. This should be your original work, written in your own words, and not copied or paraphrased from some other work.

Be sure to write about the assigned topic. Please write legibly. You may not use any reference materials during the test. Remember to review what you have written and make any changes you think will improve your written response.

PART 2: THE WRITTEN ASSIGNMENT

It is important for teachers to understand that to teach students effectively, they must use a variety of assessment methods in the classroom. Imagine that the educational goal and objectives below have been established for all schools in your district.

DISTRICT EDUCATIONAL GOALS

Goal 8: **Utilize a variety of assessment methods in the classroom to gain a broader understanding of a student's performance.**

Examples of teaching objectives:

- Give groups of students opportunities for self- and peer-assessment.
- Create creative learning experiences in which students can benefit from portfolio assessment.
- Utilize methods of assessment that measure a variety of aspects of student achievement.

ASSIGNMENT: In an essay written for a group of New York State educators, frame your response by indicating which grade level or subject you are prepared to teach, then:

- explain why the utilization of many different assessment methods is an important educational goal;
- describe two strategies that you would use to foster this goal; and
- discuss how these strategies would be effective in achieving this educational goal.

Be sure to specify a grade level/subject area in your essay, and frame your ideas so that an educator certified at your level (i.e., elementary or secondary) will be able to understand the basis for your response.

15

ATS-W Practice Test Answers and Explanations

ANSWER KEY

1. C	28. A	55. A
2. C	29. B	56. D
3. A	30. B	57. A
4. B	31. A	58. A
5. B	32. B	59. C
6. C	33. A	60. C
7. B	34. B	61. C
8. A	35. B	62. C
9. C	36. A	63. A
10. A	37. D	64. A
11. D	38. D	65. C
12. B	39. A	66. C
13. A	40. B	67. B
14. B	41. C	68. D
15. B	42. D	69. C
16. D	43. C	70. A
17. A	44. B	71. D
18. B	45. B	72. D
19. C	46. B	73. C
20. D	47. B	74. A
21. A	48. A	75. B
22. C	49. B	76. A
23. A	50. B	77. B
24. D	51. B	78. D
25. C	52. B	79. A
26. B	53. C	80. C
27. D	54. C	

EXPLANATIONS FOR THE ATS-W PRACTICE TEST

Question 1: Ben's goal as stated in the question is to help Kara Jackson's confidence with math. Answer choice (A) doesn't work well because Kara's confidence isn't going to be helped if the teacher ignores her. Answer choices (B) and (D) each put Kara in front of the class with her current weaknesses in math exposed for all to see. **Answer choice (C),** however, puts Kara in a situation where she can be successful and in turn have her confidence increase.

Question 2: This question basically focuses on an appropriate response to students' claims that they have already covered something. While this of course might be true, the teacher can't assume that the students have learned all that the teacher is trying to cover. Although giving a pop quiz is too drastic a response to the claim (you don't want to stop students from giving feedback for fear of getting a quiz), having the students finish the rest of the drill with partners will allow the teacher to circulate through the class and confirm that the students know the material as well as they say they do. Therefore, the most appropriate response to this question is **answer choice (C).**

Question 3: **Answer choice (A)** is clearly not appropriate for the classroom. A video that shows how someone uses math to profit from an illegal activity should not be on any teacher's list of audiovisual aids.

Question 4: Statement I starts out correctly by claiming that norm-referenced tests are competitive, but the claim that all high school students work better under pressure is incorrect. Therefore, you can eliminate answer choices (A) and (D) since they contain statement I. You don't have to check either statement II or statement IV since both of them are included in each of the remaining answer choices. To decide between (B) and (C), you have to check statement III. Statement III is not something that is universally and objectively true, so it should not be part of your answer. The credited response is therefore **answer choice (B).**

Question 5: The students' current dramatic play indicates that they have some interest in tools and fixing things. So in this case, Dave doesn't need to worry about an initial motivating activity: The students already appear to be motivated. Because of this, you can safely select **answer choice (B)** as your response. There doesn't seem to be anything in what you are told about Dave and his class to indicate that the weather is so awful that the field trip should be postponed. Since there doesn't seem to be a good reason to postpone the field trip, answer choice (C) seems more of a case of the teacher just wanting to wait until the weather is nicer to make his own life easier. Answer choice (D) is really weird if you recall that the students in this question are in kindergarten. There aren't many topics about which kindergartners couldn't learn something new.

Question 6: In any instance where it might be at all relevant, safety is your primary concern when young schoolchildren are involved. The credited response is therefore **answer choice (C).**

Question 7: For field trips, secure the permission of the parents and the principal. Although chaperones might be required to support a field trip, their explicit permission is not required. The credited response to this question is **answer choice (B).**

Question 8: Why would Dave manage the class so it appears that the field trip was the students' idea? Conventional wisdom says that lessons are more meaningful to students and will yield better results if the students are involved in setting goals for the class. The answer that the test writers are looking for is **answer choice (A).**

Question 9: This is a great example of a question for which you want to make sure you look at the teacher's goals. One of Dave's goals is to relate the field trip to other areas of his curriculum. The only answer choice that makes any attempt to tie the field trip to other activities during the school year is **answer choice (C).**

Question 10: This is a great example of a question for which you will want to make sure you remember the students' grade level and what that implies about their development. Answer choices (C) and (D) are not at all appropriate for kindergartners, but **answer choice (A)** would work very well. Since Dave had observed the children's play before beginning his unit on tools and the hardware store, he should be able to make note of any differences in the children's play that could be attributed to the lesson.

Question 11: This is a great example of using the criteria for a "good" teacher to help you eliminate wrong answers. Answer choice (A) can be eliminated because the field trips aren't being explained in terms of achieving an objective. Answer choice (B) can be eliminated because it's inspired by the teacher's desire to get out of work. Answer choice (C) isn't appropriate for kindergartners. The credited response must therefore be **answer choice (D).** An appropriate objective for a teacher is to integrate the classroom into the community at large.

Question 12: This is a straight knowledge question. If you draw a picture of what the question is describing, you might see why the answer is **(B)** webbing.

Question 13: This question is looking for you to remember to consider the needs and feelings of every student in your class. If some students do not have bicycles, then they are going to be singled out in a negative way. Therefore, the answer that the test writers are looking for here is **answer choice (A).**

Question 14: Which answer is expressing things in terms of what's best for the students and their education? **Answer choice (B)** meets that requirement best. Higher levels of student attention will generally promote learning. The other three responses are too focused on the teacher.

Question 15: As with many other questions, if you focus on explaining the behavior in terms of how it helps the students' learning, you will be steered right into the credited response. In this case you should be picking **answer choice (B).**

Question 16: Research indicates that teacher expectations can affect student performance. If a teacher believes that a student is a low achiever, the student will often work to meet that level of performance. Joanne was likely reluctant to share her perceptions of her students with Jerry because she is aware of this. The credited response is therefore **answer choice (D).**

Question 17: This is a straight knowledge question. The credited response is **answer choice (A).** If you have no idea what the answer is when you are faced with a question like this, look for the choice that has you check with administration. If no such answer choice exists, look for the answer choice that is in the students' best interests.

Question 18: Answer choice (A) is wrong because the use of the word *only* isn't justified. Anyone who thinks that foreign languages should be taught in school would disagree with this answer. **Answer choice (B)** is the credited response. The answer is given from the perspective of what's good for the students. Answer choice (C) is just plain wrong, and answer choice (D) is a little harsh.

Question 19: Keep thinking in terms of what's good for students and what furthers their education. Mr. Augusto-Correia is certainly having students paraphrase the student who spoke before to promote the students paying attention, but the reason he does this is to promote the learning objective elaborated in **answer choice (C).**

Question 20: Recall that students' learning is enhanced when they participate in establishing their own learning goals. Assuming that the teacher's objectives can be met with a student-selected topic, then that's the best way to go. This concept is best expressed in **answer choice (D).** Answer choice (C) is a close second choice, but since the project is going to last three months, it doesn't seem to make a whole lot of sense to tie the longer project to the topic that is currently being discussed in class.

Question 21: Since the teacher is working with a group of students who have never done a long-term project before, the most appropriate assessment would be something that would make sure students don't fall behind and that they get enough support to be able to complete the project satisfactorily. While answer choice (C) sets up more frequent opportunity for student-teacher interaction, it leaves open the possibility that students might fall through the cracks. Because it explicitly helps each student manage his or her project, the best answer to this question is **answer choice (A).**

Question 22: Since no extra credit is mentioned in the text accompanying the question, you can go ahead and eliminate answer choice (A). Also, since Ms. Singh is assigning the book herself and not working in conjunction with the English department, you can also eliminate answer choice (B). Of the remaining two, **answer choice (C)** is correct because the assignment described in the question is an example of enrichment, and answer choice (D) is not expressed in terms of why the assignment serves the students' needs.

Question 23: By focusing on Ms. Singh's goals (she wants to give everyone a chance to read *The Grapes of Wrath*) and by paying attention to the information you were given before the question (Ms. Singh utilizes learning centers), the answer that seems to fit best with the information you have is **answer choice (A).**

Question 24: Because Ms. Singh wants to ask increasingly challenging questions, she will want to start with a basic question that measures a simple fact. The most simple of the three questions can be found in statement II. You can now eliminate answer choices (A) and (C) because neither of them starts off with statement II. The last question that Ms. Singh will want to ask is the most involved question. The most involved question in this case can be found in statement I (the question requires students to apply information to a new situation). So, since statement II should be listed first and statement I should be listed last, the credited response is **answer choice (D).**

Question 25: Answer choices (A) and (B) can be tossed out pretty easily here. A "good" teacher never does anything for her own convenience or ego. Answer choices (C) and (D) are both conceivably correct, but since the question is asking about a political cartoon, the answer choice that taps into that theme would be best. In this case, **answer choice (C)** is the credited response, since a political cartoon would constitute a visual element that would appeal to visual learners.

Question 26: To assess knowledge at this level of detail, Ms. Singh should assign an essay test. The prompt she should give her students would pretty much be a paraphrase of the information found in the question. The credited response to this question is **answer choice (B).**

Question 27: With the exception of the venue of the conversation (the school parking lot), each of the other three statements can be properly said to be elements of professional behavior on Mr. Patten's part. The credited response is therefore **answer choice (D).**

Question 28: Notice that at the end of the conversation Mr. St. George indicated that the two of them should talk more about the project. Mr. Patten acknowledges this in his last statement. The next step in the process, therefore, should be for these two to have a more formal discussion about the plan. So the credited response is **answer choice (A).**

Question 29: This question tests your knowledge of "education vocabulary." If you are giving students feedback as the project goes along, that is an example of *formative evaluation*. This is different from *summative evaluation*, which involves giving all the feedback at the conclusion of the project. The credited response is therefore **answer choice (B)**.

Question 30: This is another vocabulary question. When students engage in activities to develop their own understanding (rather than get the information from a lecture or a book), this is known as *inductive method*. The credited response is therefore **answer choice (B)**.

Question 31: By thinking about the teacher's goals and by remembering that good answer choices are expressed in terms of what's good for the student, you should be inclined to select **answer choice (A)** even if you don't remember this specific concept from your education courses.

Question 32: Answer choice (A) is too pushy, and answer choice (C) is too passive. When collaborating, all parties should be involved while respecting the ideas and input of others. While it might be an issue that Martha does not know sign language, this is something that she can take up with the other teacher at the first planning meeting. The most appropriate answer to this question is therefore **answer choice (B)**.

Question 33: An auditory learner learns best through hearing how to do things. This is why the best answer to the question is **answer choice (A)**.

Question 34: First of all, you can easily toss answer choice (D) out the window. This type of answer choice is never going to be rewarded on the ATS-W. The presence of the word *best* in answer choice (A) makes this a suspicious choice. Since educational law states that students with disabilities are to be accommodated in the least-restrictive environment, the presence of a teacher communicating in sign language would be a legal requirement to meet the needs of the students who are completely deaf. Therefore, the best choice in this case is **answer choice (B)**.

Question 35: Which in-service best addresses Ms. Slovava's intended goals? **Answer choice (B)** looks very strong, because it is specifically about the children in Ms. Slovava's district.

Question 36: The answer you pick here needs to be sensitive to all the students in the group, including Zachary. Neither (B) nor (C) is an appropriate response because they do not address the issue at all. Answer choice (B) does nothing to solve the problem and answer choice (C) is potentially alienating to Zachary. Answer choice (D) can also be eliminated because this is not a reasonable use of extra credit. **Answer choice (A)** is the credited response because it treats the problem as important enough to deal with yet treats Zachary as an equal in solving the problem.

Question 37: Answer choice (D) is clearly the answer here. Did you notice the presence of the word *except* in the question? Since the question is basically asking which choice is *not* going to help students learn to work cooperatively, an answer choice that has children working alone is going to be a great choice.

Question 38: What skills *could* the students use in this project? All of them. **Answer choice (D)** is the most appropriate response.

Question 39: The two primary questions a teacher needs to consider in launching a class project would be student safety and whether educational goals can be met through the project. The most appropriate answer choice would be **answer choice (A).**

Question 40: Remember, express answer choices in terms of meeting educational goals for the students. After tossing answer choice (C) out the window, you're left with having to select the answer choice that seems to best meet student learning needs. **Answer choice (B)** articulates the kind of goal that the test writers think teachers should be pursuing.

Question 41: Seating assignments are not part of formal lesson plans. Therefore, the credited response to this question is **answer choice (C).**

Question 42: To make a computer-generated color map, you are probably best off using a graphics program. Select **answer choice (D).**

Question 43: Do the students know what a whipper-in is? Sounds like the teacher might need to elaborate on some of the specific vocabulary of the fox hunt, and as a result you would be best off selecting **answer choice (C).**

Question 44: Answer choices (A) and (C) are too absolute in the way they represent students. Additionally, neither of these answer choices is expressed in a way that relates to classroom management or the achievement of learning goals. The answer choice that does express this effectively is **answer choice (B).**

Question 45: Keep your eye on the teacher's two goals. She wants to have control of the class and she wants her students to feel comfortable. Answer choices (A) and (D) could both potentially undermine her authority. Allowing the students to choose their own seats will have the students sitting with friends, and that could lead to more distractions in the class than she might want to have. Dressing in a style similar to the students will undermine her goal of establishing herself as an authority in the classroom. If the teacher keeps the same seating configuration from the previous year, she will not need to use name tags, since the students are seated in alphabetical order and therefore can be easily logged into a seating chart. The other option, **answer choice (B),** would go a long way toward making her students feel comfortable.

Question 46: Conventional teacher wisdom says that classroom rules are important and should be in place in advance of an issue that might arise. The credited response is therefore **answer choice (B).**

Question 47: To make a formal assessment of how well the students are performing, Kyung should consider using a standardized test. Performance testing is generally used to measure how students can apply a wide variety of skills to a long-term project. To make a formal assessment, it would be important to some degree to make sure that students are being measured on the same set of criteria. Hence, a standardized test is the best option. Go ahead and select **answer choice (B).**

Question 48: You should of course be expressing your answer in terms of what's best for the students. Answer choices (B) and (C) can be easily eliminated because neither of them speak in terms of student interest. Answer choice (D) can be eliminated because collaboration is something that is done at a faculty level. The credited response should therefore be **answer choice (A).**

Question 49: Keeping in mind that the ATS-W is very much against behaviors that reflect a teacher's desire to avoid work, the LEAST important consideration in this question is stated in **answer choice (B).**

Question 50: Thinking again in terms of what's best for students and their social and academic development, you should be steered toward **answer choice (B).**

Question 51: Remember, when dealing with parents you should frame things in a positive light while clearly addressing the concerns that you need to address. Answer choices (A) and (D) would put the parent on the defensive, and answer choice (C) isn't being honest. The best answer choice is therefore **answer choice (B).**

Question 52: Dina is using the clean-up song to establish an association in her students' minds between the song and the activity. The song is therefore being used to facilitate the transition from activity time to clean-up time. The credited response is **answer choice (B).**

Question 53: The students are humming the clean-up song because they have become accustomed (conditioned) to associate cleaning up with that particular song. Therefore, the theory that is being exhibited here is classical conditioning. Your most appropriate answer is therefore **answer choice (C).**

Question 54: What's the LEAST effective classroom management technique for students who finish work early? The LEAST effective technique would be **answer choice (C).** Not only will it create an increasing level of noise in the room that will make it difficult for the slower students to finish the task, but it also creates a motivation to rush through the assignment to socialize.

Question 55: The best way to get student cooperation with classroom rules is to get students involved in putting the rules together. Students are more willing to follow rules and get more out of lesson plans if they have some voice in their construction. The most appropriate response to this question is therefore **answer choice (A).**

Question 56: All four of these options would help Tom manage his large group. If the question were worded in a slightly different way, you might want to be a bit suspicious of statement IV. However, as the question is presented, the best answer choice is **answer choice (D).**

Question 57: "Every good boy does fine" is a memory aid to help students remember what notes go with what lines on a musical staff. The credited response is therefore **answer choice (A).**

Question 58: Answer choice (D) is the worst. As a teacher, you need to be careful about being perceived as imposing your own beliefs on your students. The middle two answer choices are better than answer choice (D), but are not quite good enough. The teacher needs to acknowledge that the question was asked but cannot communicate to the class that her opinions are unimportant. **Answer choice (A)** is elegant in that it communicates strong social values without introducing specific religious beliefs.

Question 59: Tom is now working mornings and works until just before he has to come to school. The test writers are looking for you to somehow associate his recent performance in class to his new job. That association is best made in **answer choice (C).**

Question 60: Statement I is much too drastic an answer choice given what you've been told. Go ahead and eliminate answer choices (B) and (D). Statement II is a true statement about students of Tom's age. Since statement II must be part of the credited response, you can now go ahead and select **answer choice (C).**

Question 61: Standards of professionalism dictate that if you have any reservations about your ability to fulfill an obligation, you should learn more about what's involved rather than accept a responsibility that you will not be able to meet. The best balance between blowing off the assignment, coming across as bossy or difficult, and blindly accepting the assignment can be found in **answer choice (C).**

Question 62: As a teacher, you need to strike a balance between respecting your students' beliefs and creating an environment in which they are not being singled out unnecessarily. This balance would best be achieved through **answer choice (C).**

Question 63: Answer choices (B) and (C) are much too centered on the teacher to be credited responses, and answer choice (D) doesn't make that much sense. **Answer choice (A)** looks really good because it reinforces the fact that the teacher is a role model for students.

Question 64: All licenses and certifications in New York State are governed by the State Department of Education. The credited response is therefore **answer choice (A).**

Question 65: How do you deal with students who have too much energy to sit still? The trick is to find an answer choice that uses that energy in pursuit of educational goals, so the best choice is going to be **answer choice (C).**

Question 66: This is a straight knowledge question requiring you to know that the law states disabled students need to be taught in the least restrictive appropriate environment. The best answer therefore is **answer choice (C).**

Question 67: The teacher makes the prereading assignment so students will be thinking of some of the important themes of the book before they start reading. The most appropriate response is **answer choice (B).** Remember, good answer choices are going to relate to the specifics of the assignment described and what is likely the teacher's objectives in giving the lesson.

Question 68: The two statements that can be attributed to a feeling of safety in Karen's classroom can be found in statements I and III. The students know that their opinions and privacy are to be respected. The presence of the metal detector might make students feel safer in school in general, but the presence of the metal detector does nothing to make Karen's classroom any safer than any other part of the school. Finally, if Karen involves the principal in conflict resolution, some students might feel that their privacy has been invaded. The most appropriate answer is therefore **answer choice (D).**

Question 69: When faced with sticky situations like this, it would be wrong to ignore the problem and it would be wrong to jump to conclusions. The appropriate step is to make school administration informed of the situation. Therefore, the best choice here is **answer choice (C).**

Question 70: Throw answer choice (C) right out the window. Thinking in terms of objectives for the lesson, it is likely that the teacher has given this assignment to foster the development of expository writing and debating skills. The most appropriate answer is therefore **answer choice (A).**

Question 71: If you are of the opinion that a student is still formulating a response, give the student a little more time. Moving on to another student will discourage Jill from participating in future discussions. The best answer to this question is therefore **answer choice (D).**

Question 72: Statement I seems reasonable enough, so you can go ahead and eliminate answer choices (A) and (B) since they don't contain statement I. Next, you should notice that each of the remaining answer choices contains both statement II and statement III. So, there's no need to check those two because they both have to be right. Finally, statement IV is correct, because the older elementary students are in the concrete operational stage and can participate in decision making given appropriate leadership by students who are at a higher level of cognitive development. The answer that the test writers are looking for is **answer choice (D).**

Question 73: Priya is engaging in speech protected by the United States Constitution. Although schools do have editorial control over student publications, schools cannot control the political speech of their students outside of school. The credited response is therefore **answer choice (C).**

Question 74: Although a teacher should recognize the good work of his or her students, it is not appropriate for a teacher to be directly meddling in the business of another school. Answer choices (C) and (D) are too intrusive, and answer choice (B) fails to recognize the work that Priya has done. Therefore, the credited response should be **answer choice (A),** provided that the teacher is careful not to take too direct a role in the protests that are being organized.

Question 75: It's not just that these things are illegal, it's that they impede some students from being as successful as they could be. The credited response is therefore **answer choice (B).**

Question 76: The students mistakenly think there are more boys than girls in the class because the boys are more spread out. This is indicative of students in the preoperational stage of development, which is characteristic of students in early grades of elementary school. The best answer choice is therefore **answer choice (A).**

Question 77: The Hawthorne effect predicts that student performance will meet a teacher's expectations. So, the average students will perform above average because the teacher thinks they are above-average students, and the above-average students will perform at an average level due to teacher expectations. These ideas are communicated in statements I and II and that makes the credited response **answer choice (B).**

Question 78: Here's a case in which statements I and II seem like they are definitely part of the answer and statement IV is definitely not. Since the only answer choice that contains the elements you want to communicate is **answer choice (D),** it's best to settle on that one from the perspective that giving students an outlet for mental and physical energy can be used to further educational objectives.

Question 79: Modeling involves teaching by demonstration. This is best described in **answer choice (A).**

Question 80: Answer choice (A) flies in the face of the goals of multicultural education. All students should be valued for their different backgrounds and perspectives. Answer choice (B) is too bossy. Andre's mother should be asked if she would like to participate; she should not be told to participate. **Answer choice (C)** looks very good. It is respectful to Andre's mother and it further uses the pottery as a vehicle to teach students more about another culture. Answer choice (D) fails to consider that there might be ways to get Andre's mother involved even if she does not speak English. Perhaps Andre or another teacher could act as a translator. Denying students exposure to other cultures and ideas out of a concern for language is not appropriate as far as the test writers are concerned.

The Princeton Review

Completely darken bubbles with a No. 2 pencil. If you make a mistake, be sure to erase mark completely. Erase all stray marks.

1. YOUR NAME:
(Print) Last   First   M.I.

SIGNATURE: _____ DATE: ____ / ____ / ____

HOME ADDRESS: _____
(Print) Number and Street

_____
City   State   Zip Code

PHONE NO.: _____
(Print)

IMPORTANT: Please fill in these boxes exactly as shown on the back cover of your test book.

2. TEST FORM

3. TEST CODE

4. REGISTRATION NUMBER

5. YOUR NAME

First 4 letters of last name				FIRST INIT.	MID INIT.

6. DATE OF BIRTH

Month	Day	Year
JAN		
FEB		
MAR	0 0	0 0
APR	1 1	1 1
MAY	2 2	2 2
JUN	3 3	3 3
JUL	4	4
AUG	5	5
SEP	7	7
OCT	8	8
NOV	9	9
DEC		

7. SEX
○ MALE
○ FEMALE

The Princeton Review
© 2005 The Princeton Review, Inc.
FORM NO. 00001-PR

Practice Test 1
Start with number 1 for each new section.
If a section has fewer questions than answer spaces, leave the extra answer spaces blank.

1. Ⓐ Ⓑ Ⓒ Ⓓ
2. Ⓐ Ⓑ Ⓒ Ⓓ
3. Ⓐ Ⓑ Ⓒ Ⓓ
4. Ⓐ Ⓑ Ⓒ Ⓓ
5. Ⓐ Ⓑ Ⓒ Ⓓ
6. Ⓐ Ⓑ Ⓒ Ⓓ
7. Ⓐ Ⓑ Ⓒ Ⓓ
8. Ⓐ Ⓑ Ⓒ Ⓓ
9. Ⓐ Ⓑ Ⓒ Ⓓ
10. Ⓐ Ⓑ Ⓒ Ⓓ
11. Ⓐ Ⓑ Ⓒ Ⓓ
12. Ⓐ Ⓑ Ⓒ Ⓓ
13. Ⓐ Ⓑ Ⓒ Ⓓ
14. Ⓐ Ⓑ Ⓒ Ⓓ
15. Ⓐ Ⓑ Ⓒ Ⓓ
16. Ⓐ Ⓑ Ⓒ Ⓓ
17. Ⓐ Ⓑ Ⓒ Ⓓ
18. Ⓐ Ⓑ Ⓒ Ⓓ
19. Ⓐ Ⓑ Ⓒ Ⓓ
20. Ⓐ Ⓑ Ⓒ Ⓓ
21. Ⓐ Ⓑ Ⓒ Ⓓ
22. Ⓐ Ⓑ Ⓒ Ⓓ
23. Ⓐ Ⓑ Ⓒ Ⓓ
24. Ⓐ Ⓑ Ⓒ Ⓓ
25. Ⓐ Ⓑ Ⓒ Ⓓ
26. Ⓐ Ⓑ Ⓒ Ⓓ
27. Ⓐ Ⓑ Ⓒ Ⓓ
28. Ⓐ Ⓑ Ⓒ Ⓓ
29. Ⓐ Ⓑ Ⓒ Ⓓ
30. Ⓐ Ⓑ Ⓒ Ⓓ

31. Ⓐ Ⓑ Ⓒ Ⓓ
32. Ⓐ Ⓑ Ⓒ Ⓓ
33. Ⓐ Ⓑ Ⓒ Ⓓ
34. Ⓐ Ⓑ Ⓒ Ⓓ
35. Ⓐ Ⓑ Ⓒ Ⓓ
36. Ⓐ Ⓑ Ⓒ Ⓓ
37. Ⓐ Ⓑ Ⓒ Ⓓ
38. Ⓐ Ⓑ Ⓒ Ⓓ
39. Ⓐ Ⓑ Ⓒ Ⓓ
40. Ⓐ Ⓑ Ⓒ Ⓓ
41. Ⓐ Ⓑ Ⓒ Ⓓ
42. Ⓐ Ⓑ Ⓒ Ⓓ
43. Ⓐ Ⓑ Ⓒ Ⓓ
44. Ⓐ Ⓑ Ⓒ Ⓓ
45. Ⓐ Ⓑ Ⓒ Ⓓ
46. Ⓐ Ⓑ Ⓒ Ⓓ
47. Ⓐ Ⓑ Ⓒ Ⓓ
48. Ⓐ Ⓑ Ⓒ Ⓓ
49. Ⓐ Ⓑ Ⓒ Ⓓ
50. Ⓐ Ⓑ Ⓒ Ⓓ
51. Ⓐ Ⓑ Ⓒ Ⓓ
52. Ⓐ Ⓑ Ⓒ Ⓓ
53. Ⓐ Ⓑ Ⓒ Ⓓ
54. Ⓐ Ⓑ Ⓒ Ⓓ
55. Ⓐ Ⓑ Ⓒ Ⓓ
56. Ⓐ Ⓑ Ⓒ Ⓓ
57. Ⓐ Ⓑ Ⓒ Ⓓ
58. Ⓐ Ⓑ Ⓒ Ⓓ
59. Ⓐ Ⓑ Ⓒ Ⓓ
60. Ⓐ Ⓑ Ⓒ Ⓓ

61. Ⓐ Ⓑ Ⓒ Ⓓ
62. Ⓐ Ⓑ Ⓒ Ⓓ
63. Ⓐ Ⓑ Ⓒ Ⓓ
64. Ⓐ Ⓑ Ⓒ Ⓓ
65. Ⓐ Ⓑ Ⓒ Ⓓ
66. Ⓐ Ⓑ Ⓒ Ⓓ
67. Ⓐ Ⓑ Ⓒ Ⓓ
68. Ⓐ Ⓑ Ⓒ Ⓓ
69. Ⓐ Ⓑ Ⓒ Ⓓ
70. Ⓐ Ⓑ Ⓒ Ⓓ
71. Ⓐ Ⓑ Ⓒ Ⓓ
72. Ⓐ Ⓑ Ⓒ Ⓓ
73. Ⓐ Ⓑ Ⓒ Ⓓ
74. Ⓐ Ⓑ Ⓒ Ⓓ
75. Ⓐ Ⓑ Ⓒ Ⓓ
76. Ⓐ Ⓑ Ⓒ Ⓓ
77. Ⓐ Ⓑ Ⓒ Ⓓ
78. Ⓐ Ⓑ Ⓒ Ⓓ
79. Ⓐ Ⓑ Ⓒ Ⓓ
80. Ⓐ Ⓑ Ⓒ Ⓓ
81. Ⓐ Ⓑ Ⓒ Ⓓ
82. Ⓐ Ⓑ Ⓒ Ⓓ
83. Ⓐ Ⓑ Ⓒ Ⓓ
84. Ⓐ Ⓑ Ⓒ Ⓓ
85. Ⓐ Ⓑ Ⓒ Ⓓ
86. Ⓐ Ⓑ Ⓒ Ⓓ
87. Ⓐ Ⓑ Ⓒ Ⓓ
88. Ⓐ Ⓑ Ⓒ Ⓓ
89. Ⓐ Ⓑ Ⓒ Ⓓ
90. Ⓐ Ⓑ Ⓒ Ⓓ

91. Ⓐ Ⓑ Ⓒ Ⓓ
92. Ⓐ Ⓑ Ⓒ Ⓓ
93. Ⓐ Ⓑ Ⓒ Ⓓ
94. Ⓐ Ⓑ Ⓒ Ⓓ
95. Ⓐ Ⓑ Ⓒ Ⓓ
96. Ⓐ Ⓑ Ⓒ Ⓓ
97. Ⓐ Ⓑ Ⓒ Ⓓ
98. Ⓐ Ⓑ Ⓒ Ⓓ
99. Ⓐ Ⓑ Ⓒ Ⓓ
100. Ⓐ Ⓑ Ⓒ Ⓓ

Completely darken bubbles with a No. 2 pencil. If you make a mistake, be sure to erase mark completely. Erase all stray marks.

1. YOUR NAME: _____
(Print)   Last   First   M.I.

SIGNATURE: _____   **DATE:** _____ / ___ / ___

HOME ADDRESS: _____
(Print)   Number and Street

_____
                City   State   Zip Code

PHONE NO.: _____
(Print)

IMPORTANT: Please fill in these boxes exactly as shown on the back cover of your test book.

2. TEST FORM
_____

6. DATE OF BIRTH

Month		Day		Year	
○ JAN					
○ FEB					
○ MAR	⓪	⓪	⓪	⓪	
○ APR	①	①	①	①	
○ MAY	②	②	②	②	
○ JUN	③	③	③	③	
○ JUL		④	④	④	
○ AUG		⑤	⑤	⑤	
○ SEP		⑦	⑦	⑦	
○ OCT		⑧	⑧	⑧	
○ NOV		⑨	⑨	⑨	
○ DEC					

3. TEST CODE

⓪ Ⓐ ⓪ ⓪ ⓪ ⓪ ⓪ ⓪ ⓪ ⓪ ⓪
① Ⓑ ① ① ① ① ① ① ① ① ①
② Ⓒ ② ② ② ② ② ② ② ② ②
③ Ⓓ ③ ③ ③ ③ ③ ③ ③ ③ ③
④ Ⓔ ④ ④ ④ ④ ④ ④ ④ ④ ④
⑤ Ⓕ ⑤ ⑤ ⑤ ⑤ ⑤ ⑤ ⑤ ⑤ ⑤
⑦ Ⓖ ⑦ ⑦ ⑦ ⑦ ⑦ ⑦ ⑦ ⑦ ⑦
⑧ ⑧ ⑧ ⑧ ⑧ ⑧ ⑧ ⑧ ⑧ ⑧
⑨ ⑨ ⑨ ⑨ ⑨ ⑨ ⑨ ⑨ ⑨ ⑨

4. REGISTRATION NUMBER

7. SEX
○ MALE
○ FEMALE

The Princeton Review
© 2005 The Princeton Review, Inc.
FORM NO. 00001-PR

5. YOUR NAME

First 4 letters of last name				FIRST INIT.	MID INIT.
Ⓐ	Ⓐ	Ⓐ	Ⓐ	Ⓐ	Ⓐ
Ⓑ	Ⓑ	Ⓑ	Ⓑ	Ⓑ	Ⓑ
Ⓒ	Ⓒ	Ⓒ	Ⓒ	Ⓒ	Ⓒ
Ⓓ	Ⓓ	Ⓓ	Ⓓ	Ⓓ	Ⓓ
Ⓔ	Ⓔ	Ⓔ	Ⓔ	Ⓔ	Ⓔ
Ⓕ	Ⓕ	Ⓕ	Ⓕ	Ⓕ	Ⓕ
Ⓖ	Ⓖ	Ⓖ	Ⓖ	Ⓖ	Ⓖ
Ⓗ	Ⓗ	Ⓗ	Ⓗ	Ⓗ	Ⓗ
Ⓘ	Ⓘ	Ⓘ	Ⓘ	Ⓘ	Ⓘ
Ⓙ	Ⓙ	Ⓙ	Ⓙ	Ⓙ	Ⓙ
Ⓚ	Ⓚ	Ⓚ	Ⓚ	Ⓚ	Ⓚ
Ⓛ	Ⓛ	Ⓛ	Ⓛ	Ⓛ	Ⓛ
Ⓜ	Ⓜ	Ⓜ	Ⓜ	Ⓜ	Ⓜ
Ⓝ	Ⓝ	Ⓝ	Ⓝ	Ⓝ	Ⓝ
Ⓞ	Ⓞ	Ⓞ	Ⓞ	Ⓞ	Ⓞ
Ⓟ	Ⓟ	Ⓟ	Ⓟ	Ⓟ	Ⓟ
Ⓠ	Ⓠ	Ⓠ	Ⓠ	Ⓠ	Ⓠ
Ⓡ	Ⓡ	Ⓡ	Ⓡ	Ⓡ	Ⓡ
Ⓢ	Ⓢ	Ⓢ	Ⓢ	Ⓢ	Ⓢ
Ⓣ	Ⓣ	Ⓣ	Ⓣ	Ⓣ	Ⓣ
Ⓤ	Ⓤ	Ⓤ	Ⓤ	Ⓤ	Ⓤ
Ⓥ	Ⓥ	Ⓥ	Ⓥ	Ⓥ	Ⓥ
Ⓦ	Ⓦ	Ⓦ	Ⓦ	Ⓦ	Ⓦ
Ⓧ	Ⓧ	Ⓧ	Ⓧ	Ⓧ	Ⓧ
Ⓨ	Ⓨ	Ⓨ	Ⓨ	Ⓨ	Ⓨ
Ⓩ	Ⓩ	Ⓩ	Ⓩ	Ⓩ	Ⓩ

Practice Test 2
Start with number 1 for each new section.
If a section has fewer questions than answer spaces, leave the extra answer spaces blank.

1. Ⓐ Ⓑ Ⓒ Ⓓ
2. Ⓐ Ⓑ Ⓒ Ⓓ
3. Ⓐ Ⓑ Ⓒ Ⓓ
4. Ⓐ Ⓑ Ⓒ Ⓓ
5. Ⓐ Ⓑ Ⓒ Ⓓ
6. Ⓐ Ⓑ Ⓒ Ⓓ
7. Ⓐ Ⓑ Ⓒ Ⓓ
8. Ⓐ Ⓑ Ⓒ Ⓓ
9. Ⓐ Ⓑ Ⓒ Ⓓ
10. Ⓐ Ⓑ Ⓒ Ⓓ
11. Ⓐ Ⓑ Ⓒ Ⓓ
12. Ⓐ Ⓑ Ⓒ Ⓓ
13. Ⓐ Ⓑ Ⓒ Ⓓ
14. Ⓐ Ⓑ Ⓒ Ⓓ
15. Ⓐ Ⓑ Ⓒ Ⓓ
16. Ⓐ Ⓑ Ⓒ Ⓓ
17. Ⓐ Ⓑ Ⓒ Ⓓ
18. Ⓐ Ⓑ Ⓒ Ⓓ
19. Ⓐ Ⓑ Ⓒ Ⓓ
20. Ⓐ Ⓑ Ⓒ Ⓓ
21. Ⓐ Ⓑ Ⓒ Ⓓ
22. Ⓐ Ⓑ Ⓒ Ⓓ
23. Ⓐ Ⓑ Ⓒ Ⓓ
24. Ⓐ Ⓑ Ⓒ Ⓓ
25. Ⓐ Ⓑ Ⓒ Ⓓ
26. Ⓐ Ⓑ Ⓒ Ⓓ
27. Ⓐ Ⓑ Ⓒ Ⓓ
28. Ⓐ Ⓑ Ⓒ Ⓓ
29. Ⓐ Ⓑ Ⓒ Ⓓ
30. Ⓐ Ⓑ Ⓒ Ⓓ

31. Ⓐ Ⓑ Ⓒ Ⓓ
32. Ⓐ Ⓑ Ⓒ Ⓓ
33. Ⓐ Ⓑ Ⓒ Ⓓ
34. Ⓐ Ⓑ Ⓒ Ⓓ
35. Ⓐ Ⓑ Ⓒ Ⓓ
36. Ⓐ Ⓑ Ⓒ Ⓓ
37. Ⓐ Ⓑ Ⓒ Ⓓ
38. Ⓐ Ⓑ Ⓒ Ⓓ
39. Ⓐ Ⓑ Ⓒ Ⓓ
40. Ⓐ Ⓑ Ⓒ Ⓓ
41. Ⓐ Ⓑ Ⓒ Ⓓ
42. Ⓐ Ⓑ Ⓒ Ⓓ
43. Ⓐ Ⓑ Ⓒ Ⓓ
44. Ⓐ Ⓑ Ⓒ Ⓓ
45. Ⓐ Ⓑ Ⓒ Ⓓ
46. Ⓐ Ⓑ Ⓒ Ⓓ
47. Ⓐ Ⓑ Ⓒ Ⓓ
48. Ⓐ Ⓑ Ⓒ Ⓓ
49. Ⓐ Ⓑ Ⓒ Ⓓ
50. Ⓐ Ⓑ Ⓒ Ⓓ
51. Ⓐ Ⓑ Ⓒ Ⓓ
52. Ⓐ Ⓑ Ⓒ Ⓓ
53. Ⓐ Ⓑ Ⓒ Ⓓ
54. Ⓐ Ⓑ Ⓒ Ⓓ
55. Ⓐ Ⓑ Ⓒ Ⓓ
56. Ⓐ Ⓑ Ⓒ Ⓓ
57. Ⓐ Ⓑ Ⓒ Ⓓ
58. Ⓐ Ⓑ Ⓒ Ⓓ
59. Ⓐ Ⓑ Ⓒ Ⓓ
60. Ⓐ Ⓑ Ⓒ Ⓓ

61. Ⓐ Ⓑ Ⓒ Ⓓ
62. Ⓐ Ⓑ Ⓒ Ⓓ
63. Ⓐ Ⓑ Ⓒ Ⓓ
64. Ⓐ Ⓑ Ⓒ Ⓓ
65. Ⓐ Ⓑ Ⓒ Ⓓ
66. Ⓐ Ⓑ Ⓒ Ⓓ
67. Ⓐ Ⓑ Ⓒ Ⓓ
68. Ⓐ Ⓑ Ⓒ Ⓓ
69. Ⓐ Ⓑ Ⓒ Ⓓ
70. Ⓐ Ⓑ Ⓒ Ⓓ
71. Ⓐ Ⓑ Ⓒ Ⓓ
72. Ⓐ Ⓑ Ⓒ Ⓓ
73. Ⓐ Ⓑ Ⓒ Ⓓ
74. Ⓐ Ⓑ Ⓒ Ⓓ
75. Ⓐ Ⓑ Ⓒ Ⓓ
76. Ⓐ Ⓑ Ⓒ Ⓓ
77. Ⓐ Ⓑ Ⓒ Ⓓ
78. Ⓐ Ⓑ Ⓒ Ⓓ
79. Ⓐ Ⓑ Ⓒ Ⓓ
80. Ⓐ Ⓑ Ⓒ Ⓓ
81. Ⓐ Ⓑ Ⓒ Ⓓ
82. Ⓐ Ⓑ Ⓒ Ⓓ
83. Ⓐ Ⓑ Ⓒ Ⓓ
84. Ⓐ Ⓑ Ⓒ Ⓓ
85. Ⓐ Ⓑ Ⓒ Ⓓ
86. Ⓐ Ⓑ Ⓒ Ⓓ
87. Ⓐ Ⓑ Ⓒ Ⓓ
88. Ⓐ Ⓑ Ⓒ Ⓓ
89. Ⓐ Ⓑ Ⓒ Ⓓ
90. Ⓐ Ⓑ Ⓒ Ⓓ

91. Ⓐ Ⓑ Ⓒ Ⓓ
92. Ⓐ Ⓑ Ⓒ Ⓓ
93. Ⓐ Ⓑ Ⓒ Ⓓ
94. Ⓐ Ⓑ Ⓒ Ⓓ
95. Ⓐ Ⓑ Ⓒ Ⓓ
96. Ⓐ Ⓑ Ⓒ Ⓓ
97. Ⓐ Ⓑ Ⓒ Ⓓ
98. Ⓐ Ⓑ Ⓒ Ⓓ
99. Ⓐ Ⓑ Ⓒ Ⓓ
100. Ⓐ Ⓑ Ⓒ Ⓓ

NOTES

NOTES

NOTES

NOTES

NOTES

NOTES

NOTES

NOTES

NOTES

NOTES

NOTES

NOTES

NOTES

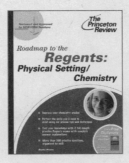

Need More?

If you want to learn more about how to excel on the NYSTCE, you're in the right place. Our expertise extends far beyond this test. But this isn't about us, it's about helping you become a certified teacher.

The Princeton Review started in 1981, helping 19 students prepare for the SAT, and over the past 20 years we have grown into the largest test preparation company in the country. We work with students at all levels to prepare them for college entrance exams, graduate school tests, and professional development exams by providing classroom and online courses, private tutoring, and a comprehensive collection of books.

Call **800-2Review** or visit *PrincetonReview.com* to learn more.

If you like our *Cracking the NYSTCE*, check out:
- *Math Smart*
- *Word Smart*
- *Writing Smart*
- *Grammar Smart*